Everyman, I will go with thee,
and be thy guide,

THE EVERYMAN BOOK
OF VICTORIAN VERSE
THE POST-ROMANTICS

Edited by
DONALD THOMAS

EVERYMAN
J. M. DENT · LONDON
CHARLES E. TUTTLE
VERMONT

for Michael Johnson

Selection, introduction and bibliography
© Donald Thomas 1992

Other critical material © J. M. Dent 1994

First published in Everyman in 1992
Reprinted 1993
This edition 1994
Reprinted 1995, 1996

J. M. Dent
Orion Publishing Group
Orion House, 5 Upper St Martin's Lane,
London WC2H 9EA
and
Charles E. Tuttle Co. Inc.
28 South Main Street,
Rutland, Vermont 05701, USA

Typeset by Deltatype Ltd, Ellesmere Port, Cheshire
Printed in Great Britain by
The Guernsey Press Co. Ltd, Guernsey, C.I.

British Library Cataloguing-in-Publication Data
is available upon request.

ISBN 0 460 87526 4

+ loss of faith *HMW*
A persistant theme in Victorian society

CONTENTS

NOTE ON THE POETS AND EDITOR

ALFRED, 1ST BARON TENNYSON (1809–92)
ROBERT BROWNING (1812–89)
MATTHEW ARNOLD (1822–88)
ARTHUR HUGH CLOUGH (1819–61)
ALGERNON CHARLES SWINBURNE (1837–1909)
Biographical notes on these poets can be found on pp. liv-lv

DONALD THOMAS is the author of two collections of poetry, including *Points of Contact* for which he won the Eric Gregory Award, as well as fiction, biography, and the history of literary censorship in *A Long Time Burning*. His recent fiction includes *Dancing in the Dark* (1992), *The Arrest of Scotland Yard* (1993) and *The Raising of Lizzie Meek* (1993). His latest biographies are *Henry Fielding* (1990) and *The Marquis de Sade* (1992). He has edited two volumes of *State Trials* and devised two series of Radio 4's *The Detectives*. His documentary crime includes *Hanged in Error?* (1994) and *Dead Giveaway* (1993), which describes the forensic detection of Cardiff's 'Body in the Carpet' murder in 1991. The complete anonymous eleven-volume diary of the Victorian philanderer, 'Walter', *My Secret Life* (1888), was published for the first time in England in his edition in 1994. Donald Thomas also holds a personal professorship in the University of Wales.

CHRONOLOGY OF THE POETS' LIVES

Year	Lives
1809	Birth of Tennyson, Somersby, Lincolnshire, 5 August
1812	Birth of Browning, Camberwell, London, 7 May
1814	Birth of Browning's sister Sarianna
1815	Tennyson begins at Louth Grammar School (until 1820)
1819	Birth of Arthur Hugh Clough, Liverpool, 1 January
1820	Browning attends school in Peckham Tennyson taught by father (until 1827)
1822	Birth of Matthew Arnold, Laleham, Middlesex, 24 December
1823	Clough taken to USA by father; lives in Charleston, South Carolina

CHRONOLOGY OF THEIR TIMES

Year	Literary Context	Historical Context
1809	Birth of Nicolai Gogol Washington Irving, *Rip Van Winkle* Birth of Edgar Allan Poe	Darwin and Abraham Lincoln born Napoleon divorces Josephine War between France and Austria Pope Pius VII taken prisoner
1812	Grimms' *Fairy Tales* Byron, *Childe Harold's Pilgrimage* Birth of Dickens Birth of I. A. Goncharov	Napoleon invades Russia; retreat from Moscow Louisiana becomes a state USA declares war on Britain Wellington enters Madrid
1814	Austen, *Mansfield Park* Scott, *Waverley* Wordsworth, *Excursion* Birth of Lermontov	Allies enter Paris Napoleon abdicates and is banished to Elba Louis XVIII takes French throne
1815	Birth of Trollope Scott, *Guy Mannering* Byron, *Hebrew Melodies* Béranger, *Chansons I*	Battle of Waterloo Napoleon banished to St Helena Birth of Bismarck Brazil declares independence
1819	Birth of George Eliot, Theodore Fontane and Walt Whitman Shelley, *The Cenci*	Singapore established Birth of Queen Victoria Peterloo massacre (Manchester) Florida purchased from Spain
1820	Keats, 'Ode to a Nightingale' Scott, *Ivanhoe* Shelley, *Prometheus Unbound*	Prince Regent succeeds as George IV Cato Street conspiracy Congress of Vienna completed
1822	Death of Shelley Birth of Edmond de Goncourt Pushkin, *Eugene Onegin* (completed 1832)	Greeks proclaim independence; Turks invade Greece Birth of Ulysses S. Grant *Sunday Times* founded
1823	Birth of Charlotte M. Yonge James Fenimore Cooper, *The Pioneers* (first of Leatherstocking novels)	Mexico becomes a republic Monroe Doctrine ends colonial settlement of America

Year	Lives
1826	Browning leaves Peckham school; educated at home (until 1828). Manuscript of *Incondita*, volume of poems, completed but later destroyed
1827	Tennyson enters Trinity College, Cambridge; with brothers Frederick and Charles publishes *Poems by Two Brothers*
1828	Browning attends London University Arthur Hallam enters Trinity College, Cambridge Clough returns to England
1829	Browning leaves London University Tennyson wins Chancellor's Gold Medal with poem 'Timbuctoo' Clough attends school at Rugby (until 1836)
1830	Tennyson, *Poems, Chiefly Lyrical*
1831	Death of Tennyson's father; Tennyson leaves Cambridge without taking degree
1832	Browning sees Edmund Kean in *Richard III* Tennyson, *Poems* (including 'The Lotos-Eaters' and 'The Lady of Shalott'); he travels with Hallam in Europe
1833	Hallam becomes engaged to Tennyson's sister Emily, but dies in Vienna, 15 September; Tennyson begins *In Memoriam* Browning's *Pauline* published anonymously
1834	Browning travels to St Petersburg Tennyson meets and falls for Rosa Baring
1835	Browning's *Paracelsus* published to critical acclaim

Year	Literary Context	Historical Context
1826	Cooper, *The Last of the Mohicans* Disraeli, *Vivian Grey* Scott, *Woodstock* Alfred de Vigny, *Cinq-Mars*	Death of Thomas Jefferson Russian war with Persia Zoological Society of London founded
1827	Hugo, *Cromwell* Heine, *Buch der Lieder* Keble, *The Christian Year* Henry Hallam, *Constitutional History of England*	Peru claims independence Battle of Navarino Russia defeats Persia and annexes Erivan (Armenia)
1828	Dumas, *Three Musketeers* Birth of Tolstoy and Jules Verne	Russo–Turkish War Wellington becomes Prime Minister Death of Goya and Schubert
1829	Balzac, *Les Chouans* Death of Schlegel	Catholic Emancipation in Britain First Oxford–Cambridge boat race
1830	Stendhal, *Le Rouge et le Noir* Birth of Emily Dickinson, Frédéric Mistral, Jules de Goncourt	France occupies Algeria Louis Philippe succeeds to French throne Death of Simón Bolívar
1831	Hugo, *Notre Dame de Paris* Peacock, *Crotchet Castle* Balzac, *La Peau de Chagrin*	Belgium separates from Netherlands First Reform Bill introduced
1832	Death of Goethe and Scott George Sand, *Indiana*	First Reform Act British occupy Falklands Birth of Manet Slavery abolished by British
1833	Carlyle, *Sartor Resartus* Lamb, *Last Essays of Elia* German translation of Shakespeare completed	Santa Ana becomes Mexican President Birth of Alfred Nobel
1834	Death of Coleridge and Lamb Pushkin, *The Queen of Spades*	Houses of Parliament burnt down Carlist Wars in Spain Quadruple Alliance formed (Britain, France, Spain, Portugal)
1835	H. C. Andersen publishes first children's stories Birth of Mark Twain and Samuel Butler	Melbourne (Australia) founded Death of Francis II, last Holy Roman Emperor Halley's Comet

Year	Literary Context	Historical Context
1836	Dickens, *Pickwick Papers* Gogol, *The Government Inspector* Birth of W. S. Gilbert	Death of Davy Crockett Texas becomes independent The Peoples' Charter (Chartism)
1837	Dickens, *Oliver Twist* Balzac, *Illusions Perdues* Pushkin killed in duel	Death of William IV; Queen Victoria succeeds Mazzini exiled in London
1838	Hugo, *Ruy Blas* E. B. Browning, *The Seraphim and Other Poems*	Victoria crowned Cobden establishes Anti-Corn Law League
1839	Poe, *Fall of the House of Usher* H. Martineau, *Deerbrook* Birth of Pater and Ouida	First Opium War (Britain–China) Grand National first run
1840	Lermontov, *A Hero of Our Times* Birth of Hardy and Zola	Queen Victoria and Prince Albert marry Frederick William IV succeeds to Prussian throne
1841	Dickens, *The Old Curiosity Shop* Poe, *The Murders in the Rue Morgue* Carlyle, *Heroes and Hero-Worship*	Hong Kong comes under British sovereignty Future Edward VII born
1842	Macaulay, *Lays of Ancient Rome* Death of Stendhal	Orange Free State founded First Opium War ends Grace Darling dies
1843	Dickens, *Martin Chuzzlewit* and *A Christmas Carol* Wordsworth Poet Laureate	Birth of Grieg *The Economist* founded
1844	Disraeli, *Coningsby* Carlyle, *Past and Present* Birth of G. M. Hopkins	Oscar I succeeds to throne of Sweden and Norway Cooperative movement founded in Rochdale (Lancashire)
1845	Disraeli, *Sybil* Prosper Mérimée, *Carmen* George Eliot begins Strauss translation	First Sikh War begins Florida and Texas become American states

1846	Lear, *Book of Nonsense*	USA annexes New Mexico
	Melville, *Typee*	Irish potato famine
	H. C. Andersen, *Fairy Tale of My Life*	Louis Napoleon escapes to London
1847	C. Brontë, *Jane Eyre*	Liberia becomes independent
	E. Brontë, *Wuthering Heights*	Start of California goldrush
	Thackeray, *Vanity Fair*	
	Dickens, *Dombey and Son*	
1848	Gaskell, *Mary Barton*	Revolutions in Europe
	Dumas, *La Dame aux Camélias*	Louis Napoleon elected President
	Chateaubriand, *Mémoires d'outre-tombe*	Second Sikh War
1849	Dickens, *David Copperfield*	Mazzini declares Rome a republic
	C. Brontë, *Shirley*	British annexe Punjab
	Strindberg born	Hungary defeated at Vilagos by Austria
1850	Hawthorne, *The Scarlet Letter*	Death of Louis Philippe and Robert Peel
	Birth of Maupassant and R. L. Stevenson	California becomes American state
	Death of Wordsworth	Peace treaty on Schleswig-Holstein (Prussia and Denmark)
	E. B. Browning, *Sonnets from the Portuguese*	
1851	Melville, *Moby-Dick*	Cuba declares independence
	Ruskin, *The Stones of Venice*	Great Exhibition in London
1852	Dickens, *Bleak House*	Second Burmese War
	Harriet Beecher Stowe, *Uncle Tom's Cabin*	Death of Wellington
	Thackeray, *Henry Esmond*	Napoleon III becomes Emperor of France

Year	Lives
1853	Birth of Tennyson's son Lionel; he moves to Farringford, Isle of Wight
	Swinburne leaves school
	Arnold, *Poems: A New Edition* (includes 'Sohrab and Rustum' and 'The Scholar Gipsy')
	Clough appointed an Examiner in Education Office, London
1854	Clough marries Blanche Smith
	Tennyson, 'The Charge of the Light Brigade'
1855	Arnold, *Poems, second series*
	Browning, *Men and Women* published without success
	Tennyson, *Maud*
1856	Browning and wife receive legacies from John Kenyon
	Swinburne at Balliol College, Oxford
1857	Arnold appointed Professor of Poetry, Oxford (to 1867)
	Death of Elizabeth Barrett Browning's father
1858	Arnold, *Merope: a Tragedy*
	Swinburne wins Taylorian scholarship
1859	Arnold tours Europe to study primary schools
	The Brownings take in Walter Savage Landor after his quarrel with family
	Clough's translation of *Plutarch's Lives* published
	Swinburne leaves Oxford without taking degree
	Tennyson, *Idylls of the King*
1860	Browning buys 'The Old Yellow Book' in Florence (to form basis of *The Ring and the Book*)
	Clough's health fails
	Swinburne moves to London
	Tennyson, *Tithonus;* he writes 'The Northern Farmer – Old Style'

Year	Literary Context	Historical Context
1853	C. Brontë, *Villette* Gaskell, *Ruth* and *Cranford* Hawthorne, *Tanglewood Tales*	Russo–Turkish War Napoleon III marries Eugénie Birth of Cecil Rhodes and Vincent van Gogh
1854	Kingsley, *Westward Ho!* Thoreau, *Walden* Dickens, *Hard Times*	Crimean War begins (to 1855) US Republican Party formed Pope Pius IX proclaims Dogma of Immaculate Conception
1855	Dickens, *Little Dorrit* Whitman, *Leaves of Grass* Trollope, *The Warden* Death of Charlotte Brontë	Sebastopol falls to Allies *Daily Telegraph* founded Tsar Nicholas I dies; succeeded by Alexander II
1856	Flaubert, *Madame Bovary* Birth of G. B. Shaw and Oscar Wilde Death of Heinrich Heine	Victoria Cross instituted Beginning of British war with China Birth of Woodrow Wilson
1857	Baudelaire, *Les Fleurs du Mal* Hughes, *Tom Brown's Schooldays* Trollope, *Barchester Towers*	Indian Mutiny begins (to 1858) Serfs emancipated in Russia Birth of Elgar
1858	Ballantyne, *Coral Island* Holmes, *The Autocrat of the Breakfast Table* G. Eliot, *Scenes of Clerical Life*	Government of India transferred to British Crown Birth of Theodore Roosevelt Assassination attempt on Napoleon III
1859	Dickens, *A Tale of Two Cities* G. Eliot, *Adam Bede* Fitzgerald, *The Rubaiyat of Omar Khayyam*	Work on Suez Canal begins Northern Italy revolts against Austria
1860	Collins, *The Woman in White* G. Eliot, *The Mill on the Floss* Birth of Chekhov	Second Maori War Lincoln elected President of USA Garibaldi marches with his 'Thousand'

Year	Lives
1861	Arnold, *On Translating Homer* (second volume 1862); also *The Popular Education of France*
	Death of Elizabeth Barrett Browning; Browning leaves Italy
	Clough writes *Mari Magno or Tales on Board;* travels in Europe; dies 13 November in Florence aged 42
	Swinburne, *The Queen Mother* and *Rosamund: Two Plays*
1862	Browning settles in London
	Clough, *Poems* (with memoir by F. T. Palgrave) published posthumously
	Swinburne stays with D. G. Rossetti and Meredith
	Tennyson visits Queen Victoria at Osborne
1863	Browning, *Poetical Works* (including 'Sordello') published in 3 volumes
	Swinburne visits Paris and meets Whistler
1864	Browning, *Dramatis Personae*
	Tennyson, *Enoch Arden and Other Poems*; he is visited by Garibaldi at Farringford
1865	Arnold, *Essays in Criticism* (1st series)
	Browning, *A Selection from the Works*
	Swinburne, *Atalanta in Calydon*
1866	Death of Browning's father
	Swinburne, *Chastelard; Poems and Ballads;* and *Byron;* he forms friendship with Adah Isaacs Menken
1867	Arnold, *On the Study of Celtic Literature; New Poems* (including 'Dover Beach'); and *Thyrsis* (on death of Clough)
	Oxford University awards Browning honorary MA
	Swinburne, *A Song of Italy* and *An Appeal to England*
1868	Browning, *Poetical Works* (6 volumes)
	Swinburne, *William Blake* and *Notes on the Royal Academy*
1869	Arnold, *Culture and Anarchy*
	Browning, *The Ring and the Book* published in four monthly volumes (beginning 1868); he is presented to Queen Victoria
	Swinburne, *Christabel and the Poems of Coleridge*
	Tennyson, *The Holy Grail and Other Poems*

Year	Literary Context	Historical Context
1861	Dickens, *Great Expectations* G. Eliot, *Silas Marner* Dostoevsky, *The House of the Dead*	American Civil War begins Death of Prince Albert
1862	Hugo, *Les Misérables* Turgenev, *Fathers and Sons* Birth of Edith Wharton	Bismarck appointed Prussian Premier First English cricket tour of Australia
1863	Kingsley, *The Water Babies* Death of Thackeray	Edward, Prince of Wales, marries Alexandra
1864	Dickens, *Our Mutual Friend* Tolstoy, *War and Peace* (to 1869) Trollope, *Can You Forgive Her?*	Grant becomes C. in C. of Union armies Lincoln re-elected President of USA
1865	Carroll, *Alice in Wonderland* Birth of Kipling and Yeats Death of Mrs Gaskell	American Civil War ends Lincoln assassinated Birth of Sibelius
1866	G. Eliot, *Felix Holt* Dostoevsky, *Crime and Punishment* A. Daudet, *Lettres de mon Moulin*	Atlantic telegraph cable laid Nobel invents dynamite Last cholera epidemic in Britain
1867	Trollope, *Last Chronicles of Barset* Zola, *Thérèse Raquin*	Second Reform Act Alaska sold to USA by Russia Garibaldi begins march on Rome
1868	Alcott, *Little Women* Collins, *The Moonstone* Dostoevsky, *The Idiot*	Grant becomes President of USA Gladstone replaces Disraeli as Prime Minister First TUC meeting, Manchester
1869	Blackmore, *Lorna Doone* Flaubert, *L'Education Sentimentale* Twain, *The Innocents Abroad*	Empress Eugénie opens Suez Canal Birth of Gandhi

Year	Literary Context	Historical Context
1870	Disraeli, *Lothair* Verne, *Twenty Thousand Leagues under the Sea* D. G. Rossetti, *Poems* Death of Dickens	Franco–Prussian War Italians enter Rome and declare it capital
1871	G. Eliot, *Middlemarch* Carroll, *Through the Looking Glass* Darwin, *The Descent of Man*	Wilhelm I becomes first Emperor of Germany Trade Unions legalised in UK Bank Holidays introduced in UK Paris Commune
1872	Samuel Butler, *Erewhon* Hardy, *Under the Greenwood Tree* Turgenev, *A Month in the Country*	Civil War in Spain; Carlists defeated First soccer international (England–Scotland)
1873	Tolstoy, *Anna Karenina* Death of Alessandro Manzoni Death of J. S. Mill	Ashanti War Lawn Tennis introduced Death of David Livingstone Gladstone government resigns
1874	Hardy, *Far from the Madding Crowd* Birth of Robert Frost, Somerset Maugham and Gertrude Stein	Disraeli becomes Prime Minister Birth of Winston Churchill Gold Coast annexed
1875	G. Eliot, *Daniel Deronda* Mark Twain, *Tom Sawyer* Birth of Thomas Mann Death of H. C. Andersen	Britain purchases controlling shares in Suez Canal Captain Webb swims Channel
1876	Henry James, *Roderick Hudson* Birth of Jack London Death of George Sand	Telephone invented Turks massacre Hungarians Victoria proclaimed Empress of India
1877	Zola, *l'Assommoir* James, *The American*	Russo–Turkish War First Kaffir War
1878	Hardy, *Return of the Native* Fontane, *Vor dem Sturm* Birth of John Masefield and Carl Sandburg	Greco–Turkish War Congress of Berlin Umberto I succeeds to Italian throne CID (Scotland Yard) formed

Year	Lives
1879	Arnold, *Mixed Essays*
	Browning, *Dramatic Idyls*
	Tennyson, *The Falcon*
	Swinburne moves to The Pines, Putney, under the care of Theodore Watts-Dunton
1880	Browning, *Dramatic Idyls: Second Series*
	Swinburne, *Modern Heptalogia: Studies in Song; A Study of Shakespeare* and *Songs of the Springtide*
	Tennyson, *Ballads and Other Poems*
1881	The Browning Society founded
	Swinburne, *Mary Stuart: a Tragedy*
	Tennyson, *The Cup*
1882	Arnold, *Irish Essays and Others*
	Swinburne meets Victor Hugo; his *Tristram of Lyonesse* published
	Tennyson, *The Promise of May* (play)
1883	Arnold lectures in America (until 1884)
	Browning, *Jocoseria*
	Swinburne, *A Century of Roundels*
	Tennyson elevated to peerage
1884	Browning, *Feristah's Fancies*
	Swinburne, *A Midsummer Holiday*
	Tennyson, *Becket* (play)
1885	Arnold, *Discourses in America*
	Swinburne, *Marino Faliero: a Tragedy*
	Tennyson, *Balin and Balan* and *Tiresias and Other Poems*
1886	Arnold again lectures in America
	Swinburne, *A Study of Victor Hugo* and *Miscellanies*
	Tennyson, *Locksley Hall Sixty Years After*
1887	Browning, *Parleyings with Certain People of Importance in Their Day*
	Swinburne, *Locrine*

Year	Literary Context	Historical Context
1879	Meredith, *The Egoist* Stevenson, *Travels with a Donkey* Strindberg, *The Red Room* Birth of E. M. Forster	Zulu War begins; Prince Imperial killed Birth of Stalin and Trotsky Germany incorporates Alsace-Lorraine
1880	Dostoevsky, *The Brothers Karamazov* Lew Wallace, *Ben Hur* Zola, *Nana* Death of George Eliot and Flaubert	Boers declare independent Transvaal republic First England–Australia Test in England
1881	James, *Portrait of a Lady* Ibsen, *Ghosts* Birth of P. G. Wodehouse Death of Dostoevsky and Carlyle	President Garfield inaugurated Death of Disraeli
1882	Shaw, *Cashel Byron's Profession* Birth of Virginia Woolf and James Joyce Death of Trollope and Longfellow	First Boer War ends Triple Alliance (Italy–Austria–Germany) Birth of F. D. Roosevelt
1883	Stevenson, *Treasure Island* Birth of Kafka Death of Turgenev	Kruger becomes South African President Birth of Mussolini
1884	Twain, *Huckleberry Finn* Birth of Damon Runyon and Sean O'Casey Ibsen, *The Wild Duck*	Grover Cleveland elected President of USA Third Reform Act Birth of Harry S. Truman
1885	Rider Haggard, *King Solomon's Mines* Tolstoy, *The Power of Darkness* Death of Victor Hugo	Gordon killed in Khartoum Germany annexes Tanganyika and Zanzibar Death of Ulysses S. Grant
1886	Stevenson, *Dr Jekyll and Mr Hyde* James, *The Bostonians* Death of Emily Dickinson	Irish Home Rule Bill introduced by Gladstone Indian National Congress first meets
1887	Conan Doyle, *A Study in Scarlet* Strindberg, *The Father* Ibsen, *Rosmersholm* Hardy, *The Woodlanders*	Queen Victoria's Golden Jubilee Birth of Chiang Kai-shek Esperanto language devised

Year	Literary Context	Historical Context

1888	Strindberg, *Miss Julie*
	Zola, *La Terre*
	Wilde, *The Happy Prince*
	Birth of T. S. Eliot
		Wilhelm II succeeds as
		  German Emperor
		Jack the Ripper murders in
		  London

1889	Jerome K. Jerome, *Three Men
	  in a Boat*
	Stevenson, *The Master of
	  Ballantrae*
	Death of G. M. Hopkins and
	  Wilkie Collins
		Suicide of Crown Prince
		  Rudolf at Mayerling
		Birth of Adolf Hitler

1890	Wilde, *Picture of Dorian
	  Gray*
	Hamsun, *Hunger*
	Tolstoy, *The Kreutzer Sonata*
		Bismarck dismissed
		First underground railway in
		  London
		Forth Bridge opened

1891	Hardy, *Tess of the
	  d'Urbervilles*
	Shaw, *Quintessence of
	  Ibsenism*
		Triple Alliance renewed
		Young Turk movement
		  founded
		Pan–Germany League
		  founded

1892	Wilde, *Lady Windermere's
	  Fan*
	Shaw, *Mrs Warren's
	  Profession*
		Keir Hardie first Labour MP
		Birth of Tito and Haile
		  Selassie
		Grover Cleveland President of
		  USA

1893	Wilde, *A Woman of No
	  Importance*
	Pinero, *The Second Mrs
	  Tanqueray*
	Death of Maupassant
		Second Irish Home Rule Bill
		  passed
		Hawaii becomes a republic
		Nansen begins attempt on
		  North Pole

1894	Kipling, *The First Jungle
	  Book*
	Shaw, *Arms and the Man*
	George & Weedon
	  Grossmith, *Diary of a
	  Nobody*
		Dreyfus arrested and
		  convicted
		Nicholas II succeeds as Tsar
		Birth of Macmillan and
		  Khrushchev

1895	Conrad, *Almayer's Folly*
	Wells, *The Time Machine*
	Wilde, *The Importance of
	  Being Earnest*
		Jameson raid into Transvaal
		Marconi invents wireless
		  telegraph

Year	Literary Context	Historical Context
1896	Chekhov, *The Seagull*	Klondike goldrush
	Housman, *A Shropshire Lad*	Madagascar annexed by
	Ibsen, *John Gabriel Borkman*	France
	Death of Harriet Beecher Stowe and Paul Verlaine	Abyssinians defeat Italians at Adowa
1897	Conrad, *The Nigger of the Narcissus*	Russia occupies Port Arthur
		Queen Victoria's Diamond
	Strindberg, *Inferno*	Jubilee
	Rostand, *Cyrano de Bergerac*	Zionist Congress, Basle
1898	James, *The Turn of the Screw*	Battle of Omdurman
	Wilde, *The Ballad of Reading Gaol*	Radium discovered by Curies
		Death of Bismarck and
	Shaw, *Caesar and Cleopatra*	Gladstone
1899	Kipling, *Stalky and Co.*	Boer War begins
	Tolstoy, *Resurrection*	First Hague Peace Conference
	Pinero, *Trelawney of the Wells*	Philippines claim independence from USA
1890	Conrad, *Lord Jim*	Boxer rising in China
	Chekhov, *Uncle Vanya*	Umberto I of Italy
	Death of Oscar Wilde	assassinated
		Australian Commonwealth founded
1901	Kipling, *Kim*	Death of Queen Victoria
	Mann, *Buddenbrooks*	President McKinley
	Strindberg, *Dance of Death*	assassinated
		Panama Canal treaty
		Boxer rising ends
1902	Conrad, *Youth*	Boer War ends
	Conan Doyle, *The Hound of the Baskervilles*	USA gains perpetual control of Panama Canal
	Chekhov, *Three Sisters*	Triple Alliance further renewed
1903	Butler, *The Way of All Flesh*	Franco–British Entente
	James, *The Ambassadors*	Cordiale
	Strindberg, *Queen Christina*	First Tour de France (cycling)
		Ford Motor Company founded
1904	Barrie, *Peter Pan*	Russo–Japanese War begins
	Chekhov, *The Cherry Orchard*	Theodore Roosevelt elected President of USA
1905	Edith Wharton, *The House of Mirth*	Russia defeated by Japan
	Orczy, *The Scarlet Pimpernel*	Norway separates from Sweden
	Wells, *Kipps*	Einstein's Special Theory of Relativity
		Tangier crisis

Year	Literary Context	Historical Context
1906	Galsworthy, *The Man of Property* Death of Ibsen 'Everyman's Library' begins	Algeciras Conference Dreyfus rehabilitated San Francisco earthquake
1907	Conrad, *The Secret Agent* Birth of Auden, Moravia and Christopher Fry Kipling wins Nobel Prize	Boy Scout movement founded Hague Peace Conference New Zealand becomes a dominion
1908	Bennett, *The Old Wives' Tale* Kenneth Grahame, *The Wind in the Willows* Forster, *A Room with a View*	Union of South Africa formed Austria occupies Bosnia–Herzegovina Jack Johnson becomes first black world heavyweight champion
1909	Synge, *Deirdre of the Sorrows* Maeterlinck, *The Bluebird* Death of Meredith Birth of Stephen Spender	W. H. Taft inaugurated as President of USA Bethmann-Hollweg becomes German Chancellor

INTRODUCTION

I

Few chronological divisions extend as far as the term 'Victorian Literature'. By creeping annexation it may include most English writing from the early Tennyson and Dickens to the later Hardy and Kipling. Even by literal chronology, it is equivalent to a period that would include both Shakespeare and Dryden, or Pope and Wordsworth, or Emily Brontë and Ezra Pound.

Victorian poetry can be variously divided. By chronology or style, the first period is that of the post-romantics, the major individual figures in a generation which was the heir to the Romantic Revival. Some of its members, like Tennyson, held sway for more than half a century. Others, like Browning, exerted an influence that was delayed but perhaps the more potent for that. Arnold and Clough were, more briefly, poets of that first Victorian generation. Swinburne, born in the year of the Queen's accession, was at his best as a poet of the 1860s and one of the truest disciples of a darker European romanticism. If Tennyson seemed at first the heir of Keats, Browning the admirer of Shelley, Arnold the Wordsworthian, it was left to Swinburne to boast the anarchic hedonism of Sade and to recognise in Baudelaire or Gautier the great themes of the moderns.

Romanticism itself was a phenomenon whose definition proved elusive but whose presence was easily recognised. It was – and it remains – a living force rather than a laboratory specimen. Historically, the great romantic achievement had existed as an historical episode in England between the publication of *Lyrical*

Ballads by Wordsworth and Coleridge in 1798 and the death of Byron in 1824. It was not, of course, an unchallenged description of the age. There was a good deal of English writing, including Jane Austen's fiction and even Byron's *Don Juan*, which might more easily have shared, with architecture and furnishing, the term 'Regency'.

At Byron's death, when Tennyson and Browning were in their teens, the best English poetry had less of medievalism or natural simplicity and more of subversion, blasphemy and open rebellion than at the beginning of the century. Madame de Staël in *De l'Allemagne*, in 1810–13, had still been able to write of romanticism as modernity growing out of 'our own soil' of the Middle Ages, unlike the classical antiquity admired since the Renaissance. By 1834, the exiled German poet Heinrich Heine denounced such views as reactionary. The revival of the culture of the Middle Ages was in reality, 'An attempt by priests and gentlemen who had conspired against the religious and political freedom of Europe.' Young people, wrote Heine, would first be seduced by the charm of the Middle Ages and would then find, too late, that such charm was the means employed by theological and political reactionaries to enslave them.

As the first generation of Victorian poets came of age, Tennyson and Browning foremost among them in the 1830s, romanticism had undergone a political change. Wordsworth, in his Preface to *Lyrical Ballads*, had written of 'the spontaneous overflow of powerful feelings' as a touchstone of true poetry. Such feelings, when they embodied benevolence towards nature and common humanity, might seem safe enough. Suppose, instead, there were powerful feelings of hatred, ridicule and contempt, aimed at the government, the monarchy or God. In 1824 Byron's publisher was convicted for the poet's verses on the death of the blind and mad George III.

> A better farmer ne'er brushed dew from lawn;
> A worse king never left a realm undone!
> He died – but left his subjects still behind,
> One half as mad – and t'other no less blind.

Was it for such writing as this that the gospel of nature had been preached so earnestly at the dawn of the century? There was worse to come. Byron's publishers were prosecuted for blasphemy when his poem *Cain* appeared, as Shelley's were for *Queen Mab*. As for Shelley's description of European monarchs as 'privileged gangs of murderers and swindlers', no publisher would put that into print for seventy years.

By 1824, it seemed that English romanticism, in whatever form, might have run its course. Keats, Shelley and Byron were dead. Wordsworth and Coleridge were burnt-out stars. 'They are all going or gone,' said the *Westminster Review* unkindly in 1831. Perhaps English poetry faced an interregnum. Yet in France and Germany the shading of European romanticism into post-romanticism showed greater continuity. Increasingly, the term 'modern' appeared as preferable to 'romantic'. But what was 'modern' in the new century? Victor Hugo offered a definition in 1827 in a famous passage from the preface to his play *Cromwell*.

Hugo saw both the classicism of the Renaissance and mere medievalism as outmoded. Europe had now embarked on what he called its 'third civilisation'. 'Another era is about to begin for the world and for poetry.' Yet it was not merely to be a world where romantic imperfection took precedence over classical perfection. The great subject of the moderns was to be the grotesque, as a rival to the sublime. Indeed, the grotesque was a necessary complement to the beautiful in modern art. 'Everything tends to show its close creative alliance with the beautiful in the so-called "romantic age",' Hugo wrote. 'Even among the simplest popular legends there are none which do not somewhere, with an admirable instinct, solve this mystery of modern art. Antiquity could not have produced *Beauty and the Beast*.'

Time seemed to prove Hugo right. Homer, in Book XVIII of the *Iliad*, describes the shield of Achilles, made for the warrior by Hepaestos, armourer of the gods. The 'glittering armour', as Homer calls it, is adorned with designs on the shield showing the stars and the heavens, peaceful cities and their inhabitants, vineyards, fields and a dance of youths and maidens. Like the rest of Achilles's weaponry, it is a thing of classical beauty which prompts no moral qualms. Compare it with Browning's poem 'A Forgiveness', published in 1876. Swords, whips and daggers are intended to inflict death or pain. Why, then, are they embellished with such loving art, as if they were the finest expression of the human spirit?

> I think there never was such – how express?
> Horror coquetting with voluptuousness,
> As in those arms of Eastern workmanship –
> Yataghan, kandjar, things that rend and rip,
> Gash rough, slash smooth, help hate so many ways,
> Yet ever keep a beauty that betrays
> Love still at work with the artificer
> Throughout his quaint devising. Why prefer,
> Except for love's sake, that a blade should writhe
> And bicker like a flame?

'Horror coquetting with voluptuousness' seems like a direct descendant of Hugo's *Beauty and the Beast* almost fifty years before. The nineteenth century was not, perhaps, the most illustrious in the history of European culture. Yet, morally and aesthetically, it was the most uneasy.

In 1843, in the *Revue des Deux Mondes*, Sainte-Beuve identi-fied two sources of inspiration in modern literature. 'I dare to affirm, without any fear of being contradicted, that Byron and Sade (forgive me for putting them together) have perhaps been the two great inspirations of the moderns. One of them is well-advertised and visible, the other is hidden – but not too hidden.' Editions of Sade were available, even in England, where George Cannon was prosecuted for publishing *Juliette* in 1830. Byron's volumes circulated more widely, though the young W. H. Smith was quick to apologise to a concerned citizen who saw a copy of *Don Juan* displayed on one of Smith's railway bookstalls.

That the flamboyant hedonism of Lord Byron and the dark spirit of Sade should be thought of as the major sources of inspiration for modern literature cast a shadow on the more gentle romantic landscape of Wordsworth and Coleridge. If the art of the past offers a mirror in which the mood of the present is reflected, that reflection was seldom more telling than in Walter Pater's reaction to the Mona Lisa, Leonardo's smiling 'Giaconda', in whom the virtues of classical humanism were embodied. Could this generous beauty be the same picture which Pater described in his book *The Renaissance* in 1873, a portrait of 'strange thoughts and fantastic reveries and exquisite passions'? The face remained the same but the 'Giaconda' now beckoned the world into darkness and decay. 'She is older than the rocks among which she sits; like the vampire, she has been dead many times, and learned the secrets of the grave.' She seemed, in other words, the goddess of post-romanticism in its decadence, a fit heroine for the poems of Swinburne or Baudelaire. Indeed, both Swinburne and Baudelaire ensured that she did not lack rivals.

II

Against this European background, a brief but invigorating movement in English culture appeared to be at a sudden end in 1824. Yet the great names of Victorian poetry were not the immediate successors of the first romantics. When Byron died, Tennyson, Browning, Clough and Arnold were children. Swinburne was not yet born. What was their inheritance to be?

There was indeed an interregnum until new forces gave momentum to English poetry again. The romantic heroes themselves suffered eclipse. Byron was taboo, in part for his treatment of his wife and for fathering a daughter on his half-sister; in part for the role of the amoral dandy in *Don Juan*. Shelley was to be read in carefully chosen poems about skylarks or the west wind. His collected poems were the subject of a successful prosecution for blasphemous libel in 1840–41. Keats was not truly popular until rescued by Richard Monckton Milnes's *Life and Letters of John Keats* in 1848, as Browning was to acknowledge in his own poem 'Popularity'. Wordsworth, at least, was safe. He had repented of his early enthusiasms and was to be made Poet Laureate in 1843. Browning also summed him up in 'The Lost Leader'.

> Just for a handful of silver he left us,
> Just for a riband to stick in his coat . . .

Though the great stream of romanticism might seem to be dribbling away in the sand, the vitality of writing during the

1830s was not in question. The example of the Regency was one of self-confident animal spirits, often characterised by a section of English society that was sporting, patrician, gallant and military. From this came the mocking and wistful *vers de société* of Winthrop Mackworth Praed (1802–39) and the *Ingoldsby Legends* of Richard Barham (1788–1845). The poetry of Praed in his verse letter of 1831, 'The Talented Man', captured the tone and rhythm of chatter in pampered society in a manner whose energy and wit anticipate Browning's monologues and the verse novels of Clough.

> Dear Alice, you'll laugh when you know it, –
>   last week at the Duchess's ball,
> I danced with the clever new poet,
>   You've heard of him – Tully St Paul.
> Miss Jonquil was perfectly frantic;
>   I wish you had seen Lady Anne!
> It really was very romantic:
>   He is such a talented man!

Society, as much in Praed as in Byron, became the subject of poetry. Yet romanticism had also nourished a Gothick theme, sometimes sentimental, often macabre. Thomas Hood (1799–1845) exploited this and wrote narrative poems of which the murder and detection described in 'Eugene Aram' remain graphic and compellingly readable. His taste for the bizarre inspired the epic-length social comedy *Miss Kilmansegg and her Precious Leg*, the story of a rich young lady who lost a leg and had a gold one fitted. Courted by men for the wealth of this artificial limb, Miss Kilmansegg married a foreign nobleman who at last beat her to death with it. The verdict was suicide because her own leg had killed her. More popular still was *Hood's Annual* and its verses, comic and macabre, like 'Mary's Ghost', with the apparition of a girl whose fresh corpse has been dug up by body-snatchers for an anatomy class. Eager children opened the *Annual* on Christmas morning and chuckled over its dark humour.

> You thought that I was buried deep,
>   Quite decent like and chary,

> But from her grave in Mary-bone
> They've come and bon'd your Mary.

For children and adults alike there were few collections to rival R.
H. Barham's *Ingoldsby Legends* with its poems like 'The Execu-
tion. A Sporting Anecdote', in which a group of young swells
make an all-night party to see a man hanged in the morning.

> My Lord Tomnoddy jump'd up at the news,
> 'Run to M'Fuse. And Lieutenant Tregooze,
> And run to Sir Carnaby Jenks of the Blues.
> Rope-dancers a score I've seen before—
> Madame Sacchi, Antonio, and Master Black-more;
> But to see a man swing at the end of a string,
> With his neck in a noose, will be quite a new thing.'

Hood, Barham and Praed exemplified the energy of English
writing in the raffish and turbulent period of the 1830s and early
1840s. Indeed, the young Charles Dickens was demonstrating a
parallel energy in prose, a similar blend of the grotesque and the
sentimental in *Oliver Twist* and *Nicholas Nickleby*. Hood, in his
most outlandish whimsy, kept alive one important strain of
romanticism. It also appeared in Thomas Lovell Beddoes (1803–
49) who worked on his poetic drama *Death's Jest-Book* for many
years until his suicide. His leg had been amputated as a result of
self-inflicted injuries and, before taking a fatal dose of curari,
Beddoes the medical man wrote, 'I ought to have been, among a
variety of other things, a good poet. Life was too great a bore on
one peg, and that a bad one.' The slangy Regency exterior
concealed a poetic intelligence whose echoes were woken in
Tennyson and Hardy.

> The wind dead leaves and snow
> Doth hurry to and fro
> And, once, a day shall break
> O'er the wave,
> When a storm of ghosts shall shake
> The dead, until they wake
> In the grave.

In a different sphere of English poetry, the 'peasant-poet' John Clare (1793–1864) wrote poems of rural life and personal reflection so limpid and easy that they made Wordsworth seem burdened by bourgeois self-consciousness. 'Graves of Infants', which came a little later in 1844, is a subject booby-trapped for the unwary by sentimentality and sermonising. Not so for John Clare. He never appears lugubrious or sententious.

> Infants have nought to weep for ere they die;
> All prayers are needless, beads they need not tell,
> White flowers their mourners are, nature their passing-bell.

The immediate successors of Byron and Shelley provided poetry whose panache made it, in the popular phrase, entertainment for all the family. Yet Hood or Praed scarcely seemed like figures of a new movement. Though they wrote of the modern world and contemporary society, they lacked true modernity. As Baudelaire remarked in his *Salon of 1846*, such writing was deficient in a most important respect. They looked outside themselves for the poetic landscape of human mentality and conduct, 'but it was only to be found within.'

III

A greater literary preoccupation with this inner landscape had been evident in the *Confessions* of Jean-Jacques Rousseau, published in 1782, and Wordsworth's long poem *The Prelude, or Growth of a Poet's Mind*, completed in 1805 though not published until 1850. Poetry as mood or state of mind was important equally to the interpretation of landscape in Tennyson or the personal debate on faith and doubt in Arnold or Clough. It was crucial to the mental analysis of moral character, which Browning practised upon his subjects.

As a modern development, this introspection characterised society as well as imaginative literature. John Henry Newman's *Apologia Pro Vita Sua* (1864) was as vivid a portrayal of the soul's progress as the poems of Clough and Arnold, though mingled with autobiography and polemic. But long before this, the science of mental analysis had changed under the impact of cultural and political revolution. The revolutionary regime in France after 1789 thought it intolerable that patients in asylums should be mocked like exhibits at a freak show. Moral therapy was pioneered by Philippe Pinel in his *Treatise on Insanity*, which appeared in an English translation in 1806. Pinel advocated the understanding of the minds and thoughts of the mentally sick. As so often, poetry represented one aspect of an intellectual development that was common to contemporary culture as a whole. By no means all mental states portrayed in post-romantic poetry were of madness, uncertainty, delusion or alienation. Yet these seemed to be characteristic of the new style, as its critics pointed out in the case of Tennyson's *Maud*, Browning's dramatic monologues or even the interior debates of Clough's poetry.

In that respect, innovations in poetry during the 1830s were less the work of the popular Hood or Praed than of the newcomer Tennyson and the unknown Browning. When Tennyson's *Poems, Chiefly Lyrical* appeared in 1830 he was twenty-one, a clever young man who had lately won the Chancellor's Medal at Cambridge for a poem on Timbuctoo. Even twelve years later, Leigh Hunt dismissed him as a literary dandy with 'a drawl of Bond Street' and reminded him sharply that he was not a boy any longer. But what struck an earlier reviewer, W. J. Fox in the *Westminster Review* in 1831, was Tennyson's scientific modernity. Fox allowed that the poems were 'very graceful', but that was nothing compared with their value to 'metaphysical science'. Tennyson's poetry represented a revolution 'in the analysis of particular states of mind; a work which is now performed with ease, power and utility as much increased, as in the grosser dissections of the anatomical lecturer.' The science of mental alienation, the most modern of all sciences at the time, formed an intellectual framework for Tennyson's lyricism. His landscapes were, to Fox, the landscapes of the mind. 'He climbs the pineal gland as if it were a hill.' A previous generation had regarded that gland as the seat of thought. There was no reason why the landscape should not be that of the healthy mind. Yet the alienist, by profession, investigated minds that were out of balance. There was certainly to be madness in Tennyson's great monodrama *Maud* and a drama of spiritual torment healed in *In Memoriam*.

In January 1836, Fox also published two anonymous poems in

his own magazine *The Monthly Repository*. They were paired as *Madhouse Cells*, when published in *Dramatic Lyrics*, six years later. One cell contained a frighteningly convincing theologian, 'Johannis Agricola in Meditation', who rejoiced that many good and virtuous people were to be tortured throughout eternity because God had predestined them to be damned. Though they had striven to be virtuous on earth, 'all their striving turned to sin', and their present agonies were a tribute to divine power. The next cell contained 'Porphyria's Lover', who had strangled Porphyria the night before and felt entirely at ease with his conscience and with God. The self-righteous cruelty of both speakers would have stamped them fifty years later as psychopaths, a term not used in 1836. They were among the first creations of the young Robert Browning.

Within a dozen years of Byron's death, English poetry in the hands of Tennyson and Browning had taken a giant stride into the modern world, though the wider public for poets like Hood was scarcely aware of this as yet. The strangler and the sadistic theologian were certainly not entertainment for all the family. Browning was to fight a thirty-year battle for critical recognition and then to be condemned for 'morbid anatomy'. Tennyson was more fortunate, if only because many of his poems appealed by their lyricism or, in the case of *In Memoriam*, by bringing comfort to an age in which mortality came frequently to families and relatively early in individual life.

In Arnold and Clough, the poetic landscape was to be that of the individual mind under the stress of faith and doubt. Arnold's vignettes of the external world, whether Rugby Chapel, or Dover Beach, or the Oxford idyll of 'The Scholar-Gipsy' were suffused by a mixture of elegiac resignation and moral energy. Swinburne represented a still younger generation. He was, as Edmund Gosse remembered him, the *enfant terrible* of the 1860s. 'He was not merely a poet but a flag; and not merely a flag but the Red Flag incarnate.' With him, post-romanticism seemed to run its course. The science which Fox had seen in Tennyson more than thirty-five years earlier was now applied to the analysis of sexual compulsions. Lesbianism, bisexuality, sado-masochism, rape and its revenge were served up with lyric brilliance to the drawing-room

and the deanery in *Poems and Ballads* (1866). It might seem a
long way since the more clinical use of 'moral therapy', by which
Philippe Pinel had endeavoured to enter the minds of his patients
at the Bicêtre asylum and lead them back to rationality. Yet it was
not entirely inappropriate, in the light of Swinburne's own
predilections, that one of his inmates should have been the
imprisoned Marquis de Sade.

The self-conscious modernity of some post-romantics made
Wordsworth or Coleridge seem as remote as Milton or Spenser.
Even under the most accomplished lyricism or elegiac landscape
there lay a hint of a mind ill at ease. If there was a single creed to
which this new generation might subscribe, it was voiced by
Browning's Bishop Blougram.

> Our interest's on the dangerous edge of things.
> The honest thief, the tender murderer,
> The superstitious atheist, demireps
> That love and save their souls in new French books –
> We watch while these in equilibrium keep
> The giddy line midway: one step aside,
> They're classed and done with.

The progress of the Victorian post-romantic soul was no longer to
be a steep and rocky ascent with a reward at the top for the
persistent and the virtuous. It seemed more often a mad caper on a
tightrope stretched above a Niagara of doubt and destruction.

IV

If the early 1830s paid direct homage to the figures of the
Romantic Revival, then Browning began as a self-proclaimed
disciple of Shelley, while Tennyson seemed to owe much to Keats.
Among the early poems, 'Mariana' has the air of a Keatsean ode,
though also evoking the flat fenland of Tennyson's boyhood, the
water-courses draining down to a windy shore and the cold line of
the North Sea. A minute pictorial vividness suggests the example
of the 'Ode to Autumn'.

> With blackest moss the flower-plots
>   Were thickly crusted, one and all:
> The rusted nails fell from the knots
>   That held the pear to the garden wall.

The early poems are characteristic of Tennyson as 'lord of landscape', in John Betjeman's phrase. But landscape was the means rather than the fulfilment of poetic sensibility. Like Keats, Tennyson also revisited the myths of chivalry and of the ancient world. Yet the voice and perception were those of the industrial age. He writes of 'Lady Godiva' from the perspective of a Victorian railway station, in a manner that might have been John Betjeman's own a century later.

> I waited for the train at Coventry:
> I hung with grooms and porters on the bridge,
> To watch the three tall spires; and there I shaped
> The city's ancient legend into this . . .

Even the hot-house voyeurism is that of Victorian prudery, Godiva naked on her horse, the walls full of chinks and holes, the gables overhead.

His reputation was secured by the publication in 1842 of his collected two-volume *Poems* 'by Alfred Tennyson'. In 1845, the prime minister, Sir Robert Peel, recommended him to the queen for a civil list pension as 'a poet of whose powers of imagination and expression many competent judges think highly'. In 1850, Lord John Russell, the new prime minister, told Prince Albert that 'Mr Tennyson is a fit person to be Poet Laureate.'

In the following year reputation swelled to fame with *In Memoriam*. The poem revealed a soul torn by the agony of religious doubt after the death of his greatest friend. Indeed, he seemed to care more for the death of Arthur Hallam than the possible death of God. Neither Wordsworth nor Baudelaire, let alone Shelley in *Adonais*, ever revealed the intensity of fear and longing displayed to the world in the fiftieth section of the great poem.

> Be near me when my light is low.
> When the blood creeps, and the nerves prick

> And tingle; and the heart is sick,
> And all the wheels of Being slow.

Fear and sorrow, faith overwhelmed by doubt, are the torments of the soul in the face of death and extinction. The interior landscape showed a desolation beyond anything in the Augustans or the Romantics. Here, if anywhere, was the precipice of the mind's destruction. Gerard Manley Hopkins recalled it in his sonnets of 1885.

> O the mind, mind has mountains; cliffs of fall
> Frightful, sheer, no-man-fathomed. Hold them cheap
> May who n'er hung there.

Yet faith triumphed and the Queen was among thousands who found consolation and hope in Tennyson's poem. After Prince Albert's death, Victoria recorded in her journal for 14 April 1862 a meeting on the Isle of Wight.

> I went down to see Tennyson, who is very peculiar-looking, tall, dark, with a fine head, long black flowing hair and a beard; oddly dressed but there is no affectation about him. I told him how much I admired his glorious lines to my precious Albert, and how much comfort I found in his *In Memoriam*. He was full of unbounded appreciation of beloved Albert. When he spoke of my own loss, of that to the nation, his eyes quite filled with tears.

Tennyson also had a taste for the macabre, as if to control his natural melancholy by reason and wit. A good many well-fleshed Victorian tenors had sung 'Come into the garden, Maud', with its lines, 'My heart would hear her and beat/ Were it earth in an earthy bed,' as a figure of speech. But those who read the whole poem knew the dark irony by which the lover in these lines was to be entombed in his madness. 'O me, why have they not buried me deep enough?' is the cry of a man who can still see and hear while the living tomb of the madhouse engulfs him.

As Poet Laureate after 1851, Tennyson was a great public voice of the age and the creator of Arthurian fantasy in *Idylls of the King*. Among his poetry for state occasions, the 'Ode on the Death of the Duke of Wellington' is a superb evocation of that chill and silent day when the hero of Waterloo and the Peninsula was borne through the packed streets of London to his resting place in St Paul's. Tennyson catches the mood, the sights and sounds, in a manner that any radio or television commentator might envy. From the booming of the minute-guns to the wintry light on the golden cross of the cathedral dome, the picture is complete.

He became the first popular poet in an age of mass-publishing. He could not walk in the summer gardens of his home at Farringford on the Isle of Wight without the heads of trippers gawping over the hedge. His verse was set to music and sung round thousands of drawing-room pianos. 'Crossing the Bar' was carved on tombstones and memorials. *The Tennyson Birthday Book* had an inspirational verse for each day of the year. He was chosen by Thomas Edison as a famous English voice to be recorded on wax. He died 1892 as the first Lord Tennyson and his funeral in Westminster Abbey was an all-ticket event.

v

Tennyson and Browning chose different paths through the post-romantic world. Yet they shared a central interest in the uneasy and the aberrant, the curious and the unbalanced. Both poets exploited legends and history, while remaining more modern in thought and expression than most novelists. Indeed, the novel usually tailored its material to what was suitable for children as well as adults. Poetry was less impeded by this restraint.

Of the major poets after 1824, Robert Browning was most self-consciously the heir of the first romantics. Shelley was his idol, to whom he paid tribute by such youthful poems as *Pauline* and *Paracelsus*. Yet it was also Browning who showed the most uncompromising modernist. In *Pippa Passes* (1843), he saw the world of northern Italy with the technique of a camera's eye that suggests the naturalism of European cinema more than a hundred years later. Naturalistically, he picks up the ordinary objects and decoration in the lovers' bedroom as the morning light comes through the shutter's chink. Ottima, from the bed, nags Sebald in play as he gets up.

Mind how you grope your way, though! How these tall
Naked geraniums straggle! Push the lattice –
Behind that frame! – Nay, do I bid you? – Sebald,
It shakes the dust down on me! Why, of course
The slide-bolt catches. – Well, are you content,
Or must I find you something else to spoil?

The couple have murdered Ottima's elderly husband. Sebald recalls the peasants laughing at the shutters of the bedroom still closed suggestively at noon, imagining how, 'The old man sleeps with the young wife!' Ottima draws to Sebald, her back naked against him, just inside the window to point out the black streak on the morning horizon that is the campanile of St Mark's in Venice. 'Look o'er my shoulder – follow my finger.'

Compared with the fiction of the 1840s, this poetry seemed to have leap-frogged into another century. Yet Browning's fame was long delayed. His poetry was thought obscure and his plays were failures. At last he combined dramatic dialogue and poetic realism in poems whose speakers seemed to step from the pages into life and to evoke the worlds they lived in, their holiness, sadism, art or treachery and above all their sexual love. Browning, more systematically than his contemporaries, anatomised those troubled saints and self-righteous tricksters, or lovers at the moment of falling in love or parting for ever. Some, like Porphyria's lover, speak with the patient and inflexible logic of the morally insane. Guido Franceschini in *The Ring and the Book* never doubts that he was right to kill Pompilia, whom he bought at twelve years old when she was still playing with her toys. She betrayed him with another man. To put such a wife to death was as much his right as to dispose of anything else he had purchased and found defective. Browning's preoccupation was, as he said in his poem 'Gold Hair. A Legend of Pornic',

> Original Sin,
> The Corruption of Man's Heart.

He must let his monsters – and his saints – speak for themselves. The author would not intervene to reassure or comfort the reader.

Not surprisingly, Julia Wedgwood and others among

Browning's friends found his interest in 'morbid anatomy' repellent. He had taken Hugo's belief in the grotesque to its limit. But he also exemplified perfectly the post-romantic as the modern. He would anticipate the cinema in *Pippa Passes*, or he might rival Zola and Maupassant in a bizarre modern tale of sexual infatuation and religious guilt, *Red Cotton Night-Cap Country*, in 1873.

Not a single copy of his first book *Pauline* was sold. *Paracelsus*, published in 1835 was a little better received. In 1840, Browning published what was intended to be his masterwork, the long poem *Sordello*. The press regarded it with dismay and exasperation. Most could not begin to understand the poem. It was a public disaster which sank Browning's uncertain reputation and tagged him with 'obscurity' for the rest of his life. Five hundred copies were printed. Fifteen years later only 157 had been sold. The publisher Edward Moxon agreed to issue his books so long as the poet's father paid the costs. By the time that Browning published *Men and Women*, one of the most splendid collections in the whole of English poetry, he was forty-three. He had still earned nothing from his work and the critical reception of the book was tepid. Even nine years later, in 1864 when he was fifty-two, his royalty payment amounted to only £15.

Recognition was so long delayed that when it came, in the 1860s, he seemed like a new poet and a successor to the fame of Tennyson. He appeared as a truly 'modern' writer. The great drama of his 'Roman murder case' in *The Ring and the Book* (1868–9) made his reputation at last. Based on a trial of 1698, when Guido Franceschini defended his right to kill his supposedly adulterous wife, it was a dark-coloured story of wickedness and nobility in which the participants themselves were the voices. Even his old enemy, the *Athenaeum*, conceded that this tale of murder and virtue, brutality and humanity, was 'the most precious and profound spiritual treasure that England has produced since the days of Shakespeare'. Contrary to the notion that all true art is non-commercial, Browning began to make some money from his writing.

He shrugged off criticism of his interest in morbidity and pursued a curiosity over objects 'that have helped great murderers to their purposes'. The 'devilishness' of human beings fascinated him. He lavished imaginative skill on the subtle Genoese daggers, whose teeth ripped a wound wider as the blade was drawn from its victim. He noted the moral paradox of embellishing knives and whips as if to add art to pain and murder. Yet he was one of the first and most vociferous opponents of the use of animals for medical experiments. He was a convinced Liberal in politics and a Christian in religion. When he was buried in Westminster Abbey, Henry James wrote, 'A good many oddities and a good many great writers have been entombed in the Abbey, but none of the odd ones have been so great and none of the great ones so odd.'

Browning never received adulation to match Tennyson. For years he remained in eclipse, emerging at last as a great modernist of the Victorian period and certainly the great post-romantic. It was not his Victorianism that made him so but his affinity with Europeanism, past and present. To read him was to recall Florence and the Medici, but also Byron and Sade, Hugo and Baudelaire.

VI

Arnold lacked the range and intensity of his two great predecessors. He had an elegiac gift and could evoke the pastoral beauty of Victorian Oxford or the sublime austerity of Rugby Chapel with a skill that also owed something to the example of Keats. In 'The Scholar-Gipsy' the sound of Oxford river water running against the boat's movement is conveyed with the immediacy of Keats.

> Crossing the stripling Thames at Bab-lock-hithe,
> Trailing in the cool stream thy fingers wet,
> As the punt's rope chops round.

Yet Arnold was a meditative philosopher in verse and, of all the major Victorians, perhaps the most obvious descendant of Wordsworth. Like Wordsworth, he was a poet of proclaimed human sympathies, which appeared as much in his 'Shakespeare' sonnet as in 'A Gipsy Child by the Seashore'. Perhaps of all his contemporaries he came closest to embodying the philosopher-poet in his pursuit of poetry as 'a criticism of life'.

In Arnold, the personal debate is decorous and subdued. He is the voice of honest doubt but not of desperation. There are no fervent outbursts as there had been during *In Memoriam*. Arnold is agreeable and intelligent. His nerves do not prick and tingle, nor is his heart sick at the thought of death and extinction, as Tennyson claimed to be. Arnold's spiritual struggle is civilised and urbane. His poems are a beautiful place to be. The dreaming spires and the Oxford countryside are a heaven in the mind, without God or angels, as if to compensate for the Christian heaven that Arnold cannot allow himself.

He does not seem to suffer as much as a Christian believer like Gerard Manley Hopkins in the so-called 'Sonnets of Desolation'. As T. S. Eliot remarked in 1933, Arnold had 'neither walked in hell nor been rapt to heaven'. But he shows a humanity and an ability to capture character and nature as a painter might. He combines the influences of romanticism with an anticipation of modernity. In a poem like 'A Summer Night', there are lines and phrases that look forward to the urban scenes of English poetry in the 1920s.

Arnold's education at Rugby and Balliol left him with every classical verse-form and metre at his disposal. When Charles Kingsley reviewed *The Strayed Reveller and Other Poems* in 1849, he remarked that the author, known only as 'A', was evidently 'a scholar, a gentleman, and a true poet. The short pieces which it contains show care and thought, delicate finish, and an almost faultless severity of language and metre.'

VII

Friendship and intellectual preoccupation linked Arnold and Clough. Both were the products of Rugby School as reformed by Thomas Arnold, the earnest and questioning Christian father of the poet. Both were at Balliol in the first years of Benjamin Jowett's influence as Fellow. Both were doubters in the religious debate of mid-century. But Arnold's 'high seriousness' gave way in Clough to apparent moments of cynicism, amusement, and downright flippancy.

Clough died at forty-two, in 1861, commemorated by Arnold

in 'Thyrsis'. At one extreme, he was a poet of spiritual drama in 'Easter Day', his realisation while walking 'the great sinful streets of Naples', that, 'Christ is not risen.' But in the second part of the poem 'Hope conquers cowardice.' Christ is risen, after all, in 'the true creed', which Clough does not precisely define.

Clough represented what his biographer Lady Chorley was to call, 'the uncommitted mind'. But a life of open-minded doubt proved more destructive to poetry than either Browning's firm Christian belief or Shelley's doctrinaire atheism. Clough practised the poetry of disengagement, as Byron sometimes did. Like Byron, he became a gifted and amused observer of fashionable society. His long poems are novels of character in verse. *The Bothie of Tober-na-Vuolich* is a laconic account of an Oxford reading-party and a romance in the Highlands during the long vacation. *Amours de Voyage* is an exchange of letters describing an English family in Rome. He wrote them in the metre of Latin hexametres, a rhythm that rarely gives solemnity to English poetry.

Clough at his best was urbane and sophisticated, an acute and witty observer of humanity. In his major poems, like 'Dipsychus', he allows sceptical and religious arguments their separate voices. He might almost have believed either voice, though he was assumed to be Faust fighting off Mephistopheles. He gave the impression of himself as a man who had been to the 'dangerous edge of things' and had no intention of taking the plunge. There was, of course, little intellectual difficulty in the social comedy of *The Bothie of Tober-na-Vuolich*, or *Amours de Voyage*, which represented the polished voice of Clough's writing. Elsewhere Clough presented a simple yet confounding problem to a good many readers. Did he mean what he said? Or, how far did he mean it?

In the poetry of intellectual debate, on matters of religion and morality, Clough was Jekyll and Hyde. Indeed he indulged in what Stevenson's Dr Jekyll would have recognised as intellectual and spiritual 'dualism'. In a long poem like 'Dipsychus' or the shorter poem 'Easter Day', Clough alternates voices and moods. In one voice, atheism or immorality is freely advocated. A second voice may contradict them, but they are stated without reservation.

> Christ is not risen, no—
> > He lies and moulders low;
> Christ is not risen!

Other heresies appear when, against all the instincts of high-minded Victorian philanthropy, the morality of human indifference is urged upon Dipsychus by the Spirit in 'How pleasant it is to have money'. Is a man always to deny himself pleasure because there is somewhere a poor man who cannot afford it?

> Who's to enjoy at all, pray let us hear?
> You won't; he can't! Oh, no more fuss!
> What's it to him, or he to us?

The rich man who enjoys his pleasure and pays for it spreads his wealth. Is that not better than puritanical abstinence?

Was this a dramatic device, as Milton put blasphemy into the mouths of the fallen angels in *Paradise Lost*? Or did Clough allow a real possibility of truth which denied religious and moral orthodoxy? He seemed an upholder of established values, though with that hint of moral ambiguity appropriate to a post-romantic age. It recalls Baudelaire's 'Les Litanies de Satan' in *Fleurs du Mal*, 'O Satan, prends pitié de ma longue misère!' In Clough too the reader feels at times the rock of moral absolutism shifting beneath the feet.

VIII

To a new generation, the philosophising of Clough and the earnestness of Matthew Arnold had grown unappealing. Swinburne, whom Arnold called a 'pseudo-Shelley', pronounced its epitaph, dismissing Arnold as a 'pseudo-Wordsworth' for good measure.

> Literary history will hardly care to remember or to register the fact that there was a bad poet named Clough, whom his friends found it useless to puff: for the public, if dull, has not quite such a skull as belongs to believers in Clough.

Swinburne was born in 1837, the year of Victoria's accession, a good quarter of a century after Tennyson and Browning. Educated at Eton and Balliol, son of an admiral, he had the patrician credentials of a true revolutionary. In lyricism, colour and imagery, rhythm and language, he was a born poet. Coming of age in the 1860s, he put his gifts at the service of a rebellion that was political, social, moral and – not least – sexual. He worshipped Mazzini's revolution and the fight for Italian independence. He proclaimed the beauty of female bisexuality in Gautier's *Mademoiselle de Maupin* and the splendour of the condemned poems in Baudelaire's *Fleurs du Mal*. More loudly, he announced the genius and example of the Marquis de Sade, though without having read much of Sade. The whiff of Bohemia became a pungent odour in his own life and work.

Murder and rape and sado-masochism were thrust upon startled readers of *Poems and Ballads* in 1866. Even the most innocuous-sounding poems, like 'Itylus', were booby-trapped with mythological references to make any young lady and her mama blush to the roots of their hair if they understood them. The outraged response of Victorian moralists was the stuff of life to the shrill-voiced poet with bright red hair that gave him the look of a cockatoo. Privately, he circulated his novelettes in which Queen Victoria proved to be the twin of a Haymarket prostitute, while Victoria herself confessed to having been seduced by William Wordsworth. She revealed that her sexual passion had been inflamed by Wordsworth's reading of his poem *The Excursion*, safely short-listed among the most tedious in the English language.

In his other pornographic writing, Swinburne sought to turn the schoolroom into a brothel. He nearly killed himself by chronic brandy-drinking. But the *enfant terrible* became a tame middle-aged poet. He had a lyric gift and a pure brilliance that he squandered as if in a nursery tantrum. But there were passages in *Atalanta in Calydon* and pieces in *Poems and Ballads* that deserved all the praise of his followers. Like Wordsworth and Coleridge, he was burnt out long before his death in 1909 but he burnt with a flame in which many contemporaries saw the brightest falling star of the age.

It was characteristic of Swinburne that in the debate on religious faith and doubt he generated more heat than light. Not for him Tennyson's self-torment in *In Memoriam* nor the elegiac wistfulness of Arnold, certainly not the fine dramatic ironies of Browning in poems like 'Bishop Blougram's Apology', or 'Cleon', or 'Karshish'. Browning was, as he said, 'very sure of God'. Swinburne claimed to be the opposite and swung into vigorous verse in his 'Hymn to Proserpine', marking the proclamation of the Christian faith in Rome.

> Thou hast conquered, O pale Galilean; the world has
>   grown grey from thy breath;
> We have drunken of things Lethean, and fed on the
>   fullness of death.
> Laurel is green for a season, and love is sweet for
>   a day;
> But love grows bitter with treason, and laurel outlives
>   not May.
> Sleep, shall we sleep after all? For the world is not
>   sweet in the end;
> For the old faiths loosen and fall, the new years ruin
>   and rend.
> Fate is a sea without shore, and the soul is a rock that
>   abides;
> But her ears are vexed with the roar and her face with
>   the foam of the tides.
> O lips that the live blood faints in, the leavings of
>   racks and rods!
> O ghastly glories of saints, dead limbs of gibbeted
>   Gods!
> Though all men abase them before you in spirit, and
>   all knees bend,
> I kneel not neither adore you, but standing look to
>   the end.

Swinburne's iconoclastic verse was splendid and spirited stuff, chanted by Cambridge undergraduates in the 1860s as they swept in rebellion, arm-in-arm along the pavements, scattering their startled elders. But it carried the philosophical debate no further in any direction. It was perhaps appropriate that the youthful Swinburne should regard God primarily as yet another figure of authority to be defied, the Deity as an unsympathetic public school housemaster, or Thomas Arnold of Rugby on a celestial scale.

With Swinburne's death in 1909, it seemed that a great post-romantic age had run its course. Arnold Bennett, at the beginning of his own fame as a novelist, stood with the crowds outside the house in Putney during the last hours of the poet's life. He reported the scene with a sense of occasion.

A few yards beyond where the autobuses turned was a certain house with lighted upper windows, and in that house the greatest lyric versifier that England ever had, and one of the great poets of the whole world and of all ages, was dying . . . The next day all the shops were open and hundreds of fatigued assistants were pouring out their exhaustless patience on thousands of urgent and bright women; and flags waved on high, and the gutters were banked with yellow and white flowers, and the air was brisk and the roadways were clean. The very vital spirit of energy seemed to have scattered the breath of life generously, so that all were intoxicated by it in the gay sunshine. He was dead then. The waving posters said it.

DONALD THOMAS

BIOGRAPHICAL NOTES

TENNYSON, Alfred, 1st Baron Tennyson (1809–92) Born Somersby, Lincolnshire; friendship with Arthur Hallam at Trinity College, Cambridge; Chancellor's Medal for English Verse, 1829; *Poems by Two Brothers*, 1827; *Poems, Chiefly Lyrical*, 1830; death of Hallam, 1833; collected *Poems*, 1842; Civil List Pension on recommendation of Sir Robert Peel, 1845; *In Memoriam*, 1850; marriage to Emily Sellwood after long engagement, 1850; Poet Laureate, 1850; home at Farringford, Isle of Wight, 1853; *Maud*, 1855; *Enoch Arden*, 1864; second home at Aldworth, 1869; created Baron Tennyson, 1883; *Death of Oenone*, 1892; died at Aldworth, 1892

BROWNING, Robert (1812–89) Born Camberwell, London; privately educated; *Pauline*, 1832; *Paracelsus*, 1835; plays include *Strafford*, an historical tragedy produced at Covent Garden, 1837; failure of *Sordello*, 1840; marriage to Elizabeth Barrett, 1846; life in Italy, 1846–61; *Christmas Eve and Easter Day*, 1850; *Men and Women*, 1855; death of Elizabeth Barrett Browning and Browning's return to England, 1861; *Dramatis Personae*, 1864; *The Ring and the Book*, 1868–9; *Red Cotton Night-Cap Country*, 1873; *Parleyings with Certain People of Importance in their Day*, 1887; died at Venice, 1889

ARNOLD, Matthew (1822–88) Son of Thomas Arnold, headmaster of Rugby; educated Rugby, Winchester, and Balliol; Newdigate prize for English Verse, 1843; Fellow of Oriel, 1845; *The Strayed Reveller, and other Poems*, 1849; Inspector of Schools, 1851; *Empedocles on Etna and other Poems*, 1852; *Poems*, 1853; *Poems, Second Series*, 1855; Professor of Poetry at Oxford, 1857–67; *Essays in Criticism*, 1865; *New Poems*, 1867; *Culture and Anarchy*, 1869; *Essays in Criticism: Second Series*, 1888; died suddenly of heart failure, 1888

CLOUGH, Arthur Hugh (1819–61) Born Liverpool; educated Rugby and Balliol; Fellow of Oriel, 1841–8; *The Bothie of Tober-na-Vuolich*, 1848; Principal, University Hall, London, 1849–52; *Ambarvalia* [with Thomas Burbidge], 1849; Examiner in the Education Office, 1853; died at Florence, 1861; commemorated by Matthew Arnold in 'Thyrsis'; posthumous publications included *Poems*, 1862, and *Letters and Remains of Arthur Hugh Clough*, 1865

SWINBURNE, Algernon Charles (1837–1909) Born Grosvenor Place, London; educated Eton and Balliol; early friendships with William Morris, Dante Gabriel Rossetti and George Meredith; *Atalanta in Calydon*, 1865; *Poems and Ballads*, 1866, published by John Camden Hotton after being withdrawn by Moxon for fear of prosecution; *A Song of Italy*, 1867; support for Mazzini and Italian independence; *Songs Before Sunrise*, 1871; *Poems and Ballads: Second Series*, 1878; *Tristram of Lyonesse*, 1882; under the superintendence of Theodore Watts-Dunton at 2, The Pines, Putney, 1879–1909, death at Putney, 1909

TENNYSON

MARIANA

First published in *Poems, Chiefly Lyrical*, 1830, 'Mariana' was described by Arthur Hallam in 1831 as a study of 'desolate loneliness' on the part of a woman waiting for her lover and a 'transition of the poet into Mariana's feelings'. The Duke in Shakespeare's *Measure for Measure*, III, i, 278, remarks, 'I will presently to St Luke's; there at the moated grange, resides the dejected Mariana.' Somersby and the Lincolnshire fens of his childhood are Tennyson's landscape, the poem sharing the pictorial immediacy of Keats and an anticipation of Pre-Raphaelite painting.

'Mariana in the moated grange.' – *Measure for Measure*.

In the darkest of times, love prevails

With blackest moss the flower-plots
    Were thickly crusted, one and all:
The rusted nails fell from the knots
    That held the pear to the garden-wall.
The broken sheds look'd sad and strange:
    Unlifted was the clinking latch;
    Weeded and worn the ancient thatch — *roof of straw*
Upon the lonely moated grange. — *country house*
    water filled ditch
    She only said, 'My life is dreary,
      He cometh not,' she said;
    She said, 'I am aweary, aweary, – *tired*
      I would that I were dead!'

Her tears fell with the dews at even;
    Her tears fell ere the dews were dried;
She could not look on the sweet heaven,
    Either at morn or eventide.
After the flitting of the bats,
    When thickest dark did trance the sky,

She drew her casement-curtain by,
And glanced athwart the glooming flats.
 She only said, 'The night is dreary,
  He cometh not,' she said;
 She said, 'I am aweary, aweary,
  I would that I were dead!'

Upon the middle of the night,
 Waking she heard the night-fowl crow:
The cock sung out an hour ere light:
 From the dark fen the oxen's low
Came to her: without hope of change,
 In sleep she seem'd to walk forlorn,
 Till cold winds woke the grey-eyed morn
About the lonely moated grange.
 She only said, 'The day is dreary,
  He cometh not,' she said;
 She said, 'I am aweary, aweary,
  I would that I were dead!'

About a stone-cast from the wall
 A sluice with blacken'd waters slept,
And o'er it many, round and small,
 The cluster'd marish-mosses crept.
Hard by a poplar shook alway,
 All silver-green with gnarled bark:
 For leagues no other tree did mark
The level waste, the rounding grey.
 She only said, 'My life is dreary,
  He cometh not,' she said;
 She said, 'I am aweary, aweary,
  I would that I were dead!'

And ever when the moon was low,
 And the shrill winds were up and away,
In the white curtain, to and fro,
 She saw the gusty shadow sway.
But when the moon was very low,
 And wild winds bound within their cell,

The shadow of the poplar fell
Upon her bed, across her brow.
　　She only said, 'The night is dreary,
　　　He cometh not,' she said;
　　She said, 'I am aweary, aweary,
　　　I would that I were dead!'

All day within the dreamy house,
　The doors upon their hinges creak'd;
The blue fly sung in the pane; the mouse
　Behind the mouldering wainscot shriek'd,
Or from the crevice peer'd about.
　Old faces glimmer'd thro' the doors,
　Old footsteps trod the upper floors,
Old voices called her from without.
　　She only said, 'My life is dreary,
　　　He cometh not,' she said;
　　She said, 'I am aweary, aweary,
　　　I would that I were dead!'

The sparrow's chirrup on the roof,
　The slow clock ticking, and the sound
Which to the wooing wind aloof
　The poplar made, did all confound
Her sense; but most she loathed the hour
　When the thick-moted sunbeam lay
　Athwart the chambers, and the day
Was sloping toward his western bower.
　　Then, said she, 'I am very dreary,
　　　He will not come,' she said;
　　She wept, 'I am aweary, aweary,
　　　Oh God, that I were dead!'

A CHARACTER

According to Edward Fitzgerald, Tennyson as a Cambridge undergraduate was ridiculed for his rustic appearance by 'a very plausible, parliament-like, self-satisfied speaker at the Union Debating Society'. The young Tennyson struck back in verse at his smooth, pretentious and well-heeled adversary.

With a half-glance upon the sky
At night he said, 'The wanderings
Of this most intricate Universe
Teach me the nothingness of things.'
Yet could not all creation pierce
Beyond the bottom of his eye.

He spake of beauty: that the dull
Saw no divinity in grass,
Life in dead stones, or spirit in air;
Then looking as 'twere in a glass,
He smooth'd his chin and sleek'd his hair,
And said the earth was beautiful.

He spake of virtue: not the gods
More purely, when they wish to charm
Pallas and Juno sitting by:
And with a sweeping of the arm,
And a lack-lustre dead-blue eye,
Devolved his rounded periods.

Most delicately hour by hour
He canvass'd human mysteries,
And trod on silk, as if the winds
Blew his own praises in his eyes,
And stood aloof from other minds
In impotence of fancied power.

With lips depress'd as he were meek,
Himself unto himself he sold:
Upon himself himself did feed:
Quiet, dispassionate, and cold,
And other than his form of creed,
With chisell'd features clear and sleek.

THE LADY OF SHALOTT

Published in *Poems* by Alfred Tennyson, 1833, the story corresponds to the death of the Lady of Astolat from unrequited love for Sir Lancelot in Malory's *Morte d'Arthur*, and the passing of her funeral barge by the royal palace. Tennyson combines English landscape with an anticipation of Pre-Raphaelite colour and symbolism. The subject was taken for a painting by Holman Hunt and a pen and ink drawing by Elizabeth Siddal, mistress and wife of Dante Gabriel Rossetti.

PART I

On either side the river lie
Long fields of barley and of rye,
That clothe the wold and meet the sky;
And thro' the field the road runs by
  To many-tower'd Camelot;
And up and down the people go,
Gazing where the lilies blow
Round an island there below,
  The island of Shalott.

Willows whiten, aspens quiver,
Little breezes dusk and shiver
Thro' the wave that runs for ever
By the island in the river
  Flowing down to Camelot.
Four grey walls, and four grey towers,
Overlook a space of flowers,
And the silent isle imbowers
  The Lady of Shalott.

By the margin, willow-veil'd,
Slide the heavy barges trail'd
By slow horses; and unhail'd
The shallop flitteth silken-sail'd
        Skimming down to Camelot:
But who hath seen her wave her hand?
Or at the casement seen her stand?
Or is she known in all the land,
        The Lady of Shalott?

Only reapers, reaping early
In among the bearded barley,
Hear a song that echoes cheerly
From the river winding clearly,
        Down to tower'd Camelot:
And by the moon the reaper weary,
Piling sheaves in uplands airy,
Listening, whispers ''Tis the fairy
        Lady of Shalott.'

PART II

There she weaves by night and day
A magic web with colours gay.
She has heard a whisper say,
A curse is on her if she stay
        To look down to Camelot.
She knows not what the curse may be,
And so she weaveth steadily,
And little other care hath she,
        The Lady of Shalott.

And moving thro' a mirror clear
That hangs before her all the year,
Shadows of the world appear.
There she sees the highway near
        Winding down to Camelot:
There the river eddy whirls,
And there the surly village-churls,

And the red cloaks of market girls,
  Pass onward from Shalott.

Sometimes a troop of damsels glad,
An abbot on an ambling pad,
Sometimes a curly shepherd-lad,
Or long-hair'd page in crimson clad,
  Goes by to tower'd Camelot;
And sometimes thro' the mirror blue
The knights come riding two and two:
She hath no loyal knight and true,
  The Lady of Shalott.

But in her web she still delights
To weave the mirror's magic sights,
For often thro' the silent nights
A funeral, with plumes and lights,
  And music, went to Camelot:
Or when the moon was overhead,
Came two young lovers lately wed;
'I am half sick of shadows,' said
  The Lady of Shalott.

PART III

A bow-shot from her bower-eaves,
He rode between the barley-sheaves,
The sun came dazzling thro' the leaves,
And flamed upon the brazen greaves
  Of bold Sir Lancelot.
A red-cross knight for ever kneel'd
To a lady in his shield,
That sparkled on the yellow field,
  Beside remote Shalott.

The gemmy bridle glitter'd free,
Like to some branch of stars we see
Hung in the golden Galaxy.
The bridle bells rang merrily
  As he rode down to Camelot:

And from his blazon'd baldric slung
A mighty silver bugle hung,
And as he rode his armour rung,
      Beside remote Shalott.

All in the blue unclouded weather
Thick-jewell'd shone the saddle-leather,
The helmet and the helmet-feather
Burn'd like one burning flame together,
      As he rode down to Camelot.
As often thro' the purple night,
Below the starry clusters bright,
Some bearded meteor, trailing light,
      Moves over still Shalott.

His broad clear brow in sunlight glow'd;
On burnish'd hooves his war-horse trode;
From underneath his helmet flow'd
His coal-black curls as on he rode,
      As he rode down to Camelot.
From the bank and from the river
He flash'd into the crystal mirror,
'Tirra lirra,' by the river
      Sang Sir Lancelot.

She left the web, she left the loom,
She made three paces thro' the room,
She saw the water-lily bloom,
She saw the helmet and the plume,
      She look'd down to Camelot.
Out flew the web and floated wide;
The mirror crack'd from side to side;
'The curse is come upon me,' cried
      The Lady of Shalott.

PART IV

In the stormy east-wind straining,
The pale yellow woods were waning,

The broad stream in his banks complaining,
Heavily the low sky raining
           Over tower'd Camelot;
Down she came and found a boat
Beneath a willow left afloat,
And round about the prow she wrote
        The Lady of Shalott.

And down the river's dim expanse –
Like some bold seër in a trance,
Seeing all his own mischance –
With a glassy countenance
           Did she look to Camelot.
And at the closing of the day
She loosed the chain, and down she lay;
The broad stream bore her far away,
           The Lady of Shalott.

Lying, robed in snowy white
That loosely flew to left and right –
The leaves upon her falling light –
Thro' the noises of the night
           She floated down to Camelot:
And as the boat-head wound along
The willowy hills and fields among,
They heard her singing her last song,
           The Lady of Shalott.

Heard a carol, mournful, holy,
Chanted loudly, chanted lowly,
Till her blood was frozen slowly,
And her eyes were darken'd wholly,
           Turn'd to tower'd Camelot.
For ere she reach'd upon the tide
The first house by the water-side,
Singing in her song she died,
           The Lady of Shalott.

Under tower and balcony,
By garden-wall and gallery,

A gleaming shape she floated by,
Dead-pale between the houses high,
   Silent into Camelot.
Out upon the wharfs they came,
Knight and burgher, lord and dame,
And round the prow they read her name,
   The Lady of Shalott.

Who is this? and what is here?
And in the lighted palace near
Died the sound of royal cheer;
And they cross'd themselves for fear,
   All the knights at Camelot:
But Lancelot mused a little space;
He said, 'She has a lovely face;
God in his mercy lend her grace,
   The Lady of Shalott.'

THE LOTOS-EATERS

Also published in 1833, this poem is based on a passage in Homer's *Odyssey*, Book IX. Ulysses and his crew, returning to Ithaca from the Trojan War, put ashore in the land of the Lotos-Eaters. The 'honey-sweet fruit', says Homer, enchants and beguiles the man who feeds on it, sapping his resolve and making him 'forgetful of his homeward journey', to which duty should call him.

'Courage!' he said, and pointed toward the land,
'This mounting wave will roll us shoreward soon.'
In the afternoon they came unto a land
In which it seemed always afternoon.
All round the coast the languid air did swoon,
Breathing like one that hath a weary dream.
Full-faced above the valley stood the moon;
And like a downward smoke, the slender stream
Along the cliff to fall and pause and fall did seem.

A land of streams! some, like a downward smoke,
Slow-dropping veils of thinnest lawn, did go;
And some thro' wavering lights and shadows broke,
Rolling a slumbrous sheet of foam below.
They saw the gleaming river seaward flow
From the inner land: far off, three mountain-tops,
Three silent pinnacles of aged snow,
Stood sunset-flush'd: and, dew'd with showery drops,
Up-clomb the shadowy pine above the woven copse.

The charmed sunset linger'd low adown
In the red West: thro' mountain clefts the dale
Was seen far inland, and the yellow down
Border'd with palm, and many a winding vale

And meadow, set with slender galingale;
A land where all things always seem'd the same!
And round about the keel with faces pale,
Dark faces pale against that rosy flame,
The mild-eyed melancholy Lotos-eaters came.

Branches they bore of that enchanted stem,
Laden with flower and fruit, whereof they gave
To each, but whoso did receive of them,
And taste, to him the gushing of the wave
Far far away did seem to mourn and rave
On alien shores; and if his fellow spake,
His voice was thin, as voices from the grave;
And deep-asleep he seem'd, yet all awake,
And music in his ears his beating heart did make.

They sat them down upon the yellow sand,
Between the sun and moon upon the shore;
And sweet it was to dream of Fatherland,
Of child, and wife, and slave; but evermore
Most weary seem'd the sea, weary the oar,
Weary the wandering fields of barren foam.
Then some one said, 'We will return no more;'
And all at once they sang, 'Our island home
Is far beyond the wave; we will no longer roam.'

CHORIC SONG

I

There is sweet music here that softer falls
Than petals from blown roses on the grass,
Or night-dews on still waters between walls
Of shadowy granite, in a gleaming pass;
Music that gentlier on the spirit lies,
Than tir'd eyelids upon tir'd eyes;
Music that brings sweet sleep down from the blissful
  skies.
Here are cool mosses deep,

And thro' the moss the ivies creep,
And in the stream the long-leaved flowers weep,
And from the craggy ledge the poppy hangs in sleep.

II

Why are we weigh'd upon with heaviness,
And utterly consumed with sharp distress,
While all things else have rest from weariness?
All things have rest: why should we toil alone,
We only toil, who are the first of things,
And make perpetual moan,
Still from one sorrow to another thrown:
Nor ever fold our wings,
And cease from wanderings,
Nor steep our brows in slumber's holy balm;
Nor hearken what the inner spirit sings,
'There is no joy but calm!'
Why should we only toil, the roof and crown of things?

III

Lo! in the middle of the wood,
The folded leaf is woo'd from out the bud
With winds upon the branch, and there
Grows green and broad, and takes no care,
Sun-steep'd at noon, and in the moon
Nightly dew-fed; and turning yellow
Falls, and floats adown the air.
Lo! sweeten'd with the summer light,
The full-juiced apple, waxing over-mellow,
Drops in a silent autumn night.
All its allotted length of days,
The flower ripens in its place,
Ripens and fades, and falls, and hath no toil,
Fast-rooted in the fruitful soil.

IV

Hateful is the dark-blue sky,
Vaulted o'er the dark-blue sea.

Death is the end of life; ah, why
Should life all labour be?
Let us alone. Time driveth onward fast
And in a little while our lips are dumb.
Let us alone. What is it that will last?
All things are taken from us, and become
Portions and parcels of the dreadful Past.
Let us alone. What pleasure can we have
To war with evil? Is there any peace
In ever climbing up the climbing wave?
All things have rest, and ripen toward the grave
In silence; ripen, fall and cease:
Give us long rest or death, dark death, or dreamful ease.

V

How sweet it were, hearing the downward stream,
With half-shut eyes ever to seem
Falling asleep in a half-dream!
To dream and dream, like yonder amber light,
Which will not leave the myrrh-bush on the height;
To hear each other's whisper'd speech;
Eating the Lotos day by day,
To watch the crisping ripples on the beach,
And tender curving lines of creamy spray;
To lend our hearts and spirits wholly
To the influence of mild-minded melancholy;
To muse and brood and live again in memory,
With those old faces of our infancy
Heap'd over with a mound of grass,
Two handfuls of white dust, shut in an urn of brass!

VI

Dear is the memory of our wedded lives,
And dear the last embraces of our wives
And their warm tears: but all hath suffer'd change;
For surely now our household hearths are cold:
Our sons inherit us: our looks are strange:
And we should come like ghosts to trouble joy.

Or else the island princes over-bold
Have eat our substance, and the minstrel sings
Before them of the ten-years' war in Troy,
And our great deeds, as half-forgotten things.
Is there confusion in the little isle?
Let what is broken so remain.
The Gods are hard to reconcile:
'Tis hard to settle order once again.
There is confusion worse than death,
Trouble on trouble, pain on pain,
Long labour unto aged breath,
Sore tasks to hearts worn out with many wars
And eyes grown dim with gazing on the pilot-stars.

VII

But, propt on beds of amaranth and moly,
How sweet (while warm airs lull us, blowing lowly)
With half-dropt eyelids still,
Beneath a heaven dark and holy,
To watch the long bright river drawing slowly
His waters from the purple hill –
To hear the dewy echoes calling
From cave to cave thro' the thick-twined vine –
To watch the emerald-colour'd water falling
Thro' many a wov'n acanthus-wreath divine!
Only to hear and see the far-off sparkling brine,
Only to hear were sweet, stretch'd out beneath the pine.

VIII

The Lotos blooms below the barren peak:
The Lotos blows by every winding creek:
All day the wind breathes low with mellower tone:
Thro' every hollow cave and alley lone
Round and round the spicy downs the yellow Lotos-dust
    is blown.
We have had enough of action, and of motion we,
Roll'd to starboard, roll'd to larboard, when the surge
    was seething free,

Where the wallowing monster spouted his foam-fountains in
    the sea.
Let us swear an oath, and keep it with an equal mind,
In the hollow Lotos-land to live and lie reclined
On the hills like Gods together, careless of mankind.
For they lie beside their nectar, and the bolts are hurl'd
Far below them in the valleys, and the clouds are lightly curl'd
Round their golden houses, girdled with the gleaming world:
Where they smile in secret, looking over wasted lands,
Blight and famine, plague and earthquake, roaring deeps and
    fiery sands,
Clanging fights, and flaming towns, and sinking ships, and
    praying hands.
But they smile, they find a music centred in a doleful song
Steaming up, a lamentation and an ancient tale of wrong,
Like a tale of little meaning tho' the words are strong;
Chanted from an ill-used race of men that cleave the soil,
Sow the seed, and reap the harvest with enduring toil,
Storing yearly little dues of wheat, and wine and oil;
Till they perish and they suffer – some, 'tis whisper'd – down in
    hell
Suffer endless anguish, others in Elysian valleys dwell,
Resting weary limbs at last on beds of asphodel.
Surely, surely, slumber is more sweet than toil, the shore
Than labour in the deep mid-ocean, wind and wave and oar;
Oh rest ye, brother mariners, we will not wander more.

MORTE D'ARTHUR

Based on Malory's account in Book XXI of the *Morte d'Arthur*, Tennyson's poem describes the last journey of King Arthur, mortally wounded in battle in Lyoness, the fabled land submerged between Land's End and the Scilly Islands. He is borne by barge to be buried at Avalon, in reality Glastonbury. The sword Excalibur is to be returned by Sir Bedivere to the lake from which Arthur received it, when it was raised above the water by an arm clad in white samite, or silk. The three queens in crowns of gold on the funeral barge are Arthur's sister, Morgan le Fay, the Queen of Northgallia, or Wales, and the Queen of the Waste Lands. An introduction to the poem reveals that it is a modern Christmas story told in the wistful hope that Arthur may come again.

So all day long the noise of battle roll'd
Among the mountains by the winter sea;
Until King Arthur's table, man by man,
Had fall'n in Lyonness about their Lord,
King Arthur: then, because his wound was deep,
The bold Sir Bedivere uplifted him,
Sir Bedivere, the last of all his knights,
And bore him to a chapel nigh the field,
A broken chancel with a broken cross,
That stood on a dark strait of barren land.
On one side lay the Ocean, and on one
Lay a great water, and the moon was full.
    Then spake King Arthur to Sir Bedivere:
'The sequel of to-day unsolders all
The goodliest fellowship of famous knights
Whereof this world holds record. Such a sleep
They sleep — the men I loved. I think that we
Shall never more, at any future time,

Delight our souls with talk of knightly deeds,
Walking about the gardens and the halls
Of Camelot, as in the days that were.
I perish by this people which I made, –
Tho' Merlin sware that I should come again
To rule once more – but let what will be, be,
I am so deeply smitten thro' the helm
That without help I cannot last till morn.
Thou therefore take my brand Excalibur,
Which was my pride: for thou rememberest how
In those old days, one summer noon, an arm
Rose up from out the bosom of the lake,
Clothed in white samite, mystic, wonderful,
Holding the sword – and how I row'd across
And took it, and have worn it, like a king:
And, wheresoever I am sung or told
In aftertime, this also shall be known:
But now delay not: take Excalibur,
And fling him far into the middle mere:
Watch what thou seëst, and lightly bring me word.'
      To him replied the bold Bedivere:
'It is not meet, Sir King, to leave thee thus,
Aidless, alone, and smitten thro' the helm.
A little thing may harm a wounded man.
Yet I thy hest will all perform at full,
Watch what I see, and lightly bring thee word.'
      So saying, from the ruin'd shrine he stept
And in the moon athwart the place of tombs,
Where lay the mighty bones of ancient men,
Old knights, and over them the sea-wind sang
Shrill, chill, with flakes of foam. He, stepping down
By zig-zag paths, and juts of pointed rock,
Came on the shining levels of the lake.
      There drew he forth the brand Excalibur,
And o'er him, drawing it, the winter moon,
Brightening the skirts of a long cloud, ran forth
And sparkled keen with frost against the hilt:
For all the haft twinkled with diamond sparks,

Myriads of topaz-lights, and jacinth-work
Of subtlest jewellery. He gazed so long
That both his eyes were dazzled, as he stood,
This way and that dividing the swift mind,
In act to throw: but at the last it seem'd
Better to leave Excalibur conceal'd
There in the many-knotted waterflags,
That whistled stiff and dry about the marge.
So strode he back slow to the wounded King.

   Then spake King Arthur to Sir Bedivere:
'Hast thou perform'd my mission which I gave?
What is it thou hast seen? or what hast heard?'

   And answer made the bold Sir Bedivere:
'I heard the ripple washing in the reeds,
And the wild water lapping on the crag.'

   To whom replied King Arthur, faint and pale:
'Thou hast betray'd thy nature and thy name,
Not rendering true answer, as beseem'd
Thy fëalty, nor like a noble knight:
For surer sign had follow'd, either hand,
Or voice, or else a motion of the mere.
This is a shameful thing for men to lie.
Yet now, I charge thee, quickly go again
As thou art lief and dear, and do the thing
I bad thee, watch, and lightly bring me word.'

   Then went Sir Bedivere the second time
Across the ridge, and paced beside the mere,
Counting the dewy pebbles, fix'd in thought;
But when he saw the wonder of the hilt,
How curiously and strangely chased, he smote
His palms together, and he cried aloud.

   'And if indeed I cast the brand away,
Surely a precious thing, one worthy note,
Should thus be lost for ever from the earth,
Which might have pleased the eyes of many men.
What good should follow this, if this were done?
What harm, undone? deep harm to disobey,
Seeing obedience is the bond of rule.

Were it well to obey then, if a king demand
An act unprofitable, against himself?
The King is sick, and knows not what he does.
What record, or what relic of my lord
Should be to aftertime, but empty breath
And rumours of a doubt? but were this kept,
Stored in some treasure-house of mighty kings,
Some one might show it at a joust of arms,
Saying, 'King Arthur's sword, Excalibur,
Wrought by the lonely maiden of the Lake.
Nine years she wrought it, sitting in the deeps
Upon the hidden bases of the hills.'
So might some old man speak in the aftertime
To all the people, winning reverence.
But now much honour and much fame were lost.'

   So spake he, clouded with his own conceit,
And hid Excalibur the second time,
And so strode back slow to the wounded King.

   Then spoke King Arthur, breathing heavily:
'What is it thou hast seen? or what hast heard?'

   And answer made the bold Sir Bedivere:
'I heard the water lapping on the crag,
And the long ripple washing in the reeds.'
To whom replied King Arthur, much in wrath:
'Ah, miserable and unkind, untrue,
Unknightly, traitor-hearted! Woe is me!
Authority forgets a dying king,
Laid widow'd of the power in his eye
That bow'd the will. I see thee what thou art,
For thou, the latest-left of all my knights,
In whom should meet the offices of all,
Thou wouldst betray me for the precious hilt;
Either from lust of gold, or like a girl
Valuing the giddy pleasure of the eyes.
Yet, for a man may fail in duty twice,
And the third time may prosper, get thee hence:
But, if thou spare to fling Excalibur,
I will arise and slay thee with my hands.'

Then quickly rose Sir Bedivere, and ran,
And, leaping down the ridges lightly, plunged
Among the bulrush-beds, and clutch'd the sword,
And strongly wheel'd and threw it. The great brand
Made lightnings in the splendour of the moon,
And flashing round and round, and whirl'd in an arch,
Shot like a streamer of the northern morn,
Seen where the moving isles of winter shock
By night, with noises of the northern sea.
So flash'd and fell the brand Excalibur:
But ere he dipt the surface, rose an arm
Clothed in white samite, mystic, wonderful,
And caught him by the hilt, and brandish'd him
Three times, and drew him under in the mere.
And lightly went the other to the King.

Then spoke King Arthur, drawing thicker breath:
'Now see I by thine eyes that this is done.
Speak out: what is it thou hast heard, or seen?'

And answer made the bold Sir Bedivere:
'Sir King, I closed mine eyelids, lest the gems
Should blind my purpose, for I never saw,
Nor shall see, here or elsewhere, till I die,
Not tho' I live three lives of mortal men,
So great a miracle as yonder hilt.
Then with both hands I flung him, wheeling him;
But when I look'd again, behold an arm,
Clothed in white samite, mystic, wonderful,
That caught him by the hilt, and brandish'd him
Three times, and drew him under in the mere.'

And answer made King Arthur, breathing hard:
'My end draws nigh; 'tis time that I were gone.
Make broad thy shoulders to receive my weight,
And bear me to the margin; yet I fear
My wound hath taken cold, and I shall die.'

So saying, from the pavement he half rose,
Slowly, with pain, reclining on his arm,
And looking wistfully with wide blue eyes
As in a picture. Him Sir Bedivere

Remorsefully regarded thro' his tears,
And would have spoken, but he found not words,
Then took with care, and kneeling on one knee,
O'er both his shoulders drew the languid hands,
And rising bore him thro' the place of tombs.

But, as he walk'd, King Arthur panted hard,
Like one that feels a nightmare on his bed
When all the house is mute. So sigh'd the King,
Muttering and murmuring at his ear, 'Quick, quick!
I fear it is too late, and I shall die.'
But the other swiftly strode from ridge to ridge,
Clothed with his breath, and looking, as he walk'd,
Larger than human on the frozen hills.
He heard the deep behind him, and a cry
Before. His own thought drove him like a goad.
Dry clash'd his harness in the icy caves
And barren chasms, and all to left and right
The bare black cliff clang'd round him, as he based
His feet on juts of slippery crag that rang
Sharp-smitten with the dint of armed heels —
And on a sudden, lo! the level lake,
And the long glories of the winter moon.

Then saw they how there hove a dusky barge,
Dark as a funeral scarf from stem to stern,
Beneath them; and descending they were ware
That all the decks were dense with stately forms
Black-stoled, black-hooded, like a dream — by these
Three Queens with crowns of gold — and from them rose
A cry that shiver'd to the tingling stars,
And, as it were one voice, an agony
Of lamentation, like a wind, that shrills
All night in a waste land, where no one comes,
Or hath come, since the making of the world.

Then murmur'd Arthur, 'Place me in the barge,'
And to the barge they came. There those three Queens
Put forth their hands, and took the King, and wept.
But she, that rose the tallest of them all
And fairest, laid his head upon her lap,

And loosed the shatter'd casque, and chafed his hands,
And call'd him by his name, complaining loud,
And dropping bitter tears against his brow
Striped with dark blood: for all his face was white
And colourless, and like the wither'd moon
Smote by the fresh beam of the springing east;
And all his greaves and cuisses dash'd with drops
Of onset; and the light and lustrous curls –
That made his forehead like a rising sun
High from the daïs-throne – were parch'd with dust;
Or, clotted into points and hanging loose,
Mix'd with the knightly growth that fringed his lips.
So like a shatter'd column lay the King;
Not like that Arthur who, with lance in rest,
From spur to plume a star of tournament,
Shot thro' the lists at Camelot, and charged
Before the eyes of ladies and of kings.

  Then loudly cried the bold Sir Bedivere,
'Ah! my Lord Arthur, whither shall I go?
Where shall I hide my forehead and my eyes?
For now I see the true old times are dead,
When every morning brought a noble chance,
And every chance brought out a noble knight.
Such times have been not since the light that led
The holy Elders with the gift of myrrh.
But now the whole ROUND TABLE is dissolved
Which was an image of the mighty world;
And I, the last, go forth companionless,
And the days darken round me, and the years,
Among new men, strange faces, other minds.'

  And slowly answered Arthur from the barge:
'The old order changeth, yielding place to new,
And God fulfils Himself in many ways,
Lest one good custom should corrupt the world.
Comfort thyself: what comfort is in me?
I have lived my life, and that which I have done
May He within Himself make pure! but thou,
If thou shouldst never see my face again,

Pray for my soul. More things are wrought by prayer
Than this world dreams of. Wherefore, let thy voice
Rise like a fountain for me night and day.
For what are men better than sheep or goats
That nourish a blind life within the brain,
If, knowing God, they lift not hands of prayer
Both for themselves and those who call them friend?
For so the whole round earth is every way
Bound by gold chains about the feet of God.
But now farewell. I am going a long way
With these thou seëst – if indeed I go –
(For all my mind is clouded with a doubt)
To the island-valley of Avilion;
Where falls not hail, or rain, or any snow,
Nor ever wind blows loudly; but it lies
Deep-meadow'd, happy, fair with orchard-lawns
And bowery hollows crown'd with summer sea,
Where I will heal me of my grievous wound.'
    So said he, and the barge with oar and sail
Moved from the brink, like some full-breasted swan
That, fluting a wild carol ere her death,
Ruffles her pure cold plume, and takes the flood
With swarthy webs. Long stood Sir Bedivere
Revolving many memories, till the hull
Look'd one black dot against the verge of dawn,
And on the mere the wailing died away.

———————————

    Here ended Hall, and our last light, that long
Had wink'd and threaten'd darkness, flared and fell:
At which the Parson, sent to sleep with sound,
And waked with silence, grunted 'Good!' but we
Sat rapt: it was the tone with which he read –
Perhaps some modern touches here and there
Redeem'd it from the charge of nothingness –
Or else we loved the man, and prized his work;
I know not: but we sitting, as I said,
The cock crew loud; as at that time of year

The lusty bird takes every hour for dawn:
Then Francis, muttering, like a man ill used,
'There now – that's nothing!' drew a little back.
And drove his heel into the smoulder'd log,
That sent a blast of sparkles up the flue:
And so to bed; where yet in sleep I seem'd
To sail with Arthur under looming shores,
Point after point, till on to dawn, when dreams
Begin to feel the truth and stir of day
To me, methought, who waited with a crowd,
There came a bark that, blowing forward, bore
King Arthur, like a modern gentleman
Of stateliest port; and all the people cried,
'Arthur is come again: he cannot die.'
Then those that stood upon the hills behind
Repeated – 'Come again, and thrice as fair;'
And, further inland, voices echoed – 'Come
With all good things, and war shall be no more.'
At this a hundred bells began to peal,
That with the sound I woke, and heard indeed
The clear church-bells ring in the Christmas morn.

ULYSSES

First published in the 1842 collection, the poem was written soon
after the death of Tennyson's friend Arthur Hallam in 1833. Its
subject, Tennyson told his son, was 'my feeling about the need of
going forward and braving the struggle of life.' In this case, after
the Trojan War, Ulysses prepares to leave his home in Ithaca and
seek his fate, to see again the great Achilles, even in death.

It little profits that an idle king,
By this still hearth, among these barren crags,
Match'd with an aged wife, I mete and dole
Unequal laws unto a savage race,
That hoard, and sleep, and feed, and know not me.
I cannot rest from travel: I will drink
Life to the lees: all times I have enjoy'd
Greatly, have suffer'd greatly, both with those
That loved me, and alone; on shore, and when
Thro' scudding drifts the rainy Hyades
Vext the dim sea: I am become a name;
For always roaming with a hungry heart
Much have I seen and known; cities of men
And manners, climates, councils, governments,
Myself not least, but honour'd of them all;
And drunk delight of battle with my peers,
Far on the ringing plains of windy Troy.
I am a part of all that I have met;
Yet all experience is an arch wherethro'
Gleams that untravell'd world, whose margin fades
For ever and for ever when I move.
How dull it is to pause, to make an end,
To rust unburnish'd, not to shine in use!
As tho' to breathe were life. Life piled on life

Were all too little, and of one to me
Little remains: but every hour is saved
From that eternal silence, something more,
A bringer of new things; and vile it were
For some three suns to store and hoard myself,
And this grey spirit yearning in desire
To follow knowledge like a sinking star,
Beyond the utmost bound of human thought.

   This is my son, mine own Telemachus,
To whom I leave the sceptre and the isle –
Well-loved of me, discerning to fulfil
This labour, by slow prudence to make mild
A rugged people, and thro' soft degrees
Subdue them to the useful and the good.
Most blameless is he, centred in the sphere
Of common duties, decent not to fail
In offices of tenderness, and pay
Meet adoration to my household gods,
When I am gone. He works his work, I mine.

   There lies the port: the vessel puffs her sail:
There gloom the dark broad seas. My mariners,
Souls that have toil'd, and wrought, and thought with me –
That ever with a frolic welcome took
The thunder and the sunshine, and opposed
Free hearts, free foreheads – you and I are old;
Old age hath yet his honour and his toil;
Death closes all: but something ere the end,
Some work of noble note, may yet be done,
Not unbecoming men that strove with Gods.
The lights begin to twinkle from the rocks:
The long day wanes: the slow moon climbs: the deep
Moans round with many voices. Come, my friends,
'Tis not too late to seek a newer world.
Push off, and sitting well in order smite
The sounding furrows; for my purpose holds
To sail beyond the sunset, and the baths
Of all the western stars, until I die.
It may be that the gulfs will wash us down:

It may be we shall touch the Happy Isles,
And see the great Achilles, whom we knew.
Tho' much is taken, much abides; and tho'
We are not now that strength which in old days
Moved earth and heaven; that which we are, we are;
One equal temper of heroic hearts,
Made weak by time and fate, but strong in will
To strive, to seek, to find, and not to yield.

LOCKSLEY HALL

A poem of the 1842 volumes, this represents Tennyson's attempt to characterise his modern narrator, rather like Browning. The speaker returns to the hall where he had spent his childhood as his uncle's ward and where he had vainly loved his cousin Amy. In rebellion against such hierarchy, he contemplates an escape to colonial adventure. Seeing this as unworthy of his intellectual heritage, he seeks a truly new world of progress and social enlightenment. The poem's story has anticipations of *Maud*, though its political gospel of change reflects the more urgent social problems of the 1840s.

Comrades, leave me here a little, while as yet 'tis early morn:
Leave me here, and when you want me, sound upon the bugle-
    horn.

'Tis the place, and all around it, as of old, the curlews call,
Dreary gleams about the moorland flying over Locksley Hall;

Locksley Hall, that in the distance overlooks the sandy tracts.
And the hollow ocean-ridges roaring into cataracts.

Many a night from yonder ivied casement, ere I went to rest,
Did I look on great Orion sloping slowly to the West.

Many a night I saw the Pleiads, rising thro' the mellow shade,
Glitter like a swarm of fire-flies tangled in a silver braid.

Here about the beach I wander'd, nourishing a youth sublime
With the fairy tales of science, and the long result of Time;

When the centuries behind me like a fruitful land reposed;
When I clung to all the present for the promise that it closed:

When I dipt into the future far as human eye could see;

Saw the Vision of the world, and all the wonder that would be. –

In the Spring a fuller crimson comes upon the robin's breast;
In the Spring the wanton lapwing gets himself another crest;

In the Spring a livelier iris changes on the burnish'd dove;
In the Spring a young man's fancy lightly turns to thoughts of love.

Then her cheek was pale and thinner than should be for one so young,
And her eyes on all my motions with a mute observance hung.

And I said, 'My cousin Amy, speak, and speak the truth to me,
Trust me, cousin, all the current of my being sets to thee.'

On her pallid cheek and forehead came a colour and a light,
As I have seen the rosy red flushing in the northern night.

And she turn'd – her bosom shaken with a sudden storm of sighs –
All the spirit deeply dawning in the dark of hazel eyes –

Saying, 'I have hid my feelings, fearing they should do me wrong;'
Saying, 'Dost thou love me, cousin?' weeping, 'I have loved thee long.'

Love took up the glass of Time, and turn'd it in his glowing hands;
Every moment, lightly shaken, ran itself in golden sands.

Love took up the harp of Life, and smote on all the chords with might;
Smote the chord of Self, that, trembling, pass'd in music out of sight.

Many a morning on the moorland did we hear the copses ring,
And her whisper throng'd my pulses with the fullness of the Spring.

Many an evening by the waters did we watch the stately ships,

And our spirits rush'd together at the touching of the lips.

O my cousin, shallow-hearted! O my Amy, mine no more!
O the dreary, dreary moorland! O the barren, barren shore!

Falser than all fancy fathoms, falser than all songs have sung,
Puppet to a father's threat, and servile to a shrewish tongue!

Is it well to wish thee happy? — having known me — to decline
On a range of lower feelings and a narrower heart than mine!

Yet it shall be: thou shalt lower to his level day by day,
What is fine within thee growing coarse to sympathize with
    clay.

As the husband is, the wife is: thou art mated with a clown,
And the grossness of his nature will have weight to drag thee
    down.

He will hold thee, when his passion shall have spent its novel
    force,
Something better than his dog, a little dearer than his horse.

What is this? his eyes are heavy: think not they are glazed with
    wine.
Go to him: it is thy duty: kiss him: take his hand in thine.

It may be my lord is weary, that his brain is overwrought:
Soothe him with thy finer fancies, touch him with thy lighter
    thought.

He will answer to the purpose, easy things to understand —
Better thou wert dead before me, tho' I slew thee with my
    hand!

Better thou and I were lying, hidden from the heart's disgrace,
Roll'd in one another's arms, and silent in a last embrace.

Cursed be the social wants that sin against the strength of
    youth!
Cursed be the social lies that warp us from the living truth!

Cursed be the sickly forms that err from honest Nature's rule!
Cursed be the gold that gilds the straiten'd forehead of the fool!

Well – 'tis well that I should bluster! – Hadst thou less
    unworthy proved –
Would to God – for I had loved thee more than ever wife was
    loved.

Am I mad, that I should cherish that which bears but bitter
    fruit?
I will pluck it from my bosom, tho' my heart be at the root.

Never, tho' my mortal summers to such length of years should
    come
As the many-winter'd crow that leads the clanging rookery
    home.

Where is comfort? in division of the records of the mind?
Can I part her from herself, and love her, as I knew her, kind?

I remember one that perish'd: sweetly did she speak and move:
Such a one do I remember, whom to look at was to love.

Can I think of her as dead, and love her for the love she bore?
No – she never loved me truly: love is love for evermore.

Comfort? comfort scorn'd of devils! this is truth the poet sings,
That a sorrow's crown of sorrow is remembering happier
    things.

Drug thy memories, lest thou learn it, lest thy heart be put to
    proof,
In the dead unhappy night, and when the rain is on the roof.

Like a dog, he hunts in dreams, and thou art staring at the wall,
Where the dying night-lamp flickers, and the shadows rise and
    fall.

Then a hand shall pass before thee, pointing to his drunken
    sleep,
To thy widow'd marriage-pillows, to the tears that thou wilt
    weep.

Thou shalt hear the 'Never, never,' whisper'd by the phantom
    years,

And a song from out the distance in the ringing of thine ears;

And an eye shall vex thee, looking ancient kindness on thy
    pain.
Turn thee, turn thee on thy pillow: get thee to thy rest again.

Nay, but Nature brings thee solace; for a tender voice will cry.
'Tis a purer life than thine; a lip to drain thy trouble dry.

Baby lips will laugh me down: my latest rival brings thee rest.
Baby fingers, waxen touches, press me from the mother's
    breast.

O, the child too clothes the father with a dearness not his due.
Half is thine and half is his: it will be worthy of the two.

O, I see thee old and formal, fitted to thy petty part,
With a little hoard of maxims preaching down a daughter's
    heart.

'They were dangerous guides the feelings – she herself was not
    exempt –
Truly, she herself had suffer'd' – Perish in thy self-contempt!

Overlive it – lower yet – be happy! wherefore should I care?
I myself must mix with action, lest I wither by despair.

What is that which I should turn to, lighting upon days like
    these?
Every door is barr'd with gold, and opens but to golden keys.

Every gate is throng'd with suitors, all the markets overflow.
I have but an angry fancy: what is that which I should do?

I had been content to perish, falling on the foeman's ground,
When the ranks are roll'd in vapour, and the winds are laid
    with sound.

But the jingling of the guinea helps the hurt that Honour feels,
And the nations do but murmur, snarling at each other's heels.

Can I but relive in sadness? I will turn that earlier page.
Hide me from my deep emotion. O thou wondrous Mother-
    Age!

Make me feel the wild pulsation that I felt before the strife,
When I heard my days before me, and the tumult of my life;

Yearning for the large excitement that the coming years would
    yield,
Eager-hearted as a boy when first he leaves his father's field,

And at night along the dusky highway near and nearer drawn,
Sees in heaven the light of London flaring like a dreary dawn;

And his spirit leaps within him to be gone before him then,
Underneath the light he looks at, in among the throngs of men;

Men, my brothers, men the workers, ever reaping something
    new:
That which they have done but earnest of the things that they
    shall do:

For I dipt into the future, far as human eye could see,
Saw the Vision of the world, and all the wonder that would be;

Saw the heavens fill with commerce, argosies of magic sails,
Pilots of the purple twilight, dropping down with costly bales;

Heard the heavens fill with shouting, and there rain'd a ghastly
    dew
From the nations' airy navies grappling in the central blue;

Far along the world-wide whisper of the south-wind rushing
    warm,
With the standards of the peoples plunging thro' the
    thunder-storm;

Till the war-drum throbb'd no longer, and the battle-flags were
    furl'd
In the Parliament of man, the Federation of the world.

There the common sense of most shall hold a fretful realm in
    awe,
And the kindly earth shall slumber, lapt in universal law.

So I triumph'd ere my passion sweeping thro' me left me dry,

Left me with the palsied heart, and left me with the jaundiced
    eye;

Eye, to which all order festers, all things here are out of joint:
Science moves, but slowly slowly, creeping on from point to
    point:

Slowly comes a hungry people, as a lion, creeping nigher,
Glares at one that nods and winks behind a slowly-dying fire.

Yet I doubt not thro' the ages one increasing purpose runs,
And the thoughts of men are widen'd with the process of the
    suns.

What is that to him that reaps not harvest of his youthful joys,
Tho' the deep heart of existence beat for ever like a boy's?

Knowledge comes, but wisdom lingers, and I linger on the
    shore,
And the individual withers, and the world is more and more.

Knowledge comes, but wisdom lingers, and he bears a laden
    breast,
Full of sad experience, moving toward the stillness of his rest.

Hark, my merry comrades call me, sounding on the bugle-horn,
They to whom my foolish passion were a target for their scorn:

Shall it not be scorn to me to harp on such a moulder'd string?
I am shamed thro' all my nature to have loved so slight a thing.

Weakness to be wroth with weakness! woman's pleasure,
    woman's pain –
Nature made them blinder motions bounded in a shallower
    brain:

Woman is the lesser man, and all thy passions, match'd with
    mine,
Are as moonlight unto sunlight, and as water unto wine –

Here at least, where nature sickens, nothing. Ah, for some
    retreat
Deep in yonder shining Orient, where my life began to beat;

Where in wild Mahratta-battle fell my father evil-starr'd; —
I was left a trampled orphan, and a selfish uncle's ward.

Or to burst all links of habit — there to wander far away,
On from island unto island at the gateways of the day.

Larger constellations burning, mellow moons and happy skies,
Breadths of tropic shade and palms in cluster, knots of
    Paradise.

Never comes the trader, never floats an European flag,
Slides the bird o'er lustrous woodland, swings the trailer from
    the crag;

Droops the heavy-blossom'd bower, hangs the heavy-fruited
    tree —
Summer isles of Eden lying in dark-purple spheres of sea.

There methinks would be enjoyment more than in this march
    of mind,
In the steamship, in the railway, in the thoughts that shake
    mankind.

There the passions cramp'd no longer shall have scope and
    breathing-space;
I will take some savage woman, she shall rear my dusky race.

Iron-jointed, supple-sinew'd, they shall dive, and they shall run,
Catch the wild goat by the hair, and hurl their lances in the
    sun;

Whistle back the parrot's call, and leap the rainbows of the
    brooks,
Not with blinded eyesight poring over miserable books —

Fool, again the dream, the fancy! but I *know* my words are
    wild,
But I count the grey barbarian lower than the Christian child.

I, to herd with narrow foreheads, vacant of our glorious gains,
Like a beast with lower pleasures, like a beast with lower pains!

Mated with a squalid savage — what to me were sun or clime?

I the heir of all the ages, in the foremost files of time —

I that rather held it better men should perish one by one,
Than that earth should stand at gaze like Joshua's moon in Ajalon!

Not in vain the distance beacons. Forward, forward let us range.
Let the great world spin for ever down the ringing grooves of change.

Thro' the shadow of the globe we sweep into the younger day:
Better fifty years of Europe than a cycle of Cathay.

Mother-Age (for mine I knew not) help me as when life begun:
Rift the hills, and roll the waters, flash the lightnings, weigh the Sun —

O, I see the crescent promise of my spirit hath not set.
Ancient founts of inspiration well thro' all my fancy yet.

Howsoever these things be, a long farewell to Locksley Hall!
Now for me the woods may wither, now for me the roof-tree fall.

Comes a vapour from the margin, blackening over heath and holt,
Cramming all the blast before it, in its breast a thunder-bolt.

Let it fall on Locksley Hall, with rain or hail, or fire or snow;
For the mighty wind arises, roaring seaward, and I go.

GODIVA

In this poem from his collection of 1842, Tennyson draws on the legend of Lady Godiva, wife of Leofric, Earl of Mercia in the eleventh century. A pious woman, she asked her husband to remit certain taxes on the inhabitants of Coventry. He agreed, provided she rode naked through the city streets at noon. She took him at his word. By the seventeenth century the legend had also acquired Peeping Tom.

I *waited for the train at Coventry;*
I *hung with grooms and porters on the bridge,*
To *watch the three tall spires; and there I shaped*
The *city's ancient legend into this:*—
   Not only we, the latest seed of Time,
New men, that in the flying of a wheel
Cry down the past, not only we, that prate
Of rights and wrongs, have loved the people well,
And loathed to see them overtax'd; but she
Did more, and underwent, and overcame,
The woman of a thousand summers back,
Godiva, wife to that grim Earl, who ruled
In Coventry: for when he laid a tax
Upon his town, and all the mothers brought
Their children, clamouring, 'If we pay, we starve!'
She sought her lord, and found him, where he strode
About the hall, among his dogs, alone,
His beard a foot before him, and his hair
A yard behind. She told him of their tears,
And pray'd him, 'If they pay this tax, they starve.'
Whereat he stared, replying, half-amazed,
'You would not let your little finger ache
For such as *these?*' — 'But I would die,' said she.

He laugh'd, and swore by Peter and by Paul:
Then fillip'd at the diamond in her ear;
'O aye, aye, aye, you talk!' – 'Alas!' she said,
'But prove me what it is I would not do.'
And from a heart as rough as Esau's hand,
He answer'd, 'Ride you naked thro' the town,
And I repeal it;' and nodding, as in scorn,
He parted, with great strides among his dogs.

So left alone, the passions of her mind,
As winds from all the compass shift and blow,
Made war upon each other for an hour,
Till pity won. She sent a herald forth,
And bade him cry, with sound of trumpet, all
The hard condition; but that she would loose
The people: therefore, as they loved her well,
From then till noon no foot should pace the street,
No eye look down, she passing; but that all
Should keep within, door shut, and window barr'd.

Then fled she to her inmost bower, and there
Unclasp'd the wedded eagles of her belt,
The grim Earl's gift; but ever at a breath
She linger'd, looking like a summer moon
Half-dipt in cloud: anon she shook her head,
And shower'd the rippled ringlets to her knee;
Unclad herself in haste; adown the stair
Stole on; and, like a creeping sunbeam, slid
From pillar unto pillar, until she reach'd
The gateway; there she found her palfrey trapt
In purple blazon'd with armorial gold.

Then she rode forth, clothed on with chastity:
The deep air listen'd round her as she rode,
And all the low wind hardly breathed for fear.
The little wide-mouth'd heads upon the spout
Had cunning eyes to see: the barking cur
Made her cheek flame: her palfrey's footfall shot
Light horrors thro' her pulses: the blind walls
Were full of chinks and holes: and overhead
Fantastic gables, crowding, stared: but she

Not less thro' all bore up, till, last, she saw
The white-flower'd elder-thicket from the field
Gleam thro' the Gothic archways in the wall.

    Then she rode back, clothed on with chastity:
And one low churl, compact of thankless earth,
The fatal byword of all years to come,
Boring a little auger-hole in fear,
Peep'd — but his eyes, before they had their will,
Were shrivell'd into darkness in his head,
And dropt before him. So the Powers, who wait
On noble deeds, cancell'd a sense misused;
And she, that knew not, pass'd: and all at once,
With twelve great shocks of sound, the shameless noon
Was clash'd and hammer'd from a hundred towers,
One after one: but even then she gain'd
Her bower; whence reissuing, robed and crown'd,
To meet her lord, she took the tax away,
And built herself an everlasting name.

THE VISION OF SIN

Finally, in the 1842 volumes, Tennyson allowed himself a dream-vision of humanity as he hoped it was not. Cynical, avaricious, sceptical, the voice of the poem sounds over a landscape of desolation. Even the hope of evolution has gone into reverse. Men and horses pass, through death, into lower forms of life. Much of the poem describes the progress of a soul which does not improve with time, as the youth of the first section becomes the cynic of the sequel. It is also the romantic perception, as in *Maud* and *Enoch Arden*, of early hope betrayed by time. However, in Tennyson's note, the final landscape reaffirms 'God, Law, and the future life.'

I

I had a vision when the night was late:
A youth came riding toward a palace-gate.
He rode a horse with wings, that would have flown,
But that his heavy rider kept him down.
And from the palace came a child of sin,
And took him by the curls, and led him in,
Where sat a company with heated eyes,
Expecting when a fountain should arise:
A sleepy light upon their brows and lips —
As when the sun, a crescent of eclipse,
Dreams over lake and lawn, and isles and capes —
Suffused them, sitting, lying, languid shapes,
By heaps of gourds, and skins of wine, and piles of grapes.

II

Then methought I heard a mellow sound,
Gathering up from all the lower ground;
Narrowing in to where they sat assembled
Low voluptuous music winding trembled,
Wov'n in circles: they that heard it sigh'd,

Panted hand in hand with faces pale,
Swung themselves, and in low tones replied;
Till the fountain spouted, showering wide
Sleet of diamond-drift and pearly hail;
Then the music touch'd the gates and died;
Rose again from where it seem'd to fail,
Storm'd in orbs of song, a growing gale;
Till thronging in and in, to where they waited,
As 'twere a hundred-throated nightingale,
The strong tempestuous treble throbb'd and palpitated;
Ran into its giddiest whirl of sound,
Caught the sparkles, and in circles,
Purple gauzes, golden hazes, liquid mazes,
Flung the torrent rainbow round:
Then they started from their places,
Moved with violence, changed in hue,
Caught each other with wild grimaces,
Half-invisible to the view,
Wheeling with precipitate paces
To the melody, till they flew,
Hair, and eyes, and limbs, and faces,
Twisted hard in fierce embraces,
Like to Furies, like to Graces,
Dash'd together in blinding dew:
Till, kill'd with some luxurious agony,
The nerve-dissolving melody
Flutter'd headlong from the sky.

III

And then I look'd up toward a mountain-tract,
That girt the region with high cliff and lawn:
I saw that every morning, far withdrawn
Beyond the darkness and the cataract,
God made Himself an awful rose of dawn,
Unheeded: and detaching, fold by fold,
From those still heights, and, slowly drawing near,
A vapour heavy, hueless, formless, cold,
Came floating on for many a month and year,

Unheeded: and I thought I would have spoken,
And warn'd that madman ere it grew too late:
But, as in dreams, I could not. Mine was broken,
When that cold vapour touch'd the palace-gate,
And link'd again. I saw within my head
A grey and gap-tooth'd man as lean as death,
Who slowly rode across a wither'd heath,
And lighted at a ruin'd inn, and said:

IV

'Wrinkled ostler, grim and thin!
    Here is custom come your way;
Take my brute, and lead him in,
    Stuff his ribs with mouldy hay.

'Bitter barmaid, waning fast!
    See that sheets are on my bed;
What! the flower of life is past:
    It is long before you wed.

'Slip-shod waiter, lank and sour,
    At the Dragon on the heath!
Let us have a quiet hour,
    Let us hob-and-nob with Death.

'I am old, but let me drink;
    Bring me spices, bring me wine;
I remember, when I think,
    That my youth was half divine.

'Wine is good for shrivell'd lips,
    When a blanket wraps the day,
When the rotten woodland drips,
    And the leaf is stamp'd in clay.

'Sit thee down, and have no shame,
    Cheek by jowl, and knee by knee:
What care I for any name?
    What for order or degree?

'Let me screw thee up a peg:
   Let me loose thy tongue with wine:
Callest thou that thing a leg?
   Which is thinnest? thine or mine?

'Thou shalt not be saved by works:
   Thou hast been a sinner too:
Ruin'd trunks on wither'd forks,
   Empty scarecrows, I and you!

'Fill the cup, and fill the can:
   Have a rouse before the morn:
Every moment dies a man,
   Every moment one is born.

'We are men of ruin'd blood;
   Therefore comes it we are wise.
Fish are we that love the mud,
   Rising to no fancy-flies.

'Name and fame! to fly sublime
   Thro' the courts, the camps, the schools,
Is to be the ball of Time,
   Bandied by the hands of fools.

'Friendship! – to be two in one –
   Let the canting liar pack!
Well I know, when I am gone,
   How she mouths behind my back.

'Virtue! – to be good and just –
   Every heart, when sifted well,
Is a clot of warmer dust,
   Mix'd with cunning sparks of hell.

'O! we two as well can look
   Whited thought and cleanly life
As the priest, above his book
   Leering at his neighbour's wife.

'Fill the cup, and fill the can:
   Have a rouse before the morn:
Every moment dies a man,
   Every moment one is born.

'Drink, and let the parties rave:
   They are fill'd with idle spleen;
Rising, falling, like a wave,
   For they know not what they mean.

'He that roars for liberty
   Faster binds a tyrant's power;
And the tyrant's cruel glee
   Forces on the freer hour.

'Fill the can, and fill the cup:
   All the windy ways of men
Are but dust that rises up,
   And is lightly laid again.

'Greet her with applausive breath,
   Freedom, gaily doth she tread;
In her right a civic wreath,
   In her left a human head.

'No, I love not what is new;
   She is of an ancient house:
And I think we know the hue
   Of that cap upon her brows.

'Let her go! her thirst she slakes
   Where the bloody conduit runs:
Then her sweetest meal she makes
   On the first-born of her sons.

'Drink to lofty hopes that cool –
   Visions of a perfect State:
Drink we, last, the public fool,
   Frantic love and frantic hate.

'Chant me now some wicked stave,
   Till thy drooping courage rise,
And the glow-worm of the grave
   Glimmer in thy rheumy eyes.

'Fear not thou to loose thy tongue;
   Set thy hoary fancies free;
What is loathsome to the young
   Savours well to thee and me.

'Change, reverting to the years,
    When thy nerves could understand
What there is in loving tears,
    And the warmth of hand in hand.

'Tell me tales of thy first love –
    April hopes, the fools of chance;
Till the graves begin to move,
    And the dead begin to dance.

'Fill the can, and fill the cup:
    All the windy ways of men
Are but dust that rises up,
    And is lightly laid again.

'Trooping from their mouldy dens
    The chap-fallen circle spreads:
Welcome, fellow-citizens,
    Hollow hearts and empty heads!

'You are bones, and what of that?
    Every face, however full,
Padded round with flesh and fat,
    Is but modell'd on a skull.

'Death is king, and Vivat Rex!
    Tread a measure on the stones,
Madam – if I know your sex,
    From the fashion of your bones.

'No, I cannot praise the fire
    In your eye – nor yet your lip:
All the more do I admire
    Joints of cunning workmanship.

'Lo! God's likeness – the ground-plan –
    Neither modell'd, glazed, or framed:
Buss me, thou rough sketch of man,
    Far too naked to be shamed!

'Drink to Fortune, drink to Chance,
    While we keep a little breath!
Drink to heavy Ignorance!
    Hob-and-nob with brother Death!

'Thou art mazed, the night is long,
    And the longer night is near:
What! I am not all as wrong
    As a bitter jest is dear.

'Youthful hopes, by scores, to all,
    When the locks are crisp and curl'd;
Unto me my maudlin gall
    And my mockeries of the world.

'Fill the cup, and fill the can!
    Mingle madness, mingle scorn!
Dregs of life, and lees of man:
    Yet we will not die forlorn.'

v

The voice grew faint: there came a further change:
Once more uprose the mystic mountain-range:
Below were men and horses pierced with worms,
And slowly quickening into lower forms;
By shards and scurf of salt, and scum of dross,
Old plash of rains, and refuse patch'd with moss.
Then some one spake: 'Behold! it was a crime
Of sense avenged by sense that wore with time.'
Another said: 'The crime of sense became
The crime of malice, and is equal blame.'
And one: 'He had not wholly quench'd his power;
A little grain of conscience made him sour.'
At last I heard a voice upon the slope
Cry to the summit, 'Is there any hope?'
To which an answer peal'd from that high land,
But in a tongue no man could understand;
And on the glimmering limit far withdrawn
God made Himself an awful rose of dawn.

From IN MEMORIAM A. H. H.

In memory of ....

In Memoriam was the poem by which Tennyson became a central figure of Victorian culture. It consists of one hundred and thirty-one short sections with prefatory and concluding verses. It was written between the death of his close friend Arthur Hallam in 1833 and the year of the poem's publication, 1850. Hallam died in Vienna. His body was brought back to the churchyard by the sea at Clevedon, where the Severn widens into the Bristol Channel, opposite the Wye on the Welsh coast. Tennyson called his elegy the 'Way of the Soul', though insisting that it was not autobiography. It moves from grief and longing at the opening to questioning and reaffirmation of faith in God and humanity. It ends with a marriage-song for the wedding of Tennyson's sister Cecilia to Edward Lushington.

The following sections describe in the prefatory verses a steadfast faith despite what follows; grief and doubt at Hallam's loss (I–III); the emptiness of familiar scenes and the return of Hallam's body (VII–IX); the resting-place at Clevedon (XIX); the sadness of Christmas alone (XXVIII); the spiritual agony of loss made worse by the thought of a world without faith or meaning (L–LVII); the recovery of trust in divine and human love with the spiritual presence of his dead friend (CXXVI–CXXXI); the concluding marriage verses.

In this poem Tennyson touched the humanity of Victorian England, its universal hopes and griefs, its spiritual ordeals and triumphs of faith, its vision of a nobler future. The consolation found in it by the queen and thousands of her subjects was balanced, in the view of Hallam Tennyson the poet's son, by those critics who thought that Tennyson 'had made a definite step towards the unification of the highest religion and philosophy with the progressive science of the day.' The image of men rising 'on stepping-stones / Of their dead selves to higher things' seemed to anticipate Darwin's *Origin of Species* (1859) in the context of religious faith. That such faith had come only after the dark night of the soul added to the power of the work.

In Memoriam A. H. H.

OBIIT MDCCCXXXIII

Strong Son of God, immortal Love,
    Whom we, that have not seen thy face,
    By faith, and faith alone, embrace,
Believing where we cannot prove;

Thine are these orbs of light and shade;
    Thou madest Life in man and brute;
    Thou madest Death; and lo, thy foot
Is on the skull which thou hast made.

Thou wilt not leave us in the dust:
    Thou madest man, he knows not why;
    He thinks he was not made to die;
And thou hast made him: thou art just.

Thou seemest human and divine,
    The highest, holiest manhood, thou:
    Our wills are ours, we know not how;
Our wills are ours, to make them thine.

Our little systems have their day;
    They have their day and cease to be:
    They are but broken lights of thee,
And thou, O Lord, art more than they.

We have but faith: we cannot know;
    For knowledge is of things we see;
    And yet we trust it comes from thee,
A beam in darkness: let it grow.

Let knowledge grow from more to more,
    But more of reverence in us dwell;
    That mind and soul, according well,
May make one music as before,

But vaster. We are fools and slight;
    We mock thee when we do not fear:
    But help thy foolish ones to bear;
Help thy vain worlds to bear thy light.

Forgive what seem'd my sin in me;
　　What seem'd my worth since I began;
　　For merit lives from man to man,
And not from man, O Lord, to thee.

Forgive my grief for one removed,
　　Thy creature, whom I found so fair.
　　I trust he lives in thee, and there
I find him worthier to be loved.

Forgive these wild and wandering cries,
　　Confusions of a wasted youth;
　　Forgive them where they fail in truth,
And in thy wisdom make me wise.

1849.

I

I held it truth, with him who sings
　　To one clear harp in divers tones,
　　That men may rise on stepping-stones
Of their dead selves to higher things.

But who shall so forecast the years
　　And find in loss a gain to match?
　　Or reach a hand thro' time to catch
The far-off interest of tears?

Let Love clasp Grief lest both be drown'd,
　　Let darkness keep her raven gloss:
　　Ah, sweeter to be drunk with loss,
To dance with death, to beat the ground,

Than that the victor Hours should scorn
　　The long result of love, and boast,
　　'Behold the man that loved and lost,
But all he was is overworn.'

II

Old Yew, which graspest at the stones
　　That name the under-lying dead,
　　Thy fibres net the dreamless head,
Thy roots are wrapt about the bones.

The seasons bring the flower again,
  And bring the firstling to the flock;
  And in the dusk of thee, the clock
Beats out the little lives of men.

O not for thee the glow, the bloom,
  Who changest not in any gale,
  Nor branding summer suns avail
To touch thy thousand years of gloom:

And gazing on thee, sullen tree,
  Sick for thy stubborn hardihood,
  I seem to fail from out my blood
And grow incorporate into thee.

III

O Sorrow, cruel fellowship,
  O Priestess in the vaults of Death,
  O sweet and bitter in a breath,
What whispers from thy lying lip?

'The stars,' she whispers, 'blindly run;
  A web is wov'n across the sky;
  From out waste places comes a cry,
And murmurs from the dying sun:

'And all the phantom, Nature, stands —
  With all the music in her tone,
  A hollow echo of my own, —
A hollow form with empty hands.'

And shall I take a thing so blind,
  Embrace her as my natural good;
  Or crush her, like a vice of blood,
Upon the threshold of the mind?

   * * *

Methaphor

VII

Dark house, by which once more I stand
    Here in the long unlovely street,
    Doors, where my heart was used to beat
So quickly, waiting for a hand,

emptiness, then rain. the day is empty and blank.

A hand that can be clasp'd no more –
    Behold me, for I cannot sleep,
    And like a guilty thing I creep
At earliest morning to the door.

He is not here; but far away
    The noise of life begins again,
    And ghastly thro' the drizzling rain
On the bald street breaks the blank day.

VIII

A happy lover who has come
    To look on her that loves him well,
    Who 'lights and rings the gateway bell,
And learns her gone and far from home;

He saddens, all the magic light
    Dies off at once from bower and hall,
    And all the place is dark, and all
The chambers emptied of delight:

So find I every pleasant spot
    In which we two were wont to meet,
    The field, the chamber and the street,
For all is dark where thou art not.

Yet as that other, wandering there
    In those deserted walks, may find
    A flower beat with rain and wind,
Which once she foster'd up with care;

So seems it in my deep regret,
    O my forsaken heart, with thee
    And this poor flower of poesy
Which little cared for fades not yet.

this poetry is like this attempt at life (a struggling flower)

But since it pleased a vanish'd eye,
   I go to plant it on his tomb,
   That if it can it there may bloom,
Or dying, there at least may die.

thre is his prayer, his poetry is his last attempt, his last faith in life.

IX

Fair ship, that from the Italian shore
   Sailest the placid ocean-plains
   With my lost Arthur's loved remains,
Spread thy full wings, and waft him o'er.

So draw him home to those that mourn
   In vain; a favourable speed
   Ruffle thy mirror'd mast, and lead
Thro' prosperous floods his holy urn.

All night no ruder air perplex
   Thy sliding keel, till Phosphor, bright
   As our pure love, thro' early light
Shall glimmer on the dewy decks.

Sphere all your lights around, above;
   Sleep, gentle heavens, before the prow;
   Sleep, gentle winds, as he sleeps now,
My friend, the brother of my love;

My Arthur, whom I shall not see
   Till all my widow'd race be run;
   Dear as the mother to the son,
More than my brothers are to me.

*   *   *

XIX

The Danube to the Severn gave
   The darken'd heart that beat no more;
   They laid him by the pleasant shore,
And in the hearing of the wave.

There twice a day the Severn fills;
    The salt sea-water passes by,
    And hushes half the babbling Wye,
And makes a silence in the hills.

The Wye is hush'd nor moved along,
    And hush'd my deepest grief of all,
    When fill'd with tears that cannot fall,
I brim with sorrow drowning song.

The tide flows down, the wave again
    Is vocal in its wooded walls;
    My deeper anguish also falls,
And I can speak a little then.

Steady rythm (handwritten annotation)

*   *   *

XXVIII

The time draws near the birth of Christ:
    The moon is hid; the night is still;
    The Christmas bells from hill to hill
Answer each other in the mist.

Four voices of four hamlets round,
    From far and near, on mead and moor,
    Swell out and fail, as if a door
Were shut between me and the sound:

It is a lovely and cheerful time but he is blocked from the happiness by a door. (handwritten annotation)

Each voice four changes on the wind,
    That now dilate, and now decrease,
    Peace and goodwill, goodwill and peace,
Peace and goodwill, to all mankind.

This year I slept and woke with pain,
    I almost wish'd no more to wake,
    And that my hold on life would break
Before I heard those bells again:

contradiction he doesn't fall these feelings. (handwritten annotation)

But they my troubled spirit rule,
    For they controll'd me when a boy;

They bring me sorrow touch'd with joy,
The merry merry bells of Yule.

bells are wake up call

* * *

L

Be near me when my light is low,
    When the blood creeps, and the nerves prick
    And tingle; and the heart is sick,
And all the wheels of Being slow.

Be near me when the sensuous frame
    Is rack'd with pangs that conquer trust;
    And Time, a maniac scattering dust,
And Life, a Fury slinging flame.

Be near me when my faith is dry,
    And men the flies of latter spring,
    That lay their eggs, and sting and sing,
And weave their petty cells and die.

Be near me when I fade away,
    To point the term of human strife,
    And on the low dark verge of life
The twilight of eternal day.

LI

Do we indeed desire the dead
    Should still be near us at our side?
    Is there no baseness we would hide?
No inner vileness that we dread?

do we really want death at our side

Shall he for whose applause I strove,
    I had such reverence for his blame,
    See with clear eye some hidden shame
And I be lessen'd in his love?

I wrong the grave with fears untrue:
    Shall love be blamed for want of faith?
    There must be wisdom with great Death:
The dead shall look me thro' and thro'.

Be near us when we climb or fall:
    Ye watch, like God, the rolling hours
    With larger other eyes than ours,
To make allowance for us all.

LII

I cannot love thee as I ought,
    For love reflects the thing beloved;
    My words are only words, and moved
Upon the topmost froth of thought.

'Yet blame not thou thy plaintive song,'
    The Spirit of true love replied;
    'Thou canst not move me from thy side,
Nor human frailty do me wrong.

'What keeps a spirit wholly true
    To that ideal which he bears?
    What record? not the sinless years
That breathed beneath the Syrian blue:

'So fret not, like an idle girl,
    That life is dash'd with flecks of sin.
    Abide: thy wealth is gather'd in,
When Time hath sunder'd shell from pearl.'

LIII

How many a father have I seen,
    A sober man, among his boys,
    Whose youth was full of foolish noise,
Who wears his manhood hale and green:

And dare we to this fancy give,
    That had the wild oat not been sown,
    The soil, left barren, scarce had grown
The grain by which a man may live?

Or, if we held the doctrine sound
    For life outliving heats of youth,

Yet who would preach it as a truth
To those that eddy round and round?

Hold thou the good: define it well:
    For fear divine Philosophy
    Should push beyond her mark, and be
Procuress to the Lords of Hell.

LIV

Oh yet we trust that somehow good
    Will be the final goal of ill,
    To pangs of nature, sins of will,
Defects of doubt, and taints of blood;

That nothing walks with aimless feet;
    That not one life shall be destroy'd,
    Or cast as rubbish to the void,
When God hath made the pile complete;

That not a worm is cloven in vain;
    That not a moth with vain desire
    Is shrivell'd in a fruitless fire,
Or but subserves another's gain.

Behold, we know not anything;
    I can but trust that good shall fall
    At last – far off – at last, to all,
And every winter change to spring.

So runs my dream: but what am I?
    An infant crying in the night:
    An infant crying for the light:
And with no language but a cry.

LV

The wish, that of the living whole
    No life may fail beyond the grave,
    Derives it not from what we have
The likest God within the soul?

[handwritten margin notes:]
Even if there is evil good will come out of it

despite appearances nothing of good is lost

not even the moth or worm dies in vain

We cannot die because God is immortal

Are God and Nature then at strife,
That Nature lends such evil dreams?
So careful of the type she seems,
So careless of the single life;

That I, considering everywhere
Her secret meaning in her deeds,
And finding that of fifty seeds
She often brings but one to bear,

[handwritten: nature is very wasteful]

I falter where I firmly trod,
And falling with my weight of cares
Upon the great world's altar-stairs
That slope thro' darkness up to God,

I stretch lame hands of faith, and grope,
And gather dust and chaff, and call
To what I feel is Lord of all,
And faintly trust the larger hope.

LVI

'So careful of the type?' but no.
From scarped cliff and quarried stone
She cries 'A thousand types are gone:
I care for nothing, all shall go.

[handwritten: contrasting hope and reality]

'Thou makest thine appeal to me:
I bring to life, I bring to death:
The spirit does but mean the breath:
I know no more.' And he, shall he,

[handwritten: Contradiction]

Man, her last work, who seem'd so fair,
Such splendid purpose in his eyes,
Who roll'd the psalm to wintry skies,
Who built him fanes of fruitless prayer,

Who trusted God was love indeed
And love Creation's final law —
Tho' Nature, red in tooth and claw
With ravine, shriek'd against his creed —

[handwritten: His friend trusted God. The whole of nature exists to destroy or be destroyed.]

Who loved, who suffer'd countless ills,
  Who battled for the True, the Just,
  Be blown about the desert dust,
Or seal'd within the iron hills?

No more? A monster then, a dream,
  A discord. Dragons of the prime,
  That tare each other in their slime,
Were mellow music match'd with him.

O life as futile, then, as frail!
  O for thy voice to soothe and bless!
  What hope of answer, or redress?
Behind the veil, behind the veil.

LVII

Peace; come away: the song of woe
  Is after all an earthly song:
  Peace; come away: we do him wrong
To sing so wildly: let us go.

Come; let us go: your cheeks are pale;
  But half my life I leave behind:
  Methinks my friend is richly shrined;
But I shall pass; my work will fail.

Yet in these ears, till hearing dies,
  One set slow bell will seem to toll
  The passing of the sweetest soul
That ever look'd with human eyes.

I hear it now, and o'er and o'er,
  Eternal greetings to the dead;
  And 'Ave, Ave, Ave,' said,
'Adieu, adieu' for evermore.

* * *

CXXVI

Love is and was my Lord and King,
    And in his presence I attend
    To hear the tidings of my friend,
Which every hour his couriers bring.

Love is and was my King and Lord,
    And will be, tho' as yet I keep
    Within his court on earth, and sleep
Encompass'd by his faithful guard,

And hear at times a sentinel
    Who moves about from place to place,
    And whispers to the worlds of space,
In the deep night, that all is well.

His friend is gone but his love is still with him

CXXVII

And all is well, tho' faith and form
    Be sunder'd in the night of fear;
    Well roars the storm to those that hear
A deeper voice across the storm,

Proclaiming social truth shall spread,
    And justice, ev'n tho' thrice again
    The red fool-fury of the Seine
Should pile her barricades with dead.

But ill for him that wears a crown,
    And him, the lazar, in his rags:
    They tremble, the sustaining crags;
The spires of ice are toppled down,

And molten up, and roar in flood;
    The fortress crashes from on high,
    The brute earth lightens to the sky,
And the great Aeon sinks in blood,

And compass'd by the fires of Hell;
    While thou, dear spirit, happy star,
    O'erlook'st the tumult from afar,
And smilest, knowing all is well.

CXXVIII

The love that rose on stronger wings,
    Unpalsied when he met with Death,
    Is comrade of the lesser faith
That sees the course of human things.

No doubt vast eddies in the flood
    Of onward time shall yet be made,
    And throned races may degrade;
Yet O ye mysteries of good,

Wild Hours that fly with Hope and Fear,
    If all your office had to do
    With old results that look like new;
If this were all your mission here,

To draw, to sheathe a useless sword,
    To fool the crowd with glorious lies,
    To cleave a creed in sects and cries,
To change the bearing of a word,

To shift an arbitrary power,
    To cramp the student at his desk,
    To make old bareness picturesque
And tuft with grass a feudal tower;

Why then my scorn might well descend
    On you and yours. I see in part
    That all, as in some piece of art,
Is toil cöoperant to an end.

CXXIX

Dear friend, far off, my lost desire,
    So far, so near in woe and weal;
    O loved the most, when most I feel
There is a lower and a higher;

Known and unknown; human, divine;
    Sweet human hand and lips and eye;
    Dear heavenly friend that canst not die,
Mine, mine, for ever, ever mine;

Strange friend, past, present, and to be; *He will be his friend forever*
    Loved deeplier, darklier understood;
    Behold, I dream a dream of good,
And mingle all the world with thee.

CXXX

Thy voice is on the rolling air;
    I hear thee where the waters run;
    Thou standest in the rising sun,
And in the setting thou art fair.

What art thou then? I cannot guess;
    But tho' I seem in star and flower
    To feel thee some diffusive power,
I do not therefore love thee less:

My love involves the love before;
    My love is vaster passion now;
    Tho' mix'd with God and Nature thou,
I seem to love thee more and more.

Far off thou art, but ever nigh;
    I have thee still, and I rejoice;
    I prosper, circled with thy voice;
I shall not lose thee tho' I die. *I wont lose you even when I die*

CXXXI

O living will that shalt endure
    When all that seems shall suffer shock,
    Rise in the spiritual rock,
Flow thro' our deeds and make them pure,

That we may lift from out of dust
    A voice as unto him that hears,
    A cry above the conquer'd years
To one that with us works, and trust,

With faith that comes of self-control,
    The truths that never can be proved
    Until we close with all we loved,
And all we flow from, soul in soul.

*   *   *

O true and tried, so well and long,
    Demand not thou a marriage lay;
    In that it is thy marriage day
Is music more than any song.

Nor have I felt so much of bliss
    Since first he told me that he loved
    A daughter of our house; nor proved
Since that dark day a day like this;

Tho' I since then have number'd o'er
    Some thrice three years: they went and came,
    Remade the blood and changed the frame,
And yet is love not less, but more;

No longer caring to embalm
    In dying songs a dead regret,
    But like a statue solid-set,
And moulded in colossal calm.

Regret is dead, but love is more
    Than in the summers that are flown,
    For I myself with these have grown
To something greater than before;

Which makes appear the songs I made
    As echoes out of weaker times,
    As half but idle brawling rhymes,
The sport of random sun and shade.

But where is she, the bridal flower,
    That must be made a wife ere noon?
    She enters, glowing like the moon
Of Eden on its bridal bower:

On me she bends her blissful eyes
    And then on thee; they meet thy look
    And brighten like the star that shook
Betwixt the palms of paradise.

O when her life was yet in bud,
    He too foretold the perfect rose.
    For thee she grew, for thee she grows
For ever, and as fair as good.

And thou art worthy; full of power;
    As gentle; liberal-minded, great,
    Consistent; wearing all that weight
Of learning lightly like a flower.

But now set out: the noon is near,
    And I must give away the bride;
    She fears not, or with thee beside
And me behind her, will not fear:

For I that danced her on my knee,
    That watch'd her on her nurse's arm,
    That shielded all her life from harm
At last must part with her to thee;

Now waiting to be made a wife,
    Her feet, my darling, on the dead;
    Their pensive tablets round her head,
And the most living words of life

Breathed in her ear. The ring is on,
    The 'wilt thou' answer'd, and again
    The 'wilt thou' ask'd, till out of twain
Her sweet 'I will' has made ye one.

Now sign your names, which shall be read,
    Mute symbols of a joyful morn,
    By village eyes as yet unborn;
The names are sign'd, and overhead

Begins the clash and clang that tells
    The joy to every wandering breeze;
    The blind wall rocks, and on the trees
The dead leaf trembles to the bells.

O happy hour, and happier hours
    Await them. Many a merry face

Wedding symbolises the
kingdom of God.

Salutes them — maidens of the place,
That pelt us in the porch with flowers.

O happy hour, behold the bride
    With him to whom her hand I gave.
    They leave the porch, they pass the grave
That has to-day its sunny side.

To-day the grave is bright for me,
    For them the light of life increased,
    Who stay to share the morning feast,
Who rest to-night beside the sea.

Let all my genial spirits advance
    To meet and greet a whiter sun;
    My drooping memory will not shun
The foaming grape of eastern France.

It circles round, and fancy plays,
    And hearts are warm'd and faces bloom,
    As drinking health to bride and groom
We wish them store of happy days.

Nor count me all to blame if I
    Conjecture of a stiller guest,
    Perchance, perchance, among the rest,
And, tho' in silence, wishing joy.

But they must go, the time draws on,
    And those white-favour'd horses wait;
    They rise, but linger; it is late;
Farewell, we kiss, and they are gone.

A shade falls on us like the dark
    From little cloudlets on the grass,
    But sweeps away as out we pass
To range the woods, to roam the park,

Discussing how their courtship grew,
    And talk of others that are wed,
    And how she look'd, and what he said,
And back we come at fall of dew.

Again the feast, the speech, the glee,
    The shade of passing thought, the wealth
    Of words and wit, the double health,
The crowning cup, the three-times-three,

And last the dance; – till I retire:
    Dumb is that tower which spake so loud,
    And high in heaven the streaming cloud,
And on the downs a rising fire:

And rise, O moon, from yonder down,
    Till over down and over dale
    All night the shining vapour sail
And pass the silent-lighted town,

The white-faced halls, the glancing rills,
    And catch at every mountain head,
    And o'er the friths that branch and spread
Their sleeping silver thro' the hills;

And touch with shade the bridal doors,
    With tender gloom the roof, the wall;
    And breaking let the splendour fall
To spangle all the happy shores

By which they rest, and ocean sounds,
    And, star and system rolling past,
    A soul shall draw from out the vast
And strike his being into bounds,

And, moved thro' life of lower phase,
    Result in man, be born and think,
    And act and love, a closer link
Betwixt us and the crowning race

Of those that, eye to eye, shall look
    On knowledge; under whose command
    Is Earth and Earth's, and in their hand
Is Nature like an open book;

No longer half-akin to brute,
    For all we thought and loved and did.

And hoped, and suffer'd, is but seed
Of what in them is flower and fruit;

Whereof the man, that with me trod
    This planet, was a noble type
    Appearing ere the times were ripe,
That friend of mine who lives in God,

That God, which ever lives and loves,
    One God, one law, one element,
    And one far-off divine event,
To which the whole creation moves.

seed of learning, coming clear and closer to the truth

From MAUD: A MONODRAMA

Tennyson's 'little *Hamlet*' as he called this verse novel, appeared in 1855. Its narrator is another study of a mind on the dangerous edge of self-analysis. The apparent suicide of his ruined father and hostility of the old lord of the Hall is the prelude to his falling in love with Maud, the old lord's daughter. Yet the affection and possibility of love between them in childhood and youth is worsted by the arrival of the 'new-made lord' whom the girl is to marry. There is a quarrel in which the narrator strikes Maud's brother an apparently fatal blow and escapes abroad. His reason is tormented, uncertain whether the brother is dead or not, though believing Maud herself to have died. In this state he is entombed alive in the madhouse. At length, though his life has 'crept so long on a broken wing/Thro' cells of madness, haunts of horror and fear', he recovers his sanity and goes to fight his country's war in the Crimea.

> For the peace, that I deem'd no peace, is over and done,
> And now by the side of the Black and the Baltic deep,
> And deathful-grinning mouths of the fortress, flames
> The blood-red blossom of war with a heart of fire.

The theme of childhood love doomed to despair in adult life also runs through 'Locksley Hall' in the *Poems* of 1842 and *Enoch Arden* (1864). There is a poignant irony in *Maud* between the lover's lyric cliché, 'My heart would hear her and beat,/Were it earth in an earthy bed,' and the living burial of the madhouse, 'O me, why have they not buried me deep enough,' where he longs to escape the sounds above his head. The self-pity and disjointed thoughts of Tennyson's mad-scene made a powerful climax to the monodrama.

The following sections describe the narrator's childhood and the thought of war as an escape from mental anguish; his first suspicion of both Maud and her military brother; his belief that he had triumphed over the young lord; a lyric outburst at what proved their last meeting; and a living death in the madhouse.

PART I

I

I

I hate the dreadful hollow behind the little wood,
Its lips in the field above are dabbled with blood-red heath,
The red-ribb'd ledges drip with a silent horror of blood,
And Echo there, whatever is ask'd her, answers 'Death'.

II

For there in the ghastly pit long since a body was found,
His who had given me life – O father! O God! was it well? –
Mangled, and flatten'd, and crush'd, and dinted into the
    ground:
There yet lies the rock that fell with him when he fell.

III

Did he fling himself down? who knows? for a vast speculation
    had fail'd,
And ever he mutter'd and madden'd, and ever wann'd with
    despair,
And out he walk'd when the wind like a broken worldling
    wail'd,
And the flying gold of the ruin'd woodlands drove thro' the air.

IV

I remember the time, for the roots of my hair were stirr'd
By a shuffled step, by a dead weight trail'd, by a whisper'd
    fright,
And my pulses closed their gates with a shock on my heart as I
    heard
The shrill-edged shriek of a mother divide the shuddering night.

V

Villany somewhere! whose? One says, we are villains all.
Not he: his honest fame should at least by me be maintain'd:
But that old man, now lord of the broad estate and the Hall,

Dropt off gorged from a scheme that had left us flaccid and
    drain'd.

VI

Why do they prate of the blessings of Peace? we have made
    them a curse,
Pickpockets, each hand lusting for all that is not its own;
And lust of gain, in the spirit of Cain, is it better or worse
Than the heart of the citizen hissing in war on his own
    hearthstone?

VII

But these are the days of advance, the works of the men of
    mind,
When who but a fool would have faith in a tradesman's ware
    or his word?
Is it peace or war? Civil war, as I think, and that of a kind
The viler, as underhand, not openly bearing the sword.

VIII

Sooner or later I too may passively take the print
Of the golden age — why not? I have neither hope nor trust;
May make my heart as a millstone, set my face as a flint,
Cheat and be cheated, and die: who knows? we are ashes and
    dust.

IX

Peace sitting under her olive, and slurring the days gone by,
When the poor are hovell'd and hustled together, each sex, like
    swine,
When only the ledger lives, and when only not all men lie;
Peace in her vineyard — yes! — but a company forges the wine.

X

And the vitriol madness flushes up in the ruffian's head,
Till the filthy by-lane rings to the yell of the trampled wife,
While chalk and alum and plaster are sold to the poor for
    bread,

And the spirit of murder works in the very means of life,

XI

And Sleep must lie down arm'd, for the villainous centre-bits
Grind on the wakeful ear in the hush of the moonless nights,
While another is cheating the sick of a few last gasps, as he sits
To pestle a poison'd poison behind his crimson lights.

XII

When a Mammonite mother kills her babe for a burial fee,
And Timour-Mammon grins on a pile of children's bones,
Is it peace or war? better, war! loud war by land and by sea,
War with a thousand battles, and shaking a hundred thrones.

XIII

For I trust if an enemy's fleet came yonder round by the hill,
And the rushing battle-bolt sang from the three-decker out of
  the foam,
That the smooth-faced snubnosed rogue would leap from his
  counter and till,
And strike, if he could, were it but with his cheating yardwand,
  home.——

XIV

What! am I raging alone as my father raged in his mood?
Must *I* too creep to the hollow and dash myself down and die
Rather than hold by the law that I made, nevermore to brood
On a horror of shatter'd limbs and a wretched swindler's lie?

XV

Would there be sorrow for *me*? there was *love* in the passionate
  shriek,
Love for the silent thing that had made false haste to the
  grave —
Wrapt in a cloak, as I saw him, and thought he would rise and
  speak
And rave at the lie and the liar, ah God, as he used to rave.

XVI

I am sick of the Hall and the hill, I am sick of the moor and the
main.
Why should I stay? can a sweeter chance ever come to me here?
O, having the nerves of motion as well as the nerves of pain,
Were it not wise if I fled from the place and the pit and the
fear?

XVII

Workmen up at the Hall! – they are coming back from abroad;
The dark old place will be gilt by the touch of a millionaire:
I have heard, I know not whence, of the singular beauty of
Maud;
I play'd with the girl when a child; she promised then to be fair.

XVIII

Maud with her venturous climbings and tumbles and childish
escapes,
Maud the delight of the village, the ringing joy of the Hall,
Maud with her sweet purse-mouth when my father dangled the
grapes,
Maud the beloved of my mother, the moon-faced darling of
all, –

XIX

What is she now? My dreams are bad. She may bring me a
curse.
No, there is fatter game on the moor; she will let me alone.
Thanks, for the fiend best knows whether woman or man be
the worse.
I will bury myself in myself, and the Devil may pipe to his own.

II

Long have I sigh'd for a calm: God grant I may find it at last!
It will never be broken by Maud, she has neither savour nor
    salt,
But a cold and clear-cut face, as I found when her carriage past,
Perfectly beautiful: let it be granted her: where is the fault?
All that I saw (for her eyes were downcast, not to be seen)
Faultily faultless, icily regular, splendidly null,
Dead perfection, no more; nothing more, if it had not been
For a chance of travel, a paleness, an hour's defect of the rose,
Or an underlip, you may call it a little too ripe, too full,
Or the least little delicate acquiline curve in a sensitive nose,
From which I escaped heart-free, with the least little touch of
    spleen.

III

Cold and clear-cut face, why come you so cruelly meek,
Breaking a slumber in which all spleenful folly was drown'd,
Pale with the golden beam of an eyelash dead on the cheek,
Passionless, pale, cold face, star-sweet on a gloom profound;
Womanlike, taking revenge too deep for a transient wrong
Done but in thought to your beauty, and ever as pale as before
Growing and fading and growing upon me without a sound,
Luminous, gemlike, ghostlike, deathlike, half the night long
Growing and fading and growing, till I could bear it no more,
But arose, and all by myself in my own dark garden ground,
Listening now to the tide in its broad-flung ship-wrecking roar,
Now to the scream of a madden'd beach dragg'd down by the
    wave,
Walk'd in a wintry wind by a ghastly glimmer, and found
The shining daffodil dead, and Orion low in his grave.

*   *   *

VI

I

Morning arises stormy and pale,
No sun, but a wannish glare
In fold upon fold of hueless cloud,
And the budded peaks of the wood are bow'd
Caught and cuff'd by the gale:
I had fancied it would be fair.

II

Whom but Maud should I meet
Last night, when the sunset burn'd
On the blossom'd gable-ends
At the head of the village street,
Whom but Maud should I meet?
And she touch'd my hand with a smile so sweet,
She made me divine amends
For a courtesy not return'd.

III

And thus a delicate spark
Of glowing and growing light
Thro' the livelong hours of the dark
Kept itself warm in the heart of my dreams,
Ready to burst in a colour'd flame;
Till at last when the morning came
In a cloud, it faded, and seems
But an ashen-grey delight.

IV

What if with her sunny hair,
And smile as sunny as cold,
She meant to weave me a snare
Of some coquettish deceit,
Cleopatra-like as of old
To entangle me when we met,
To have her lion roll in a silken net
And fawn at a victor's feet.

V

Ah, what shall I be at fifty
Should Nature keep me alive,
If I find the world so bitter
When I am but twenty-five?
Yet, if she were not a cheat,
If Maud were all that she seem'd,
And her smile were all that I dream'd,
Then the world were not so bitter
But a smile could make it sweet.

VI

What if tho' her eye seem'd full
Of a kind intent to me,
What if that dandy-despot, he,
That jewell'd mass of millinery,
That oil'd and curl'd Assyrian Bull
Smelling of musk and of insolence,
Her brother, from whom I keep aloof,
Who wants the finer politic sense
To mask, tho' but in his own behoof,
With a glassy smile his brutal scorn —
What if he had told her yestermorn
How prettily for his own sweet sake
A face of tenderness might be feign'd,
And a moist mirage in desert eyes,
That so, when the rotten hustings shake
In another month to his brazen lies,
A wretched vote may be gain'd.

VII

For a raven ever croaks, at my side,
Keep watch and ward, keep watch and ward,
Or thou wilt prove their tool.
Yea, too, myself from myself I guard,
For often a man's own angry pride
Is cap and bells for a fool.

VIII

Perhaps the smile and tender tone
Came out of her pitying womanhood,
For am I not, am I not, here alone
So many a summer since she died,
My mother, who was so gentle and good?
Living alone in an empty house,
Here half-hid in the gleaming wood,
Where I hear the dead at midday moan,
And the shrieking rush of the wainscot mouse,
And my own sad name in corners cried,
When the shiver of dancing leaves is thrown
About its echoing chambers wide,
Till a morbid hate and horror have grown
Of a world in which I have hardly mixt,
And a morbid eating lichen fixt
On a heart half-turn'd to stone.

IX

O heart of stone, are you flesh, and caught
By that you swore to withstand?
For what was it else within me wrought
But, I fear, the new strong wine of love,
That made my tongue so stammer and trip
When I saw the treasured splendour, her hand,
Come sliding out of her sacred glove,
And the sunlight broke from her lip?

X

I have play'd with her when a child;
She remembers it now we meet.
Ah well, well, well, I *may* be beguiled
By some coquettish deceit.
Yet, if she were not a cheat,
If Maud were all that she seem'd,
And her smile had all that I dream'd,
Then the world were not so bitter
But a smile could make it sweet.

*   *   *

XII

I

Birds in the high Hall-garden
        When twilight was falling,
Maud, Maud, Maud, Maud,
        They were crying and calling.

II

Where was Maud? in our wood;
        And I, who else, was with her,
Gathering woodland lilies,
        Myriads blow together.

III

Birds in our wood sang
        Ringing thro' the valleys,
Maud is here, here, here
        In among the lilies.

IV

I kiss'd her slender hand,
        She took the kiss sedately;
Maud is not seventeen,
        But she is tall and stately.

V

I to cry out on pride
        Who have won her favour!
O Maud were sure of Heaven
        If lowliness could save her.

VI

I know the way she went
        Home with her maiden posy,
For her feet have touch'd the meadows
        And left the daisies rosy.

VII

Birds in the high Hall-garden
    Were crying and calling to her,
Where is Maud, Maud, Maud?
    One is come to woo her.

VIII

Look, a horse at the door,
    And little King Charley snarling,
Go back, my lord, across the moor,
    You are not her darling.

*   *   *

XXII

I

Come into the garden, Maud,
    For the black bat, night, has flown,
Come into the garden, Maud,
    I am here at the gate alone;
And the woodbine spices are wafted abroad,
    And the musk of the rose is blown.

II

For a breeze of morning moves,
    And the planet of Love is on high,
Beginning to faint in the light that she loves
    On a bed of daffodil sky,
To faint in the light of the sun she loves,
    To faint in his light, and to die.

III

All night have the roses heard
    The flute, violin, bassoon;
All night has the casement jessamine stirr'd
    To the dancers dancing in tune;

Till a silence fell with the waking bird,
　And a hush with the setting moon.

IV

I said to the lily, 'There is but one
　With whom she has heart to be gay.
When will the dancers leave her alone?
　She is weary of dance and play.'
Now half to the setting moon are gone,
　And half to the rising day;
Low on the sand and loud on the stone
　The last wheel echoes away.

V

I said to the rose, 'The brief night goes
　In babble and revel and wine.
O young lord-lover, what sighs are those,
　For one that will never be thine?
But mine, but mine,' so I sware to the rose,
　'For ever and ever, mine.'

VI

And the soul of the rose went into my blood,
　As the music clash'd in the hall;
And long by the garden lake I stood,
　For I heard your rivulet fall
From the lake to the meadow and on to the wood,
　Our wood, that is dearer than all;

VII

From the meadow your walks have left so sweet
　That whenever a March-wind sighs
He sets the jewel-print of your feet
　In violets blue as your eyes,
To the woody hollows in which we meet
　And the valleys of Paradise.

VIII

The slender acacia would not shake
One long milk-bloom on the tree;
The white lake-blossom fell into the lake
As the pimpernel dozed on the lea;
But the rose was awake all night for your sake,
Knowing your promise to me;
The lilies and roses were all awake,
They sigh'd for the dawn and thee.

IX

Queen rose of the rosebud garden of girls,
Come hither, the dances are done,
In gloss of satin and glimmer of pearls,
Queen lily and rose in one;
Shine out, little head, sunning over with curls,
To the flowers, and be their sun.

X

There has fallen a splendid tear
From the passion-flower at the gate.
She is coming, my dove, my dear;
She is coming, my life, my fate;
The red rose cries, 'She is near, she is near;'
And the white rose weeps, 'She is late;'
The larkspur listens, 'I hear, I hear;'
And the lily whispers, 'I wait.'

XI

She is coming, my own, my sweet;
Were it ever so airy a tread,
My heart would hear her and beat,
Were it earth in an earthy bed;
My dust would hear her and beat,
Had I lain for a century dead;
Would start and tremble under her feet,
And blossom in purple and red.

*   *   *

V

I

Dead, long dead,
Long dead!
And my heart is a handful of dust,
And the wheels go over my head,
And my bones are shaken with pain,
For into a shallow grave they are thrust,
Only a yard beneath the street,
And the hoofs of the horses beat, beat,
The hoofs of the horses beat,
Beat into my scalp and my brain,
With never an end to the stream of passing feet,
Driving, hurrying, marrying, burying,
Clamour and rumble, and ringing and clatter,
And here beneath it is all as bad,
For I thought the dead had peace, but it is not so;
To have no peace in the grave, is that not sad?
But up and down and to and fro,
Ever about me the dead men go;
And then to hear a dead man chatter
Is enough to drive one mad.

II

Wretchedest age, since Time began,
They cannot even bury a man;
And tho' we paid our tithes in the days that are gone,
Not a bell was rung, not a prayer was read;
It is that which makes us loud in the world of the dead
There is none that does this work, not one;
A touch of their office might have sufficed,
But the churchmen fain would kill their church,
As the churches have kill'd their Christ.

III

See, there is one of us sobbing,
No limit to his distress;
And another, a lord of all things, praying
To his own great self, as I guess;
And another, a statesman there, betraying
His party-secret, fool, to the press;
And yonder a vile physician, blabbing
The case of his patient – all for what?
To tickle the maggot born in an empty head,
And wheedle a world that loves him not,
For it is but a world of the dead.

IV

Nothing but idiot gabble!
For the prophecy given of old
And then not understood,
Has come to pass as foretold;
Not let any man think for the public good,
But babble, merely for babble.
For I never whisper'd a private affair
Within the hearing of cat or mouse,
No, not to myself in the closet alone,
But I heard it shouted at once from the top of the house;
Everything came to be known:
Who told *him* we were there?

V

Not that grey old wolf, for he came not back
From the wilderness, full of wolves, where he used to lie;
He has gather'd the bones for his o'ergrown whelp to
crack;
Crack them now for yourself, and howl, and die.

VI

Prophet, curse me the blabbing lip,
And curse me the British vermin, the rat;
I know not whether he came in the Hanover ship,

But I know that he lies and listens mute
In an ancient mansion's crannies and holes:
Arsenic, arsenic, sure, would do it,
Except that now we poison our babes, poor souls!
It is all used up for that.

VII

Tell him now: she is standing here at my head;
Not beautiful now, not even kind;
He may take her now; for she never speaks her mind
But is ever the one thing silent here.
She is not of us, as I divine;
She comes from another stiller world of the dead,
Stiller, not fairer than mine.

VIII

But I know where a garden grows,
Fairer than aught in the world beside,
All made up of the lily and rose
That blow by night, when the season is good,
To the sound of dancing music and flutes:
It is only flowers, they had no fruits,
And I almost fear they are not roses, but blood;
For the keeper was one, so full of pride,
He linkt a dead man there to a spectral bride;
For he, if he had not been a Sultan of brutes,
Would he have that hole in his side?

IX

But what will the old man say?
He laid a cruel snare in a pit
To catch a friend of mine one stormy day;
Yet now I could even weep to think of it;
For what will the old man say
When he comes to the second corpse in the pit?

X

Friend, to be struck by the public foe,

Then to strike him and lay him low,
That were a public merit, far,
Whatever the Quaker holds, from sin;
But the red life spilt for a private blow —
I swear to you, lawful and lawless war
Are scarcely even akin.

XI

O me, why have they not buried me deep enough?
Is it kind to have made me a grave so rough,
Me, that was never a quiet sleeper?
Maybe still I am but half-dead;
Then I cannot be wholly dumb;
I will cry to the steps above my head,
And somebody, surely, some kind heart will come
To bury me, bury me
Deeper, ever so little deeper.

From ODE ON THE DEATH OF THE DUKE OF WELLINGTON

The funeral of the Duke of Wellington, on 18 November 1852, a day of cold sun and bitter wind, was one of the greatest ceremonial occasions that London has ever seen. Though Wellington died on 17 September, it took two months to arrange the details of his final journey from the lying-in-state in the Great Hall of Chelsea Hospital to the burial in St Paul's. Field-marshals and peers of the realm, Prince Albert in a coach-and-six, as well as three thousand foot-soldiers, eight squadrons of cavalry and three batteries of guns followed the coffin, which lay draped in crimson velvet on its towering 'funeral car'. The funeral car weighed eighteen tons and was drawn by twelve black-caparisoned dray-horses. In Pall Mall, its six huge wheels sank into the mud and it required the additional efforts of sixty men to move it. Yet the roar of central London fell silent, to be replaced by muffled drums, the solemn blasts of military bands playing the 'Dead March in Saul' and Handel's 'Old Hundred and Fourth'. The reverberations of the minute guns kept time across the parks and the river.

Tennyson evokes the scene with power and dignity, the visual detail and suggestion as specific here as in the private world of 'Mariana'. He catches the public mood with a subtlety no journalist could equal. Even the radicals and his political opponents were moved by the departure of the Iron Duke. Thomas Cooper, a Chartist, watched the coffin borne past Green Park to the slow march of the regiments, Wellington's white-plumed cocked hat and sword upon it. Far off, sunlight glinted on the golden cross of St Paul's dome. Cooper stood among silent crowds as the coffin passed. 'I stretched my neck to get the last sight of the car as it passed along Piccadilly, till it was out of sight; and then I thought the great connecting link of our national life was broken: the great actor in the scenes of the Peninsula and Waterloo – the conqueror of Napoleon – and the chief name in our home political life for many years – had disappeared. I seemed to myself now to belong to another generation of men; for my childhood was passed amid the noise of Wellington's battles, and his name and existence seemed stamped on every year of our time.'

There follow the first five of the poem's nine sections. Tennyson opens with a rhythm which suggests the muffled beat of the kettledrums and the boom of minute guns in the distance.

I

Bury the Great Duke
   With an empire's lamentation,
Let us bury the Great Duke
   To the noise of the mourning of a mighty nation,
Mourning when their leaders fall,
Warriors carry the warrior's pall,
And sorrow darkens hamlet and hall.

II

Where shall we lay the man whom we deplore?
Here, in streaming London's central roar.
Let the sound of those he wrought for,
And the feet of those he fought for,
Echo round his bones for evermore.

III

Lead out the pageant: sad and slow,
As fits an universal woe,
Let the long long procession go,
And let the sorrowing crowd about it grow,
And let the mournful martial music blow;
The last great Englishman is low.

IV

Mourn, for to us he seems the last,
Remembering all his greatness in the Past.
No more in soldier fashion will he greet
With lifted hand the gazer in the street.
O friends, our chief state-oracle is mute:
Mourn for the man of long-enduring blood,
The statesman-warrior, moderate, resolute,
Whole in himself, a common good.
Mourn for the man of amplest influence,
Yet clearest of ambitious crime,
Our greatest yet with least pretence,
Great in council and great in war,
Foremost captain of his time,
Rich in saving common-sense,
And, as the greatest only are,
In his simplicity sublime.
O good grey head which all men knew,
O voice from which their omens all men drew,
O iron nerve to true occasion true,
O fall'n at length that tower of strength
Which stood four-square to all winds that blew!
Such was he whom we deplore.
The long self-sacrifice of life is o'er.
The great World-victor's victor will be seen no more.

V

All is over and done:
Render thanks to the Giver,
England, for thy son.
Let the bell be toll'd.
Render thanks to the Giver,
And render him to the mould.
Under the cross of gold
That shines over city and river,
There he shall rest for ever
Among the wise and the bold.
Let the bell be toll'd:

And a reverent people behold
The towering car, the sable steeds:
Bright let it be with its blazon'd deeds,
Dark in its funeral fold.
Let the bell be toll'd:
And a deeper knell in the heart be knoll'd;
And the sound of the sorrowing anthem roll'd
Thro' the dome of the golden cross;
And the volleying cannon thunder his loss;
He knew their voices of old.
For many a time in many a clime
His captain's-ear has heard them boom
Bellowing victory, bellowing doom:
When he with those deep voices wrought,
Guarding realms and kings from shame;
With those deep voices our dead captain taught
The tyrant, and asserts his claim
In that dread sound to the great name,
Which he has worn so pure of blame,
In praise and in dispraise the same,
A man of well-attemper'd frame.
O civic muse, to such a name,
To such a name for ages long,
To such a name,
Preserve a broad approach of fame,
And ever-echoing avenues of song.

THE IDYLLS OF THE KING:
From MERLIN AND VIVIEN

Following his first specific treatment of Arthurian legend in the 'Morte d'Arthur' of 1842, Tennyson began an extended series of longer poems which appeared between 1859 and 1885 as *The Idylls of the King. Merlin and Vivien*, published in 1859, is the tale of the beautiful and cunning daughter of a man killed fighting against Arthur. In pursuit of revenge, she attempts to seduce Arthur himself and then accompanies the aged magician Merlin to Broceliande.

> A storm was coming, but the winds were still,
> And in the wild woods of Broceliande,
> Before an oak, so hollow, huge, and old
> It look'd a tower of ivied masonwork,
> At Merlin's feet the wily Vivien lay.

By her seductive craft she coaxes a secret charm from the wizard and leaves him imprisoned in the oak as her vengeance against the court of the 'blameless king'. The following extract shows Tennyson as the painter of a landscape of legend and of seductive qualities in primeval womanhood, owing something to the Pre-Raphaelite vision, as well as that of post-romanticism. The enchantress, like Walter Pater's recreation of the Mona Lisa, is both a figure of myth and a creature of flesh and blood, as she lies beguilingly at Merlin's feet.

> There lay she all her length and kiss'd his feet,
> As if in deepest reverence and in love.
> A twist of gold was round her hair; a robe
> Of samite without price, that more exprest
> Than hid her, clung about her lissome limbs,
> In colour like the satin-shining palm

On sallows in the windy gleams of March:
And while she kiss'd them, crying 'Trample me,
Dear feet, that I have follow'd thro' the world,
And I will pay you worship; tread me down
And I will kiss you for it;' he was mute:
So dark a forethought roll'd about his brain,
As on a dull day in an Ocean cave
The blind wave feeling round his long sea-hall
In silence: wherefore, when she lifted up
A face of sad appeal, and spake and said,
'O Merlin, do you love me?' and again,
'O Merlin, do you love me?' and once more,
'Great Master, do you love me?' he was mute.
And lissome Vivien, holding by his heel,
Writhed toward him, slided up his knee and sat,
Behind his ankle twined her hollow feet
Together, curved an arm about his neck,
Clung like a snake; and letting her left hand
Droop from his mighty shoulder, as a leaf,
Made with her right a comb of pearl to part
The lists of such a beard as youth gone out
Had left in ashes: then he spoke and said,
Not looking at her, 'Who are wise in love
Love most, say least,' and Vivien answer'd quick,
'I saw the little elf-god eyeless once
In Arthur's arras hall at Camelot:
But neither eyes nor tongue – O stupid child!
Yet you are wise who say it; let me think
Silence is wisdom: I am silent then
And ask no kiss;' then adding all at once,
'And lo, I clothe myself with wisdom,' drew
The vast and shaggy mantle of his beard
Across her neck and bosom to her knee,
And call'd herself a gilded summer fly
Caught in a great old tyrant spider's web,
Who meant to eat her up in that wild wood
Without one word. So Vivien call'd herself,
But rather seem'd a lovely baleful star

Veil'd in grey vapour; till he sadly smiled:
'To what request for what strange boon,' he said,
'Are these your pretty tricks and fooleries,
O Vivien, the preamble? yet my thanks,
For these have broken up my melancholy.'

And Vivien answer'd smiling saucily,
'What, O my Master, have you found your voice?
I bid the stranger welcome. Thanks at last!
But yesterday you never open'd lip,
Except indeed to drink: no cup had we:
In mine own lady palms I cull'd the spring
That gather'd trickling dropwise from the cleft,
And made a pretty cup of both my hands
And offer'd you it kneeling: then you drank
And knew no more, nor gave me one poor word;
O no more thanks than might a goat have given
With no more sign of reverence than a beard.
And when we halted at that other well,
And I was faint to swooning, and you lay
Foot-gilt with all the blossom-dust of those
Deep meadows we had traversed, did you know
That Vivien bathed your feet before her own?
And yet no thanks: and all thro' this wild wood
And all this morning when I fondled you:
Boon, yes, there was a boon, one not so strange —
How had I wrong'd you? surely you are wise,
But such a silence is more wise than kind.'

And Merlin lock'd his hand in hers and said:
'O did you never lie upon the shore,
And watch the curl'd white of the coming wave
Glass'd in the slippery sand before it breaks?
Ev'n such a wave, but not so pleasurable,
Dark in the glass of some presageful mood,
Had I for three days seen, ready to fall.
And then I rose and fled from Arthur's court
To break the mood. You follow'd me unask'd;
And when I look'd, and saw you following still,

My mind involved yourself the nearest thing
In that mind-mist: for shall I tell you truth?
You seem'd that wave about to break upon me
And sweep me from my hold upon the world,
My use and name and fame. Your pardon, child.
Your pretty sports have brighten'd all again.
And ask your boon, for boon I owe you thrice,
Once for wrong done you by confusion, next
For thanks it seems till now neglected, last
For these your dainty gambols: wherefore ask;
And take this boon so strange and not so strange.'

  And Vivien answer'd, smiling mournfully:
'O not so strange as my long asking it,
Nor yet so strange as you yourself are strange,
Nor half so strange as that dark mood of yours.
I ever fear'd you were not wholly mine;
And see, yourself have own'd you did me wrong.
The people call you prophet: let it be:
But not of those that can expound themselves.
Take Vivien for expounder; she will call
That three-days-long presageful gloom of yours
No presage, but the same mistrustful mood
That makes you seem less noble than yourself,
Whenever I have ask'd this very boon,
Now ask'd again: for see you not, dear love,
That such a mood as that, which lately gloom'd
Your fancy when you saw me following you,
Must make me fear still more you are not mine,
Must make me yearn still more to prove you mine,
And make me wish still more to learn this charm
Of woven paces and of waving hands,
As proof of trust. O Merlin, teach it me.
The charm so taught will charm us both to rest.
For, grant me some slight power upon your fate,
I, feeling that you felt me worthy trust,
Should rest and let you rest, knowing you mine.
And therefore be as great as you are named,

Not muffled round with selfish reticence.
How hard you look and how denyingly!
O, if you think this wickedness in me,
That I should prove it on you unawares,
To make you lose your use and name and fame,
That makes me most indignant; then our bond
Had best be loosed for ever: but think or not,
By Heaven that hears I tell you the clean truth,
As clean as blood of babes, as white as milk:
O Merlin, may this earth, if ever I,
If these unwitty wandering wits of mine,
Ev'n in the jumbled rubbish of a dream,
Have tript on such conjectural treachery —
May this hard earth cleave to the Nadir hell
Down, down, and close again, and nip me flat,
If I be such a traitress. Yield my boon,
Till which I scarce can yield you all I am;
And grant my re-reiterated wish,
The great proof of your love: because I think,
However wise, you hardly know me yet.'

TO VIRGIL

Published in the *Nineteenth Century*, in September 1882, Tennyson's poem was written 'at the request of the Mantuans for the nineteenth century of Virgil's death.' It is a fine and majestic tribute, following Virgil in references to the destruction of Troy, the mission of Aeneas to found Rome, the suicide and funeral pyre of Dido, Queen of Carthage, deserted by Aeneas in his nobler quest. Hesiod's *Works and Days*, and the shepherd Tityrus, remind us that Virgil was the poet of the pastoral *Eclogues* and *Georgics*, as well as of the great historical sweep from Troy to Rome in the *Aeneid*. Tennyson's reference to the 'doom of humankind' suggests the evocative line of the *Aeneid*, (1, 462)

> sunt lacrimae rerum et mentem mortalia tangunt.

Almost untranslatable, its literal meaning is 'There are tears of things and thoughts of mortality touch upon the mind.' Virgil was not the only Roman poet to receive Tennyson's homage. In March 1883, in the *Nineteenth Century*, he was to pay tribute to the love poetry of Catullus, whose home was not far from Virgil's Mantua, at Sirmio, on the southern shore of Lake Garda. In 'Frater Ave Atque Vale', the memorial salute 'Brother, Hail and Farewell', Tennyson recalls visiting the little peninsula of the modern Italian town of Sirmione. 'Venusta Sirmio' in Catullus is lovely or graceful Sirmio.

> Row us out from Desenzano, to your Sirmione row!
> So they row'd, and there we landed – 'O Venusta Sirmio!'
> There to me thro' all the groves of olives in the summer glow,
> There beneath the Roman ruin where the purple flowers grow,
> Came that 'Ave atque Vale' of the Poet's helpless woe,
> Tenderest of Roman poets nineteen-hundred years ago,
> 'Frater Ave atque Vale' – as we wander'd to and fro
> Gazing at the Lydian laughter of the Garda Lake below
> Sweet Catullus's all-but-island, olive-silvery Sirmio.

I

Roman Virgil, thou that singest
    Ilion's lofty temples robed in fire,
Ilion falling, Rome arising,
    wars, and filial faith, and Dido's
        pyre;

II

Landscape-lover, lord of language
    more than he that sang the Works
        and Days,
All the chosen coin of fancy
    flashing out from many a golden
        phrase;

III

Thou that singest wheat and woodland,
    tilth and vineyard, hive and horse
        and herd;
All the charm of all the Muses
    often flowering in a lonely word;

IV

Poet of the happy Tityrus
    piping underneath his beechen
        bowers;
Poet of the poet-satyr
    whom the laughing shepherd
        bound with flowers;

V

Chanter of the Pollio, glorying
    in the blissful years again to be,
Summers of the snakeless meadow,
    unlaborious earth and oarless sea;

VI

Thou that seëst Universal
    Nature moved by Universal
        Mind;
Thou majestic in thy sadness
    at the doubtful doom of human
        kind;

VII

Light among the vanish'd ages;
    star that gildest yet this phantom
        shore;
Golden branch amid the shadows,
    kings and realms that pass to rise
        no more;

VIII

Now thy Forum roars no longer,
    fallen every purple Cæsar's
        dome –
Tho' thine ocean-roll of rhythm
    sound for ever of Imperial Rome –

IX

Now the Rome of slaves hath perish'd,
    and the Rome of freemen holds
        her place,
I, from out the Northern Island
    sunder'd once from all the human
        race,

X

I salute thee, Mantovano,
    I that loved thee since my day
        began,
Wielder of the stateliest measure
    ever moulded by the lips of man.

OPENING OF THE INDIAN AND COLONIAL EXHIBITION BY THE QUEEN

Written at the Request of the Prince of Wales

Of all Tennyson's poems for public occasions, this marked one of the grandest celebrations, the Indian and Colonial Exhibition of May 1886, held in South Kensington, where the Albert Hall and the Natural History Museum had been completed, and where the Victoria and Albert Museum was under construction. The Indian Hall, the Indian Bazaar, as well as 'Old London' and the Australian Colonies were among the most popular displays. The queen, in her journal for 4 May, describes the opening ceremony in the crowded Albert Hall, where the Prince of Wales greeted her. 'We stood upon a large dais under the organ, where there was an Indian chair of state, standing on an Indian carpet. The National Anthem was sung, the second verse in Sanscrit, translated by Prof. Max Müller . . . Then followed an Ode for the occasion, with beautiful words by Tennyson, the music by Sullivan, the solo being sung by Albani. Bertie read a very long Address, to which I read an Answer. Dear Bertie, who was most kind throughout, then kissed my hand.' After 'Home Sweet Home' 'The Hallelujah Chorus', and 'Rule, Britannia' had been sung, the queen returned to Buckingham Palace to the cheers of some of the largest crowds that London had ever seen.

Tennyson's poem ought, primarily, to be read in the context of this summer of national and imperial pride. The ceremony prompted the queen to reflect on her private thoughts of the dead Prince Albert in the spirit of *In Memoriam*. 'How pleased my darling husband would have been at the whole thing, and who knows but that his pure white spirit looks down upon his poor little wife, his children and children's children, with pleasure, on the development of his work!' Against the self-righteousness of much Victorian opinion, occasions of this kind evoked an honesty and directness of emotion, which Tennyson records and which made a later generation self-conscious and uncomfortable.

Opening of the Indian and Colonial Exhibition by the Queen

Written at the Request of the Prince of Wales

I

Welcome, welcome with one voice!
In your welfare we rejoice,
Sons and brothers that have sent,
From isle and cape and continent,
Produce of your field and flood,
Mount and mine, and primal wood;
Works of subtle brain and hand,
And splendours of the morning land,
Gifts from every British zone;
    Britons, hold your own!

II

May we find, as ages run,
The mother featured in the son;
And may yours for ever be
That old strength and constancy
Which has made your fathers great
In our ancient island State,
And wherever her flag fly,
Glorying between sea and sky,
Makes the might of Britain known;
    Britons, hold your own!

III

Britain fought her sons of yore –
Britain fail'd; and never more,
Careless of our growing kin,
Shall we sin our fathers' sin,
Men that in a narrower day –
Unprophetic rulers they –
Drove from out the mother's nest
That young eagle of the West

To forage for herself alone;
  Britons, hold your own!

IV

Sharers of our glorious past,
Brothers, must we part at last?
Shall we not thro' good and ill
Cleave to one another still?
Britain's myriad voices call,
'Sons, be welded each and all,
Into one imperial whole,
One with Britain, heart and soul!
One life, one flag, one fleet, one Throne!
  Britons, hold your own!'

CROSSING THE BAR

It was Tennyson's wish that 'Crossing the Bar' should be placed at the end of all editions of his poetry. It was written in October 1889, three years before his death, when he was eighty years old and had been seriously ill. While he was crossing to the Isle of Wight on the steamer, the poem came to him 'in a moment'. It was, and is, one of the most popular and frequently borrowed sets of memorial verses. The 'moaning of the bar' is the sound of the sea against a harbour sand-bar as a storm gathers.

Sunset and evening star,
    And one clear call for me!
And may there be no moaning of the bar,
    When I put out to sea,

But such a tide as moving seems asleep,
    Too full for sound and foam,
When that which drew from out the boundless deep
    Turns again home.

Twilight and evening bell,
    And after that the dark!
And may there be no sadness of farewell,
    When I embark;

For tho' from out our bourne of Time and Place
    The flood may bear me far,
I hope to see my Pilot face to face
    When I have crost the bar.

BROWNING

PORPHYRIA'S LOVER

First published as 'Porphyria' in the *Monthly Repository* in 1836 and reprinted in *Dramatic Lyrics* in 1842, at the end of Browning's abortive career as a verse playwright, 'Porphyria's Lover' is a powerful example of Browning's early interest in 'morbid anatomy', at a time when his desk was decorated with two skulls whose owners, he thought, had come to a bad end.

The rain set early in to-night
   The sullen wind was soon awake,
It tore the elm-tops down for spite,
   And did its worst to vex the lake,
I listened with heart fit to break;
When glided in Porphyria: straight
   She shut the cold out and the storm,
And kneeled and made the cheerless grate
   Blaze up, and all the cottage warm;
Which done, she rose, and from her form
Withdrew the dripping cloak and shawl,
   And laid her soiled gloves by, untied
Her hat and let the damp hair fall,
   And last, she sate down by my side
And called me. When no voice replied,
She put my arm about her waist,
   And made her smooth white shoulder bare,
And all her yellow hair displaced,
   And, stooping, made my cheek lie there,
And spread o'er all her yellow hair,
Murmuring how she loved me; she
   Too weak, for all her heart's endeavour,
To set its struggling passion free
   From pride, and vainer ties dissever,

And give herself to me for ever:
But passion sometimes would prevail,
   Nor could to-night's gay feast restrain
A sudden thought of one so pale
   For love of her, and all in vain;
So, she was come through wind and rain.
Be sure I looked up at her eyes
   Proud, very proud; at last I knew
Porphyria worshipped me; surprise
   Made my heart swell, and still it grew
While I debated what to do.
That moment she was mine, mine, fair,
   Perfectly pure and good: I found
A thing to do, and all her hair
   In one long yellow string I wound
Three times her little throat around,
And strangled her. No pain felt she;
   I am quite sure she felt no pain.
As a shut bud that holds a bee
   I warily oped her lids; again
Laughed the blue eyes without a stain.
And I untightened next the tress
   About her neck; her cheek once more
Blushed bright beneath my burning kiss:
   I propped her head up as before,
Only, this time *my* shoulder bore
Her head, which droops upon it still:
   The smiling rosy little head,
So glad it has its utmost will,
   That all it scorned at once is fled,
And I, its love, am gained instead!
Porphyria's love: she guessed not how
   Her darling one wish would be heard.
And thus we sit together now,
   And all night long we have not stirred,
And yet God has not said a word!

From PAULINE

Pauline was Browning's first book-length poem, dated 'Richmond, October 1832', his aunt Mrs Silverthorne having paid £30 for the printing and advertising. It is his self-conscious tribute to Shelley and he later preferred to disown it. 'Will you and must you have *Pauline*?' he wrote to Elizabeth Barrett, 'It is altogether foolish and *not* boylike.' Yet some of its neo-Shelleyan landscapes held an appeal for the new painters and poets of the mid-Victorian period.

Night, and one single ridge of narrow path
Between the sullen river and the woods
Waving and muttering – for the moonless night
Has shaped them into images of life,
Like the upraising of the giant-ghosts,
Looking on earth to know how their sons fare.
Thou art so close by me, the roughest swell
Of wind in the tree-tops hides not the panting
Of thy soft breasts; no – we will pass to morning –
Morning – the rocks, and vallies, and old woods.
How the sun brightens in the mist, and here, –
Half in the air, like creatures of the place,
Trusting the element – living on high boughs
That swing in the wind – look at the golden spray,
Flung from the foam-sheet of the cataract,
Amid the broken rocks – shall we stay here
With the wild hawks? – no, ere the hot noon come
Dive we down – safe; – see this our new retreat
Walled in with a sloped mound of matted shrubs,
Dark, tangled, old and green – still sloping down
To a small pool whose waters lie asleep
Amid the trailing boughs turned water plants

And tall trees over-arch to keep us in,
Breaking the sunbeams into emerald shafts,
And in the dreamy water one small group
Of two or three strange trees are got together,
Wondering at all around – as strange beasts herd
Together far from their own land – all wildness –
No turf nor moss, for boughs and plants pave all,
And tongues of bank go shelving in the waters,
Where the pale-throated snake reclines his head,
And old grey stones lie making eddies there;
The wild mice cross them dry-shod – deeper in –
Shut thy soft eyes – now look – still deeper in:
This is the very heart of the woods – all round,
Mountain-like, heaped above us; yet even here
One pond of water gleams – far off the river
Sweeps like a sea, barred out from land; but one –
One thin clear sheet has over-leaped and wound
Into this silent depth, which gained, it lies
Still, as but let by sufferance; the trees bend
O'er it as wild men watch a sleeping girl,
And thro' their roots long creeping plants stretch out
Their twined hair, steeped and sparkling; farther on,
Tall rushes and thick flag-knots have combined
To narrow it; so, at length, a silver thread
It winds, all noiselessly, thro' the deep wood,
Till thro' a cleft way, thro' the moss and stone,
It joins its parent-river with a shout.

From SORDELLO

Sordello, a poem in six books, celebrated an Italian poet and
warrior of the thirteenth century. Published in 1840, it was
damned by the critics as incomprehensible and tagged Browning
as an 'obscure' writer for the rest of his life. At full-length, the
poem was hard reading. Even the following description of the
Castle of Goito, scene of Sordello's childhood, was less accessible
to readers in an age accustomed to plainer narrative style. In
modern terms, Browning's technique is more suggestively
imagistic, even cinematic, as in the opening of *Pippa Passes*. At
Goito, the eye seems to move like a camera through the strange
interior, through light and darkness, hazy half-lit scenes whose
silence holds a sense of menace and veiled sexuality.

    In Mantua-territory half is slough
Half pine-tree forest; maples, scarlet-oaks
Breed o'er the river-beds; even Mincio chokes
With sand the summer through; but 'tis morass
In winter up to Mantua walls. There was
(Some thirty years before this evening's coil)
One spot reclaimed from the surrounding spoil,
Goito; just a castle built amid
A few low mountains; firs and larches hid
Their main defiles and rings of vineyard bound
The rest: some captured creature in a pound,
Whose artless wonder quite precludes distress
Secure beside in its own loveliness,
So peered with airy head, below, above,
The castle at its toils the lapwings love
To glean among at grape-time. Pass within:
A maze of corridors contrived for sin,
Dusk winding-stairs, dim galleries got past,

You gain the inmost chambers, gain at last
A maple-panelled room: that haze which seems
Floating about the panel, if there gleams
A sunbeam over it will turn to gold
And in light-graven characters unfold
The Arab's wisdom everywhere; what shade
Marred them a moment, those slim pillars made,
Cut like a company of palms to prop
The roof, each kissing top entwined with top,
Leaning together; in the carver's mind
Some knot of bacchanals, flushed cheek combined
With straining forehead, shoulders purpled, hair
Diffused between, who in a goat-skin bear
A vintage; graceful sister-palms: but quick
To the main wonder now. A vault, see; thick
Black shade about the ceiling, though fine slits
Across the buttress suffer light by fits
Upon a marvel in the midst: nay, stoop –
A dullish grey-streaked cumbrous font, a group
Round it, each side of it, where'er one sees,
Upholds it – shrinking Caryatides
Of just-tinged marble like Eve's lilied flesh
Beneath her Maker's finger when the fresh
First pulse of life shot brightening the snow:
The font's edge burthens every shoulder, so
They muse upon the ground, eyelids half closed,
Some, with meek arms behind their backs disposed,
Some, crossed above their bosoms, some, to veil
Their eyes, some, propping chin and cheek so pale,
Some, hanging slack an utter helpless length
Dead as a buried vestal whose whole strength
Goes when the grate above shuts heavily;
So dwell these noiseless girls, patient to see,
Like priestesses because of sin impure
Penanced for ever, who resigned endure,
Having that once drunk sweetness to the dregs;
And every eve Sordello's visit begs
Pardon for them: constant as eve he came

To sit beside each in her turn, the same
As one of them, a certain space: and awe
Made a great indistinctness till he saw
Sunset slant cheerful through the buttress chinks,
Gold seven times globed; surely our maiden shrinks
And a smile stirs her as if one faint grain
Her load were lightened, one shade less the stain
Obscured her forehead, yet one more bead slipt
From off the rosary whereby the crypt
Keeps count of the contritions of its charge?
Then with a step more light, a heart more large,
He may depart, leave her and every one
To linger out the penance in mute stone.

MY LAST DUCHESS

'My Last Duchess' is another poem from *Dramatic Lyrics* in 1842. The speaker is no common murderer like Porphyria's lover but a powerful ruler, a Renaissance Duke of Ferrara who has had his 'last Duchess' put to death for her familiar manner with other men. 'I choose never to stoop.' It is a matter of pride and honour with him, as it was to be with the wife-murderer Guido Franceschini in *The Ring and the Book*. The moral horror in the present case is concealed until the last lines, when the person addressed is revealed as a visitor arranging the Duke's next marriage to a young and unsuspecting second bride.

FERRARA

That's my last Duchess painted on the wall,
Looking as if she were alive; I call
That piece a wonder, now: Frà Pandolf's hands
Worked busily a day, and there she stands.
Will't please you sit and look at her? I said
'Frà Pandolf' by design, for never read
Strangers like you that pictured countenance,
The depth and passion of its earnest glance,
But to myself they turned (since none puts by
The curtain I have drawn for you, but I)
And seemed as they would ask me, if they durst,
How such a glance came there; so, not the first
Are you to turn and ask thus. Sir, 'twas not
Her husband's presence only, called that spot
Of joy into the Duchess' cheek: perhaps
Frà Pandolf chanced to say 'Her mantle laps
'Over my Lady's wrist too much,' or 'Paint
'Must never hope to reproduce the faint

'Half-flush that dies along her throat;' such stuff
Was courtesy, she thought, and cause enough
For calling up that spot of joy. She had
A heart . . . how shall I say? . . . too soon made glad,
Too easily impressed; she liked whate'er
She looked on, and her looks went everywhere.
Sir, 'twas all one! My favour at her breast,
The drooping of the daylight in the West,
The bough of cherries some officious fool
Broke in the orchard for her, the white mule
She rode with round the terrace – all and each
Would draw from her alike the approving speech,
Or blush, at least. She thanked men, – good; but thanked
Somehow . . . I know not how . . . as if she ranked
My gift of a nine hundred years old name
With anybody's gift. Who'd stoop to blame
This sort of trifling? Even had you skill
In speech – (which I have not) – to make your will
Quite clear to such an one, and say 'Just this
'Or that in you disgusts me; here you miss,
'Or there exceed the mark' – and if she let
Herself be lessoned so, nor plainly set
Her wits to yours, forsooth, and made excuse,
– E'en then would be some stooping, and I chuse
Never to stoop. Oh, Sir, she smiled, no doubt,
Whene'er I passed her; but who passed without
Much the same smile? This grew; I gave commands;
Then all smiles stopped together. There she stands
As if alive. Will't please you rise? We'll meet
The company below, then. I repeat,
The Count your Master's known munificence
Is ample warrant that no just pretence
Of mine for dowry will be disallowed;
Though his fair daughter's self, as I avowed
At starting, is my object. Nay, we'll go
Together down, Sir! Notice Neptune, tho',
Taming a sea-horse, thought a rarity,
Which Claus of Innsbruck cast in bronze for me.

THE BISHOP ORDERS HIS TOMB IN ST PRAXED'S CHURCH

One of Browning's finest dramatic monologues, a Renaissance bishop on his deathbed reveals to his illegitimate sons – 'nephews' – an all too human soul torn between pious pretensions and jealousy, fear and greed, sexual nostalgia and love of classical learning. The poem appeared in *Dramatic Romances and Lyrics* in 1845. In his fourth volume of *Modern Painters* in 1856, John Ruskin noted of its central passage, 'I know no other piece of modern English, prose or poetry, in which there is so much told, as in these lines, of the Renaissance spirit, – its worldliness, inconsistency, pride, hypocrisy, ignorance of itself, love of art, of luxury, and of good Latin.'

[ROME, 15—]

Vanity, saith the preacher, vanity!
Draw round my bed: is Anselm keeping back?
Nephews – sons mine . . . ah God, I know not! Well –
She, men would have to be your mother once,
Old Gandolf envied me, so fair she was!
What's done is done, and she is dead beside,
Dead long ago, and I am bishop since,
And as she died so must we die ourselves,
-And thence ye may perceive the world's a dream.
Life, how and what is it? As here I lie
In this state-chamber, dying by degrees,
Hours and long hours in the dead night, I ask
'Do I live, am I dead?' Peace, peace seems all.
St Praxed's ever was the church for peace;
And so, about this tomb of mine. I fought
With tooth and nail to save my niche, ye know:

– Old Gandolf cozened me, despite my care;
Shrewd was that snatch from out the corner South
He graced his carrion with, God curse the same!
Yet still my niche is not so cramped but thence
One sees the pulpit o' the epistle-side,
And somewhat of the choir, those silent seats,
And up into the aery dome where live
The angels, and a sunbeam's sure to lurk:
And I shall fill my slab of basalt there,
And 'neath my tabernacle take my rest,
With those nine columns round me, two and two,
The odd one at my feet where Anselm stands:
Peach-blossom marble all, the rare, the ripe
As fresh-poured red wine of a mighty pulse
– Old Gandolf with his paltry onion-stone,
Put me where I may look at him! True peach,
Rosy and flawless: how I earned the prize!
Draw close: that conflagration of my church
– What then? So much was saved if aught were missed!
My sons, ye would not be my death? Go dig
The white-grape vineyard where the oil-press stood,
Drop water gently till the surface sinks,
And if ye find . . . Ah, God I know not, I! . . .
Bedded in store of rotton figleaves soft,
And corded up in a tight olive-frail,
Some lump, ah God, of *lapis lazuli*,
Big as a Jew's head cut off at the nape,
Blue as a vein o'er the Madonna's breast . . .
Sons, all have I bequeathed you, villas, all,
That brave Frascati villa with its bath,
So, let the blue lump poise between my knees,
Like God the Father's globe on both his hands
Ye worship in the Jesu Church so gay,
For Gandolf shall not choose but see and burst!
Swift as a weaver's shuttle fleet our years:
Man goeth to the grave, and where is he?
Did I say basalt for my slab, sons? Black –
'Twas ever antique-black I meant! How else

Shall ye contrast my frieze to come beneath?
The bas-relief in bronze ye promised me,
Those Pans and Nymphs ye wot of, and perchance
Some tripod, thyrsus, with a vase or so,
The Saviour at his sermon on the mount,
St Praxed in a glory, and one Pan
Ready to twitch the Nymph's last garment off,
And Moses with the tables . . . but I know
Ye mark me not! What do they whisper thee,
Child of my bowels, Anselm? Ah, ye hope
To revel down my villas while I gasp
Bricked o'er with beggar's mouldy travertine
Which Gandolf from his tomb-top chuckles at!
Nay, boys, ye love me – all of jasper, then!
'Tis jasper ye stand pledged to, lest I grieve
My bath must needs be left behind, alas!
One block, pure green as a pistachio-nut,
There's plenty jasper somewhere in the world –
And have I not St Praxed's ear to pray
Horses for ye, and brown Greek manuscripts,
And mistresses with great smooth marbly limbs?
—That's if ye carve my epitaph aright,
Choice Latin, picked phrase, Tully's every word,
No gaudy ware like Gandolf's second line –
Tully, my masters? Ulpian serves his need!
And then how I shall lie through centuries,
And hear the blessed mutter of the mass,
And see God made and eaten all day long,
And feel the steady candle-flame, and taste
Good strong thick stupifying incense-smoke!
For as I lie here, hours of the dead night,
Dying in state and by such slow degrees,
I fold my arms as if they clasped a crook,
And stretch my feet forth straight as stone can point,
And let the bedclothes for a mortcloth drop
Into great laps and folds of sculptor's-work:
And as yon tapers dwindle, and strange thoughts
Grow, with a certain humming in my ears,

About the life before I lived this life,
And this life too, Popes, Cardinals and Priests,
St Praxed at his sermon on the mount,
Your tall pale mother with her talking eyes,
And new-found agate urns as fresh as day,
And marble's language, Latin pure, discreet,
– Aha, ELUCESCEBAT quoth our friend?
No Tully, said I, Ulpian at the best!
Evil and brief hath been my pilgrimage.
All *lapis*, all, sons! Else I give the Pope
My villas: will ye ever eat my heart?
Ever your eyes were as a lizard's quick,
They glitter like your mother's for my soul,
Or ye would heighten my impoverished frieze,
Piece out its starved design, and fill my vase
With grapes, and add a vizor and a Term,
And to the tripod ye would tie a lynx
That in his struggle throws the thyrsus down,
To comfort me on my entablature
Whereon I am to lie till I must ask
'Do I live, am I dead?' There, leave me, there!
For ye have stabbed me with ingratitude
To death – ye wish it – God, ye wish it! Stone—
Gritstone, a-crumble! Clammy squares which sweat
As if the corpse they keep were oozing through—
And no more *lapis* to delight the world!
Well, go! I bless ye. Fewer tapers there,
But in a row: and, going, turn your backs
– Ay, like departing altar-ministrants,
And leave me in my church, the church for peace,
That I may watch at leisure if he leers –
Old Gandolf, at me, from his onion-stone,
As still he envied me, so fair she was!

A LOVERS' QUARREL

By contrast with Renaissance subjects, Browning's love poetry is of physical sexuality in modern settings. 'A Lovers' Quarrel', from *Men and Women* in 1855, is about dressing, and therefore undressing, or making love in the various rooms of the house, as the speaker remembers a snowbound winter with the mistress he has now lost. Precise modernity is specified by reading in the *Times* about Napoleon III, who had assumed his title five years before the poem's publication.

I Oh, what a dawn of day!
How the March sun feels like May!
    All is blue again
    After last night's rain,
And the south dries the hawthorn-spray.
    Only, my Love's away!
I'd as lief that the blue were grey.

II Runnels, which rillets swell,
Must be dancing down the dell
    With a foamy head
    On the beryl bed
Paven smooth as a hermit's cell;
    Each with a tale to tell,
Could my Love but attend as well.

III Dearest, three months ago!
When we lived blocked-up with snow, –
    When the wind would edge
    In and in his wedge,
In, as far as the point could go –
    Not to our ingle, though,
Where we loved each the other so!

IV Laughs with so little cause!
　　We devised games out of straws.
　　　　We would try and trace
　　　　One another's face
　　In the ash, as an artist draws;
　　　　Free on each other's flaws,
　　How we chattered like two church daws!

V What's in the 'Times'? – a scold
　　At the emperor deep and cold;
　　　　He has taken a bride
　　　　To his gruesome side,
　　That's as fair as himself is bold:
　　　　There they sit ermine-stoled,
　　And she powders her hair with gold.

VI Fancy the Pampas' sheen!
　　Miles and miles of gold and green
　　　　Where the sun-flowers blow
　　　　In a solid glow,
　　And to break now and then the screen –
　　　　Black neck and eyeballs keen,
　　Up a wild horse leaps between!

VII Try, will our table turn?
　　Lay your hands there light, and yearn
　　　　Till the yearning slips
　　　　Thro' the finger tips
　　In a fire which a few discern,
　　　　And a very few feel burn,
　　And the rest, they may live and learn!

VIII Then we would up and pace,
　　For a change, about the place,
　　　　Each with arm o'er neck.
　　　　'Tis our quarter-deck,
　　We are seamen in woeful case,
　　　　Help in the ocean-space!
　　Or, if no help, we'll embrace.

IX See, how she looks now, drest
In a sledging-cap and vest.
    'Tis a huge fur cloak –
    Like a reindeer's yoke
Falls the lappet along the breast:
    Sleeves for her arms to rest,
Or to hang, as my Love likes best.

X Teach me to flirt a fan
As the Spanish ladies can,
    Or I tint your lip
    With a burnt stick's tip
And you turn into such a man!
    Just the two spots that span
Half the bill of the young male swan.

XI Dearest, three months ago
When the mesmeriser Snow
    With his hand's first sweep
    Put the earth to sleep,
'Twas a time when the heart could show
    All – how was earth to know,
'Neath the mute hand's to-and-fro!

XII Dearest, three months ago
When we loved each other so,
    Lived and loved the same
    Till an evening came
When a shaft from the Devil's bow
    Pierced to our ingle-glow,
And the friends were friend and foe!

XIII Not from the heart beneath –
'Twas a bubble born of breath
    Neither sneer nor vaunt,
    Nor reproach nor taunt.
See a word, how it severeth!
    Oh, power of life and death
In the tongue, as the Preacher saith!

xiv Woman, and will you cast
For a word, quite off at last,
       Me, your own, your you, –
       Since, as Truth is true,
I was you all the happy past –
       Me do you leave aghast
With the memories we amassed?

xv   Love, if you knew the light
That your soul casts in my sight,
       How I look to you
       For the pure and true,
And the beauteous and the right, –
       Bear with a moment's spite
When a mere mote threats the white!

xvi What of a hasty word?
Is the fleshly heart not stirred
       By a worm's pin-prick
       Where its roots are quick?
See the eye, by a fly's foot blurred –
       Ear, when a straw is heard
Scratch the brain's coat of curd!

xvii Foul be the world or fair,
More or less, how can I care?
       'Tis the world the same
       For my praise or blame,
And endurance is easy there.
       Wrong in the one thing rare –
Oh, it is hard to bear!

xviii Here's the spring back or close,
When the almond-blossom blows;
       We shall have the word
       In that minor third
There is none but the cuckoo knows –
       Heaps of the guelder-rose!
I must bear with it, I suppose.

XIX Could but November come,
        Were the noisy birds struck dumb
            At the warning slash
            Of his driver's-lash –
        I would laugh like the valiant Thumb
            Facing the castle glum
        And the giant's fee-faw-fum!

XX Then, were the world well stript
        Of the gear wherein equipped
            We can stand apart,
            Heart dispense with heart
        In the sun, with the flowers unnipped, –
            Oh, the world's hangings ripped,
        We were both in a bare-walled crypt!

XXI Each in the crypt would cry
        'But one freezes here! and why?
            When a heart as chill
            At my own would thrill
        Back to life, and its fires out-fly?
            Heart, shall we live or die?
        The rest, ... settle it by and by!'

XXII So, she'd efface the score,
        And forgive me as before.
            Just at twelve o'clock
            I shall hear her knock
        In the worst of a storm's uproar –
            I shall pull her through the door –
        I shall have her for evermore!

LOVE IN A LIFE

In another love poem from *Men and Women*, the lover describes his mistress in terms of her clothes, her perfume and the lingering presence of her body in rooms she has just left. It is evocative and suggestive, yet still a materialistically sexual vision.

I Room after room,
   I hunt the house through
   We inhabit together.
   Heart, fear nothing, for, heart, thou shalt find her,
   Next time, herself! – not the trouble behind her
   Left in the curtain, the couch's perfume!
   As she brushed it, the cornice-wreath blossomed anew, –
   Yon looking-glass gleamed at the wave of her feather.

II Yet the day wears,
   And door succeeds door;
   I try the fresh fortune –
   Range the wide house from the wing to the centre,
   Still the same chance! she goes out as I enter.
   Spend my whole day in the quest, -- who cares?
   But 'tis twilight, you see, – with such suites to explore,
   Such closets to search, such alcoves to importune!

A TOCCATA OF GALUPPI'S

Baldassare Galuppi (1706–85) was a composer for the keyboard, as well as for churches and opera houses, whom Browning uses in this sardonic illustration of human frivolity at carnival time in Venice. Of all the poems in *Men and Women*, none has quite this quality of mordant observation as death closes upon an aimless gaiety.

I

Oh, Galuppi, Baldassaro, this is very sad to find!
I can hardly misconceive you; it would prove me deaf and blind;
But although I give you credit, 'tis with such a heavy mind!

II

Here you come with your old music, and here's all the good it brings.
What, they lived once thus at Venice, where the merchants were the kings,
Where St. Marks is, where the Doges used to wed the sea with rings?

III

Ay, because the sea's the street there; and 'tis arched by . . . what you call
. . . Shylock's bridge with houses on it, where they kept the carnival!
I was never out of England – it's as if I saw it all!

IV

Did young people take their pleasure when the sea was warm in May?

Balls and masks begun at midnight, burning ever to mid-day,
When they made up fresh adventures for the morrow, do you
    say?

V

Was a lady such a lady, cheeks so round and lips so red, –
On her neck the small face buoyant, like a bell-flower on its
    bed,
O'er the breast's superb abundance where a man might base his
    head?

VI

Well (and it was graceful of them) they'd break talk off and
    afford
– She, to bite her mask's black velvet, he to finger on his
    sword,
While you sat and played Toccatas, stately at the clavichord?

VII

What? Those lesser thirds so plaintive, sixths diminished, sigh
    on sigh,
Told them something? Those suspensions, those solutions –
    'Must we die?'
Those commiserating sevenths – 'Life might last! we can but
    try!'

VIII

'Were you happy?' – 'Yes.' – 'And are you still as happy?' –
    'Yes – And you?'
—'Then more kisses' – 'Did *I* stop them, when a million
    seemed so few?'
Hark – the dominant's persistence, till it must be answered to!

IX

So an octave struck the answer. Oh, they praised you, I dare
    say!
'Brave Galuppi! that was music! good alike at grave and gay!
I can always leave off talking, when I hear a master play.'

X

Then they left you for their pleasure: till in due time, one by
    one,
Some with lives that came to nothing, some with deeds as well
    undone,
Death came tacitly and took them where they never see the sun.

XI

But when I sit down to reason, – think to take my stand nor
    swerve
Till I triumph o'er a secret wrung from nature's close reserve,
In you come with your cold music, till I creep thro' every nerve,

XII

Yes, you, like a ghostly cricket, creaking where a house was
    burned –
'Dust and ashes, dead and done with, Venice spent what Venice
    earned!
The soul, doubtless, is immortal – where a soul can be
    discerned.

XIII

'Yours for instance, you know physics, something on geology,
Mathematics are your pastime; souls shall rise in their degree;
Butterflies may dread extinction, – you'll not die, it cannot be!

XIV

'As for Venice and its people, merely born to bloom and drop,
Here on earth they bore their fruitage, mirth and folly were the
    crop,
What of soul was left, I wonder, when the kissing had to stop?

XV

'Dust and ashes!' So you creak it, and I want the heart to scold.
Dear dead women, with such hair, too – what's become of all
    the gold
Used to hang and brush their bosoms? I feel chilly and grown
    old.

FRA LIPPO LIPPI

The first of Browning's great monologues in *Men and Women* presents the Renaissance painter and monk Filippo Lippi (1412–69) justifying the humanist character of his art. However, having been arrested by the watch, he is first obliged to explain his presence in a part of Florence 'where sportive ladies leave their doors ajar'. As a painter of the Renaissance, he has modelled the great figures of Christian history from people he meets. As a monk, he tells his captors that hunger in childhood was his only incentive to enter a religious order. Nor does he forget to remind those who detain him that his protector is the tyrant of Florence, Cosimo di Medici. He is as human and worldly as the bishop ordering his tomb in St Praxed's church, though more candid.

I am poor brother Lippo, by your leave!
You need not clap your torches to my face.
Zooks, what's to blame? you think you see a monk!
What, it's past midnight, and you go the rounds,
And here you catch me at an alley's end
Where sportive ladies leave their doors ajar.
The Carmine's my cloister: hunt it up,
Do, – harry out, if you must show your zeal,
Whatever rat, there, haps on his wrong hole,
And nip each softling of a wee white mouse,
Weke, weke, that's crept to keep him company!
Aha, you know your betters? Then, you'll take
Your hand away that's fiddling on my throat,
And please to know me likewise. Who am I?
Why, one, sir, who is lodging with a friend
Three streets off – he's a certain . . . how d'ye call?
Master – a . . . Cosimo of the Medici,
In the house that caps the corner. Boh! you were best!

Remember and tell me, the day you're hanged,
How you affected such a gullet's gripe
But you, sir, it concerns you that your knaves
Pick up a manner nor discredit you.
Zooks, are we pilchards, that they sweep the streets
And count fair prize what comes into their net?
He's Judas to a tittle, that man is!
Just such a face! why, sir, you make amends.
Lord, I'm not angry! Bid your hangdogs go
Drink out this quarter florin to the health
Of the munificent House that harbours me
(And many more beside, lads! more beside!)
And all's come square again. I'd like his face –
His, elbowing on his comrade in the door
With the pike and lantern, – for the slave that holds
John Baptist's head a-dangle by the hair
With one hand ('look you, now,' as who should say)
And his weapon in the other, yet unwiped!
It's not your chance to have a bit of chalk,
A wood-coal or the like? or you should see!
Yes, I'm the painter, since you style me so.
What, brother Lippo's doings, up and down,
You know them and they take you? like enough!
I saw the proper twinkle in your eye –
Tell you I liked your looks at very first.
Let's sit and set things straight now, hip to haunch.
Here's spring come, and the nights one makes up bands
To roam the town and sing out carnival,
And I've been three weeks shut within my mew,
A-painting for the great man, saints and saints
And saints again. I could not paint all night –
Ouf! I leaned out of window for fresh air.
There came a hurry of feet and little feet,
A sweep of lute-strings, laughs, and whiffs of song, –
Flower o' the broom,
Take away love, and our earth is a tomb!
Flower o' the quince,
I let Lisa go, and what good's in life since?

Flower o' the thyme – and so on. Round they went.
Scarce had they turned the corner when a titter,
Like the skipping of rabbits by moonlight, – three slim
shapes –
And a face that looked up . . . zooks, sir, flesh and blood,
That's all I'm made of! Into shreds it went,
Curtain and counterpane and coverlet,
All the bed furniture – a dozen knots,
There was a ladder! down I let myself,
Hands and feet, scrambling somehow, and so dropped,
And after them. I came up with the fun
Hard by St. Laurence, hail fellow, well met, –
Flower o' the rose
If I've been merry, what matter who knows?
And so as I was stealing back again
To get to bed and have a bit of sleep
Ere I rise up to-morrow and go work
On Jerome knocking at his poor old breast
With his great round stone to subdue the flesh,
You snap me of the sudden. Ah, I see!
Though your eye twinkles still, you shake your head –
Mine's shaved, – a monk, you say – the sting's in that!
If Master Cosimo announced himself,
Mum's the word naturally; but a monk!
Come, what am I a beast for? tell us, now!
I was a baby when my mother died
And father died and left me in the street.
I starved there, God knows how, a year or two
On fig-skins, melon-parings, rinds and shucks,
Refuse and rubbish. One fine frosty day
My stomach being empty as your hat,
The wind doubled me up and down I went.
Old Aunt Lapaccia trussed me with one hand,
(Its fellow was a stinger as I knew)
And so along the wall, over the bridge,
By the straight cut to the convent. Six words, there,
While I stood munching my first bread that month:
'So, boy, you're minded,' quoth the good fat father

Wiping his own mouth, 'twas refection-time, –
'To quit this very miserable world?
Will you renounce' . . . The mouthful of bread? thought I;
By no means! Brief, they made a monk of me,
I did renounce the world, its pride and greed,
Palace, farm, villa, shop and banking-house,
Trash, such as these poor devils of Medici
Have given their hearts to – all at eight years old.
Well, sir, I found in time, you may be sure,
'Twas not for nothing – the good bellyful,
The warm serge and the rope that goes all round,
And day-long blessed idleness beside!
'Let's see what the urchin's fit for' – that came next.
Not overmuch their way, I must confess.
Such a to-do! they tried me with their books.
Lord, they'd have taught me Latin in pure waste!
Flower o' the clove,
All the Latin I construe is, 'amo,' I love!
But, mind you, when a boy starves in the streets
Eight years together, as my fortune was,
Watching folk's faces to know who will fling
The bit of half-stripped grape-bunch he desires,
And who will curse or kick him for his pains –
Which gentleman processional and fine,
Holding a candle to the Sacrament
Will wink and let him lift a plate and catch
The droppings of the wax to sell again,
Or holla for the Eight and have him whipped, –
How say I? – nay, which dog bites, which lets drop
His bone from the heap of offal in the street!
– The soul and sense of him grow sharp alike,
He learns the look of things, and none the less
For admonitions from the hunger-pinch.
I had a store o' such remarks, be sure,
Which, after I found leisure, turned to use:
I drew men's faces on my copy-books,
Scrawled them within the antiphonary's marge,
Joined legs and arms to the long music-notes,

Found nose and eyes and chin for A.s and B.s,
And made a string of pictures of the world
Betwixt the ins and outs of verb and noun,
On the wall, the bench, the door. The monks looked black.
'Nay,' quoth the Prior, 'turn him out, d'ye say?
In no wise. Lose a crow and catch a lark.
What if at last we get our man of parts,
We Carmelites, like those Camaldolese
And Preaching Friars, to do our church up fine
And put the front on it that ought to be!'
And hereupon they bade me daub away.
Thank you! my head being crammed, their walls a blank,
Never was such prompt disemburdening.
First, every sort of monk, the black and white,
I drew them, fat and lean: then, folks at church,
From good old gossips waiting to confess
Their cribs of barrel-droppings, candle-ends, –
To the breathless fellow at the altar-foot,
Fresh from his murder, safe and sitting there
With the little children round him in a row
Of admiration, half for his beard and half
For that white anger of his victim's son
Shaking a fist at him with one fierce arm,
Signing himself with the other because of Christ
(Whose sad face on the cross sees only this
After the passion of a thousand years)
Till some poor girl, her apron o'er her head
Which the intense eyes looked through, came at eve
On tip-toe, said a word, dropped in a loaf,
Her pair of ear-rings and a bunch of flowers
The brute took growling, prayed, and then was gone.
I painted all, then cried ''tis ask and have –
Choose, for more's ready!' – laid the ladder flat,
And showed my covered bit of cloister-wall.
The monks closed in a circle and praised loud
Till checked, (taught what to see and not to see,
Being simple bodies) 'that's the very man!
Look at the boy who stoops to pat the dog!

That woman's like the Prior's niece who comes
To care about his asthma: it's the life!'
But there my triumph's straw-fire flared and funked –
Their betters took their turn to see and say:
The Prior and the learned pulled a face
And stopped all that in no time. 'How? what's here?
Quite from the mark of painting, bless us all!
Faces, arms, legs and bodies like the true
As much as pea and pea! it's devil's game!
Your business is not to catch men with show,
With homage to the perishable clay,
But lift them over it, ignore it all,
Make them forget there's such a thing as flesh.
Your business is to paint the souls of men –
Man's soul, and it's a fire, smoke . . . no it's not . . .
It's vapour done up like a new-born babe –
(In that shape when you die it leaves your mouth)
It's . . . well, what matters talking, it's the soul!
Give us no more of body than shows soul.
Here's Giotto, with his Saint a-praising God!
That sets you praising, – why not stop with him?
Why put all thoughts of praise out of our heads
With wonder at lines, colours, and what not?
Paint the soul, never mind the legs and arms!
Rub all out, try at it a second time.
Oh, that white smallish female with the breasts,
She's just my niece . . . Herodias, I would say, –
Who went and danced and got men's heads cut off –
Have it all out!' Now, is this sense, I ask?
A fine way to paint soul, by painting body
So ill, the eye can't stop there, must go further
And can't fare worse! Thus, yellow does for white
When what you put for yellow's simply black,
And any sort of meaning looks intense
When all beside itself means and looks nought.
Why can't a painter lift each foot in turn,
Left foot and right foot, go a double step,
Make his flesh liker and his soul more like,

Both in their order? Take the prettiest face,
The Prior's niece . . . patron-saint – is it so pretty
You can't discover if it means hope, fear,
Sorrow or joy? won't beauty go with these?
Suppose I've made her eyes all right and blue,
Can't I take breath and try to add life's flash
And then add soul and heighten them threefold?
Or say there's beauty with no soul at all –
(I never saw it – put the case the same –)
If you get simple beauty and nought else,
You get about the best thing God invents, –
That's somewhat. And you'll find the soul you have missed,
Within yourself when you return Him thanks!
'Rub all out!' well, well, there's my life, in short,
And so the thing has gone on ever since.
I'm grown a man no doubt, I've broken bounds –
You should not take a fellow eight years old
And make him swear to never kiss the girls –
I'm my own master, paint now as I please –
Having a friend, you see, in the Corner-house!
Lord, it's fast holding by the rings in front –
Those great rings serve more purposes than just
To plant a flag in, or tie up a horse!
And yet the old schooling sticks – the old grave eyes
Are peeping o'er my shoulder as I work,
The heads shake still – 'it's Art's decline, my son!
You're not of the true painters, great and old:
Brother Angelico's the man, you'll find:
Brother Lorenzo stands his single peer.
Fag on at flesh, you'll never make the third!'
Flower o' the pine,
You keep your mistr . . . manners, and I'll stick to mine!
I'm not the third, then: bless us, they must know!
Don't you think they're the likeliest to know,
They, with their Latin? so I swallow my rage,
Clench my teeth, suck my lips in tight, and paint
To please them – sometimes do, and sometimes don't,
For, doing most, there's pretty sure to come

A turn – some warm eve finds me at my saints –
A laugh, a cry, the business of the world –
(*Flower o' the peach,*
Death for us all, and his own life for each!)
And my whole soul revolves, the cup runs o'er,
The world and life's too big to pass for a dream,
And I do these wild things in sheer despite,
And play the fooleries you catch me at,
In pure rage! the old mill-horse, out at grass
After hard years, throws up his stiff heels so,
Although the miller does not preach to him
The only good of grass is to make chaff.
What would men have? Do they like grass or no –
May they or mayn't they? all I want's the thing
Settled for ever one way: as it is,
You tell too many lies and hurt yourself.
You don't like what you only like too much,
You do like what, if given you at your word,
You find abundantly detestable.
For me, I think I speak as I was taught –
I always see the Garden and God there
A-making man's wife – and, my lesson learned,
The value and significance of flesh,
I can't unlearn ten minutes afterward.

    You understand me: I'm a beast, I know.
But see, now – why, I see as certainly
As that the morning-star's about to shine,
What will hap some day. We've a youngster here
Comes to our convent, studies what I do,
Slouches and stares and lets no atom drop –
His name is Guidi – he'll not mind the monks –
They call him Hulking Tom, he lets them talk –
He picks my practice up – he'll paint apace,
I hope so – though I never live so long,
I know what's sure to follow. You be judge!
You speak no Latin more than I, belike –
However, you're my man, you've seen the world
– The beauty and the wonder and the power,

The shapes of things, their colours, lights and shades,
Changes, surprises, – and God made it all!
– For what? do you feel thankful, ay or no,
For this fair town's face, yonder river's line,
The mountain round it and the sky above,
Much more the figures of man, woman, child,
These are the frame to? What's it all about?
To be passed o'er, despised? or dwelt upon,
Wondered at? oh, this last of course, you say.
But why not do as well as say, – paint these
Just as they are, careless what comes of it?
God's works – paint any one, and count it crime
To let a truth slip. Don't object, 'His works
Are here already – nature is complete:
Suppose you reproduce her – (which you can't)
There's no advantage! you must beat her, then.'
For, don't you mark, we're made so that we love
First when we see them painted, things we have passed
Perhaps a hundred times nor cared to see;
And so they are better, painted – better to us,
Which is the same thing. Art was given for that –
God uses us to help each other so,
Lending our minds out. Have you noticed, now,
Your cullion's hanging face? A bit of chalk,
And trust me but you should, though! How much more,
If I drew higher things with the same truth!
That were to take the Prior's pulpit-place,
Interpret God to all of you! oh, oh,
It makes me mad to see what men shall do
And we in our graves! This world's no blot for us,
Nor blank – it means intensely, and means good:
To find its meaning is my meat and drink.
'Ay, but you don't so instigate to prayer,'
Strikes in the Prior! 'when your meaning's plain
It does not say to folks – remember matins –
Or, mind you fast next Friday.' Why, for this
What need of art at all? A skull and bones,
Two bits of stick nailed cross-wise, or, what's best,

A bell to chime the hour with, does as well.
I painted a St. Laurence six months since
At Prato, splashed the fresco in fine style.
'How looks my painting, now the scaffold's down?'
I ask a brother: 'Hugely,' he returns –
'Already not one phiz of your three slaves
That turn the Deacon off his toasted side,
But's scratched and prodded to our heart's content,
The pious people have so eased their own
When coming to say prayers there in a rage.
We get on fast to see the bricks beneath.
Expect another job this time next year,
For pity and religion grow i' the crowd –
Your painting serves its purpose!' Hang the fools!
   – That is – you'll not mistake an idle word
Spoke in a huff by a poor monk, God wot,
Tasting the air this spicy night which turns
The unaccustomed head like Chianti wine!
Oh, the church knows! don't misreport me, now!
It's natural a poor monk out of bounds
Should have his apt word to excuse himself:
And hearken how I plot to make amends.
I have bethought me: I shall paint a piece
. . . There's for you! Give me six months, then go, see
Something in Sant' Ambrogio's . . . (bless the nuns!
They want a cast of my office) I shall paint
God in the midst, Madonna and her babe,
Ringed by a bowery, flowery angel-brood,
Lilies and vestments and white faces, sweet
As puff on puff of grated orris-root
When ladies crowd to church at midsummer.
And then in the front, of course a saint or two –
Saint John, because he saves the Florentines,
Saint Ambrose, who puts down in black and white
The convent's friends and gives them a long day.
And Job, I must have him there past mistake,
The man of Uz, (and Us without the z,
Painters who need his patience). Well, all these

Secured at their devotions, up shall come
Out of a corner when you least expect,
As one by a dark stair into a great light,
Music and talking, who but Lippo! I! –
Mazed, motionless and moon-struck – I'm the man!
Back I shrink – what is this I see and hear?
I, caught up with my monk's things by mistake,
My old serge gown and rope that goes all round,
I, in this presence, this pure company!
Where's a hole, where's a corner for escape?
Then steps a sweet angelic slip of a thing
Forward, puts out a soft palm – 'Not so fast!'
– Addresses the celestial presence, 'nay –
He made you and devised you, after all,
Though he's none of you! Could Saint John there, draw –
His camel-hair make up a painting-brush?
We come to brother Lippo for all that,
Iste perfecit opus!' So, all smile –
I shuffle sideways with my blushing face
Under the cover of a hundred wings
Thrown like a spread of kirtles when you're gay
And play hot cockles, all the doors being shut,
Till, wholly unexpected, in there pops
The hothead husband! Thus I scuttle off
To some safe bench behind, not letting go
The palm of her, the little lily thing
That spoke the good word for me in the nick,
Like the Prior's niece . . . Saint Lucy, I would say.
And so all's saved for me, and for the church
A pretty picture gained. Go, six months hence!
Your hand, sir, and good-bye: no lights, no lights!
The street's hushed, and I know my own way back –
Don't fear me! There's the grey beginning, Zooks!

monologue

catholic priest

BISHOP BLOUGRAM'S APOLOGY
* *speaking to a journalist (atheist)*

Browning's major poem in *Men and Women* is a scarcely veiled portrait of Cardinal Nicholas Wiseman (1802–65), first Archbishop of Westminster after the restoration of the Catholic hierarchy in England. Often regarded as worldly and indulgent, too intellectually sophisticated to believe all that he should, Wiseman's obligation to eat fish on Fridays and during Lent prompted one of his aides to remark ruefully, 'There is a lobster-salad side to the Cardinal.' Wiseman as Blougram is here interviewed by an eager and hostile young journalist, Gigadibs. But in the person of Gigadibs and through the voice of Blougram, investigative journalism gets the trouncing of all time during the after-dinner interview.

In the great Victorian debate between faith and doubt, Blougram puts his creed aside but only to demonstrate in a masterly conjuring-show of paradox and argument that submission to faith is the only alternative to abject slavery. Indeed, the only alternative to believing in the latest 'winking Virgin' of modern Catholic miracles is to lapse into blind superstition. The clever young Gigadibs stumbles away defeated and emigrates to Australia to become a farmer. Wiseman, in a witty review of the poem, suggested that the Noncomformist Browning showed signs in it of a coming conversion to the Catholic faith.

Modern characters

No more wine? Then we'll push back chairs and talk.
A final glass for me, tho'; cool, i'faith!
We ought to have our Abbey back, you see.
It's different, preaching in basilicas,
And doing duty in some masterpiece
Like this of brother Pugin's, bless his heart!
I doubt if they're half baked, those chalk rosettes,
Ciphers and stucco-twiddlings everywhere; *talking about architecture*

It's just like breathing in a lime-kiln: eh?
These hot long ceremonies of our church
Cost us a little – oh, they pay the price,
You take me – amply pay it! Now, we'll talk.

So, you despise me, Mr Gigadibs.
No deprecation, – nay, I beg you, sir!
Beside 'tis our engagement: don't you know,
I promised, if you'd watch a dinner out,
We'd see truth dawn together? – truth that peeps
Over the glass's edge when dinner's done,
And body gets its sop and holds its noise
And leaves soul free a little. Now's the time –
'Tis break of day! You do despise me then.
And if I say, 'despise me,' – never fear –
I know you do not in a certain sense –
Not in my arm-chair for example: here,
I well imagine you respect my place
(Status, *entourage*, worldly circumstance)
Quite to its value – very much indeed
– Are up to the protesting eyes of you
In pride at being seated here for once –
You'll turn it to such capital account!
When somebody, through years and years to come,
Hints of the bishop, – names me – that's enough –
'Blougram? I knew him' – (into it you slide)
'Dined with him once, a Corpus Christi Day,
All alone, we two – he's a clever man –
And after dinner, – why, the wine you know, –
Oh, there was wine, and good! – what with the wine . . .
'Faith, we began upon all sorts of talk!
He's no bad fellow, Blougram – he had seen
Something of mine he relished – some review –
He's quite above their humbug in his heart,
Half-said as much, indeed – the thing's his trade –
I warrant, Blougram's sceptical at times –
How otherwise? I liked him, I confess!'
Che ch'è, my dear sir, as we say at Rome,

Don't you protest now! It's fair give and take;
You have had your turn and spoken your home-truths —
The hand's mine now, and here you follow suit.

  Thus much conceded, still the first fact stays —
You do despise me; your ideal of life
Is not the bishop's — you would not be I —
You would like better to be Goethe, now,
Or Buonaparte — or, bless me, lower still,
Count D'Orsay, — so you did what you preferred,
Spoke as you thought, and, as you cannot help,
Believed or disbelieved, no matter what,
So long as on that point, whate'er it was,
You loosed your mind, were whole and sole yourself.
— That, my ideal never can include,
Upon that element of truth and worth
Never be based! for say they make me Pope
(They can't — suppose it for our argument)
Why, there I'm at my tether's end — I've reached
My height, and not a height which pleases you.
An unbelieving Pope won't do, you say.
It's like those eerie stories nurses tell,
Of how some actor played Death on a stage
With pasteboard crown, sham orb, and tinselled dart,
And called himself the monarch of the world,
Then going in the tire-room afterward
Because the play was done, to shift himself,
Got touched upon the sleeve familiarly
The moment he had shut the closet door
By Death himself. Thus God might touch a Pope
At unawares, ask what his baubles mean,
And whose part he presumed to play just now?
Best be yourself, imperial, plain and true!

So, drawing comfortable breath again,
You weigh and find whatever more or less
I boast of my ideal realised
Is nothing in the balance when opposed
To your ideal, your grand simple life,

Of which you will not realise one jot.
I am much, you are nothing; you would be all,
I would be merely much – you beat me there.

No, friend, you do not beat me, – hearken why.
The common problem, yours, mine, every one's,
Is not to fancy what were fair in life
Provided it could be, – but, finding first
What may be, then find how to make it fair
Up to our means – a very different thing!
No abstract intellectual plan of life
Quite irrespective of life's plainest laws,
But one, a man, who is man and nothing more,
May lead within a world which (by your leave)
Is Rome or London – not Fool's-paradise.
Embellish Rome, idealise away,
Make Paradise of London if you can,
You're welcome, nay, you're wise.

                                        A simile!
We mortals cross the ocean of this world
Each in his average cabin of a life –
The best's not big, the worst yields elbow-room.
Now for our six months' voyage – how prepare?
You come on shipboard with a landsman's list
Of things he calls convenient – so they are!
An India screen is pretty furniture,
A piano-forte is a fine resource,
All Balzac's novels occupy one shelf,
The new edition fifty volumes long;
And little Greek books with the funny type
They get up well at Leipsic fill the next –
Go on! slabbed marble, what a bath it makes!
And Parma's pride, the Jerome, let us add!
'Twere pleasant could Correggio's fleeting glow
Hang full in face of one where'er one roams,
Since he more than the others brings with him
Italy's self, – the marvellous Modenese!
Yet 'twas not on your list before, perhaps.

– Alas! friend, here's the agent . . . is't the name?
The captain, or whoever's master here –
You see him screw his face up; what's his cry
Ere you set foot on shipboard? 'Six feet square!'
If you won't understand what six feet mean,
Compute and purchase stores accordingly –
And if in pique because he overhauls
Your Jerome, piano and bath, you come on board
Bare – why you cut a figure at the first
While sympathetic landsmen see you off;
Not afterwards, when, long ere half seas o'er,
You peep up from your utterly naked boards
Into some snug and well-appointed berth
Like mine, for instance (try the cooler jug –
Put back the other, but don't jog the ice)
And mortified you mutter 'Well and good –
He sits enjoying his sea-furniture –
'Tis stout and proper, and there's store of it,
Though I've the better notion, all agree,
Of fitting rooms up! hang the carpenter,
Neat ship-shape fixings and contrivances –
I would have brought my Jerome, frame and all!'
And meantime you bring nothing: never mind –
You've proved your artist-nature: what you don't,
You might bring, so despise me, as I say.

   Now come, let's backward to the starting place.
See my way: we're two college friends, suppose –
Prepare together for our voyage, then,
Each note and check the other in his work, –
Here's mine, a bishop's outfit; criticise!
What's wrong? why won't you be a bishop too?

   Why, first, you don't believe, you don't and can't,
(Not statedly, that is, and fixedly
And absolutely and exclusively)
In any revelation called divine.
No dogmas nail your faith – and what remains
But say so, like the honest man you are?

First, therefore, overhaul theology!
Nay, I too, not a fool, you please to think,
Must find believing every whit as hard,
And if I do not frankly say as much,
The ugly consequence is clear enough.

  Now, wait, my friend: well, I do not believe –
If you'll accept no faith that is not fixed,
Absolute and exclusive, as you say.
(You're wrong – I mean to prove it in due time)
Meanwhile, I know where difficulties lie
I could not, cannot solve, nor ever shall,
So give up hope accordingly to solve –
(To you, and over the wine). Our dogmas then
With both of us, tho' in unlike degree,
Missing full credence – overboard with them!
I mean to meet you on your own premise –
Good, there go mine in company with yours!

  And now what are we? unbelievers, both,
Calm and complete, determinately fixed
To-day, to-morrow, and for ever, pray?
You'll guarantee me that? Not so, I think.
In no-wise! all we've gained is, that belief,
As unbelief before, shakes us by fits,
Confounds us like its predecessor. Where's
The gain? how can we guard our unbelief,
Make it bear fruit to us? – the problem here.
Just when we are safest, there's a sunset-touch,
A fancy from a flower-bell, some one's death,
A chorus-ending from Euripides, –
And that's enough for fifty hopes and fears
As old and new at once as Nature's self,
To rap and knock and enter in our soul,
Take hands and dance there, a fantastic ring,
Round the ancient idol, on his base again, –
The grand Perhaps! we look on helplessly, –
There the old misgivings, crooked questions are –
This good God, – what he could do, if he would,

Would, if he could – then must have done long since:
If so, when, where, and how? some way must be, –
Once feel about, and soon or late you hit
Some sense, in which it might be, after all.
Why not, 'The Way, the Truth, the Life?'

                                        – That way
Over the mountain, which who stands upon
Is apt to doubt if it's indeed a road;
While if he views it from the waste itself,
Up goes the line there, plain from base to brow,
Not vague, mistakeable! what's a break or two
Seen from the unbroken desert either side?
And then (to bring in fresh philosophy)
What if the breaks themselves should prove at last
The most consummate of contrivances
To train a man's eye, teach him what is faith, –
And so we stumble at truth's very test?
What have we gained then by our unbelief
But a life of doubt diversified by faith,
For one of faith diversified by doubt?
We called the chess-board white, – we call it black.

    'Well,' you rejoin, 'the end's no worse, at least,
We've reason for both colours on the board.
Why not confess then, where I drop the faith
And you the doubt, that I'm as right as you?'

    Because, friend, in the next place, this being so,
And both things even, – faith and unbelief
Left to a man's choice, – we'll proceed a step,
Returning to our image, which I like.

    A man's choice, yes – but a cabin-passenger's –
The man made for the special life of the world –
Do you forget him? I remember though!
Consult our ship's conditions and you find
One and but one choice suitable to all,
The choice that you unluckily prefer
Turning things topsy-turvy – they or it

Going to the ground. Belief or unbelief
Bears upon life, determines its whole course,
Begins at its beginning. See the world
Such as it is, – you made it not, nor I;
I mean to take it as it is, – and you
Not so you'll take it, – though you get nought else.
I know the special kind of life I like,
What suits the most my idiosyncrasy,
Brings out the best of me and bears me fruit
In power, peace, pleasantness, and length of days.
I find that positive belief does this
For me, and unbelief, no whit of this.
– For you, it does, however – that we'll try!
'Tis clear, I cannot lead my life, at least
Induce the world to let me peaceably,
Without declaring at the outset, 'Friends,
I absolutely and peremptorily
Believe!' – I say faith is my waking life.
One sleeps, indeed, and dreams at intervals,
We know, but waking's the main point with us,
And my provision's for life's waking part.
Accordingly, I use heart, head and hands
All day, I build, scheme, study and make friends;
And when night overtakes me, down I lie,
Sleep, dream a little, and get done with it,
The sooner the better, to begin afresh.
What's midnight's doubt before the dayspring's faith?
You, the philosopher, that disbelieve,
That recognise the night, give dreams their weight –
To be consistent you should keep your bed,
Abstain from healthy acts that prove you a man,
For fear you drowse perhaps at unawares!
And certainly at night you'll sleep and dream,
Live through the day and bustle as you please.
And so you live to sleep as I to wake,
To unbelieve as I to still believe?
Well, and the common sense of the world calls you
Bed-ridden, – and its good things come to me.

Its estimation, which is half the fight,
That's the first cabin-comfort I secure –
The next . . . but you perceive with half an eye!
Come, come, it's best believing, if we can –
You can't but own that.

                    Next, concede again –
If once we choose belief, on all accounts
We can't be too decisive in our faith,
Conclusive and exclusive in its terms,
To suit the world which gives us the good things.
In every man's career are certain points
Whereon he dares not be indifferent;
The world detects him clearly, if he is,
As baffled at the game, and losing life.
He may care little or he may care much
For riches, honour, pleasure, work, repose,
Since various theories of life and life's
Success are extant which might easily
Comport with either estimate of these,
And whoso chooses wealth or poverty,
Labour or quiet, is not judged a fool
Because his fellows would choose otherwise.
We let him choose upon his own account
So long as he's consistent with his choice.
But certain points, left wholly to himself,
When once a man has arbitrated on,
We say he must succeed there or go hang.
Thus, he should wed the woman he loves most
Or needs most, whatsoe'er the love or need –
For he can't wed twice. Then, he must avouch
Or follow, at the least, sufficiently,
The form of faith his conscience holds the best,
Whate'er the process of conviction was.
For nothing can compensate his mistake
On such a point, the man himself being judge –
He cannot wed twice, nor twice lose his soul.

Well now – there's one great form of Christian faith
I happened to be born in – which to teach
Was given me as I grew up, on all hands,
As best and readiest meant of living by;
The same on examination being proved
The most pronounced moreover, fixed, precise
And absolute form of faith in the whole world –
Accordingly, most potent of all forms
For working on the world. Observe, my friend,
Such as you know me, I am free to say,
In these hard latter days which hamper one,
Myself, by no immoderate exercise
Of intellect and learning, and the tact.
To let external forces work for me,
Bid the street's stones be bread and they are bread,
Bid Peter's creed, or, rather, Hildebrand's,
Exalt me o'er my fellows in the world
And make my life an ease and joy and pride,
It does so, – which for me's a great point gained,
Who have a soul and body that exact
A comfortable care in many ways.
There's power in me and will to dominate
Which I must exercise, they hurt me else:
In many ways I need mankind's respect,
Obedience, and the love that's born of fear:
While at the same time, there's a taste I have,
A toy of soul, a titillating thing,
Refuses to digest these dainties crude.
The naked life is gross till clothed upon:
I must take what men offer, with a grace
As though I would not, could I help it, take!
A uniform to wear though over-rich –
Something imposed on me, no choice of mine;
No fancy-dress worn for pure fashion's sake
And despicable therefore! now men kneel
And kiss my hand – of course the Church's hand.
Thus I am made, thus life is best for me,
And thus that it should be I have procured;

And thus it could not be another way,
I venture to imagine.

You'll reply –
So far my choice, no doubt, is a success; *to become a bisho*
But were I made of better elements,
With nobler instincts, purer tastes, like you,
I hardly would account the thing success
Though it do all for me I say.

But, friend,
We speak of what is – not of what might be, *I have been*
And how 'twere better if 'twere otherwise. *trying to convince*
I am the man you see here plain enough – *you. I want to*
Grant I'm a beast, why beasts must lead beasts' lives? *talk to you of*
Suppose I own at once to tail and claws – *what might be*
The tailless man exceeds me; but being tailed
I'll lash out lion-fashion, and leave apes
To dock their stump and dress their haunches up.
My business is not to remake myself,
But make the absolute best of what God made.
Or – our first simile – though you proved me doomed
To a viler birth still, to the steerage-hole,
The sheep-pen or the pig-stye, I should strive *If you believe that*
To make what use of each were possible; *God made you to the*
And as this cabin gets upholstery, *best you can be, then*
That hutch should rustle with sufficient straw. *you will be the*
best you can be.

But, friend, I don't acknowledge quite so fast
I fail of all your manhood's lofty tastes
Enumerated so complacently,
On the mere ground that you forsooth can find
In this particular life I choose to lead
No fit provision for them. Can you not?
Say you, my fault is I address myself
To grosser estimators than I need, *I bow down*
And that's no way of holding up the soul –
Which, nobler, needs men's praise perhaps, yet knows
One wise man's verdict outweighs all the fools', –

Would like the two, but, forced to choose, takes that?
I pine among my million imbeciles
(You think) aware some dozen men of sense
Eye me and know me, whether I believe
In the last winking Virgin, as I vow,
And am a fool, or disbelieve in her
And am a knave, – approve in neither case,
Withhold their voices though I look their way:
Like Verdi when, at his worst opera's end
(The thing they gave at Florence, – what's its name?)
While the mad houseful's plaudits near out-bang
His orchestra of salt-box, tongs and bones,
He looks through all the roaring and the wreaths
Where sits Rossini patient in his stall.

    Nay, friend, I meet you with an answer here –
For even your prime men who appraise their kind
Are men still, catch a thing within a thing,
See more in a truth than the truth's simple self,
Confuse themselves. You see lads walk the street
Sixty the minute; what's to note in that?
You see one lad o'erstride a chimney-stack;
Him you must watch – he's sure to fall, yet stands!
Our interest's on the dangerous edge of things.
The honest thief, the tender murderer,
The superstitious atheist, demireps
That love and save their souls in new French books –
We watch while these in equilibrium keep
The giddy line midway: one step aside,
They're classed and done with. I, then, keep the line
Before your sages, – just the men to shrink
From the gross weights, coarse scales, and labels broad
You offer their refinement. Fool or knave?
Why needs a bishop be a fool or knave
When there's a thousand diamond weights between?
So I enlist them. Your picked Twelve, you'll find,
Profess themselves indignant, scandalised
At thus being held unable to explain

How a superior man who disbelieves
May not believe as well: that's Schelling's way!
It's through my coming in the tail of time,
Nicking the minute with a happy tact.
Had I been born three hundred years ago
They'd say, 'What's strange? Blougram of course believes;'
And, seventy years since, 'disbelieves of course.'
But now, 'He may believe; and yet, and yet
How can he?' – All eyes turn with interest.
Whereas, step off the line on either side –
You, for example, clever to a fault,
The rough and ready man that write apace,
Read somewhat seldomer, think perhaps even less –
You disbelieve! Who wonders and who cares?
Lord So-and-So – his coat bedropt with wax,
All Peter's chains about his waist, his back
Brave with the needlework of Noodledom,
Believes! Again, who wonders and who cares?
But I, the man of sense and learning too,
The able to think yet act, the this, the that,
I, to believe at this late time of day!
Enough; you see, I need not fear contempt.

    – Except it's yours! admire me as these may,
You don't. But what at least do you admire?
Present your own perfections, your ideal,
Your pattern man for a minute – oh, make haste!
Is it Napoleon you would have us grow?
Concede the means; allow his head and hand,
(A large concession, clever as you are)
Good! – In our common primal element
Of unbelief (we can't believe, you know –
We're still at that admission, recollect)
Where do you find – apart from, towering-o'er
The secondary temporary aims
Which satisfy the gross tastes you despise –
Where do you find his star? – his crazy trust
God knows through what or in what? it's alive

And shines and leads him and that's all we want.
Have we ought in our sober night shall point
Such ends as his were, and direct the means
Of working out our purpose straight as his,
Nor bring a moment's trouble on success,
With after-care to justify the same?
– Be a Napoleon and yet disbelieve!
Why, the man's mad, friend, take his light away.
What's the vague good of the world for which you'd dare
With comfort to yourself blow millions up?
We neither of us see it! we do see
The blown-up millions – spatter of their brains
And writhing of their bowels and so forth,
In that bewildering entanglement
Of horrible eventualities
Past calculation to the end of time!
Can I mistake for some clear word of God
(Which were my ample warrant for it all)
His puff of hazy instincts, idle talk,
'The state, that's I,' quack-nonsense about kings,
And (when one beats the man to his last hold)
The vague idea of setting things to rights,
Policing people efficaciously,
More to their profit, most of all to his own;
The whole to end that dismallest of ends
By an Austrian marriage, cant to us the Church,
And resurrection of the old *régime*.
Would I, who hope to live a dozen years,
Fight Austerlitz for reasons such and such?
No: for, concede me but the merest chance
Doubt may be wrong – there's judgment, life to come!
With just that chance, I dare not. Doubt proves right?
This present life is all? you offer me
Its dozen noisy years with not a chance
That wedding an Arch-Duchess, wearing lace,
And getting called by divers new-coined names,
Will drive off ugly thoughts and let me dine,
Sleep, read and chat in quiet as I like!

Therefore, I will not.
                    Take another case;
Fit up the cabin yet another way.
What say you to the poet's? shall we write
Hamlets, Othellos – make the world our own,
Without a risk to run of either sort?
I can't! – to put the strongest reason first.
'But try,' you urge, 'the trying shall suffice:
The aim, if reached or not, makes great the life.
Try to be Shakspeare, leave the rest to fate!'
Spare my self-knowledge – there's no fooling me!
If I prefer remaining my poor self,
I say so not in self-dispraise but praise.
If I'm a Shakspeare, let the well alone –
Why should I try to be what now I am?
If I'm no Shakspeare, as too probable, –
His power and consciousness and self-delight
And all we want in common, shall I find –
Trying for ever? while on points of taste
Wherewith, to speak it humbly, he and I
Are dowered alike – I'll ask you, I or he,
Which in our two lives realises most?
Much, he imagined – somewhat, I possess.
He had the imagination; stick to that!
Let him say 'In the face of my soul's works
Your world is worthless and I touch it not
Lest I should wrong them' – I withdraw my plea.
But does he say so? look upon his life!
Himself, who only can, gives judgment there.
He leaves his towers and gorgeous palaces
To build the trimmest house in Stratford town;
Saves money, spends it, owns the worth of things,
Giulio Romano's pictures, Dowland's lute;
Enjoys a show, respects the puppets, too,
And none more, had he seen its entry once,
Than 'Pandulph, of fair Milan cardinal.'
Why then should I who play that personage,
The very Pandulph Shakspeare's fancy made,

Be told that had the poet chanced to start
From where I stand now (some degree like mine
Being just the goal he ran his race to reach)
He would have run the whole race back, forsooth,
And left being Pandulph, to begin write plays?
Ah, the earth's best can be but the earth's best!
Did Shakspeare live, he could but sit at home
And get himself in dreams the Vatican,
Greek busts, Venetian paintings, Roman walls,
And English books, none equal to his own,
Which I read, bound in gold, (he never did).
– Terni and Naples' bay and Gothard's top –
Eh, friend? I could not fancy one of these –
But, as I pour this claret, there they are –
I've gained them – crossed St Gothard last July
With ten mules to the carriage and a bed
Slung inside; is my hap the worse for that?
We want the same things, Shakspeare and myself,
And what I want, I have; he, gifted more,
Could fancy he too had it when he liked,
But not so thoroughly that if fate allowed
He would not have it also in my sense.
We play one game. I send the ball aloft
No less adroitly that of fifty strokes
Scarce five go o'er the wall so wide and high
Which sends them back to me: I wish and get.
He struck balls higher and with better skill,
But at a poor fence level with his head,
And hit – his Stratford house, a coat of arms,
Successful dealings in his grain and wool, –
While I receive heaven's incense in my nose
And style myself the cousin of Queen Bess.
Ask him, if this life's all, who wins the game?

Believe – and our whole argument breaks up.
Enthusiasm's the best thing, I repeat;
Only, we can't command it; fire and life
Are all, dead matter's nothing; we agree:

And be it a mad dream or God's very breath,
The fact's the same, – belief's fire once in us, *The world is illusion*
Makes of all else mere stuff to show itself.
We penetrate our life with such a glow
As fire lends wood and iron – this turns steel,
That burns to ash – all's one, fire proves its power
For good or ill, since men call flare success.
But paint a fire, it will not therefore burn.
Light one in me, I'll find it food enough!
Why, to be Luther – that's a life to lead,
Incomparably better than my own.
He comes, reclaims God's earth for God, he says,
Sets up God's rule again by simple means,
bible Re-opens a shut book, and all is done.
He flared out in the flaring of mankind;
Such Luther's luck was – how shall such be mine?
If he succeeded, nothing's left to do:
And if he did not altogether – well,
Strauss is the next advance. All Strauss should be
I might be also. But to what result?
He looks upon no future: Luther did. *heal*
What can I gain on the denying side?
Ice makes no conflagration. State the facts,
Read the text right, emancipate the world –
The emancipated world enjoys itself
With scarce a thank-you – Blougram told it first
It could not owe a farthing, – not to him
More than St. Paul! 'twould press its pay, you think?
Then add there's still that plaguey hundredth chance
Strauss may be wrong. And so a risk is run –
For what gain? not for Luther's, who secured
A real heaven in his heart throughout his life,
Supposing death a little altered things!

The kingdom comes wherever you believe

        'Ay, but since really I lack faith,' you cry,
'I run the same risk really on all sides,
In cool indifference as bold unbelief.
As well be Strauss as swing 'twixt Paul and him.

It's not worth having, such imperfect faith,
Nor more available to do faith's work
Than unbelief like yours. Whole faith, or none!'

    Softly, my friend! I must dispute that point.
Once own the use of faith, I'll find you faith.
We're back on Christian ground. You call for faith;
I show you doubt, to prove that faith exists.
The more of doubt, the stronger faith, I say,
If faith o'ercomes doubt. How I know it does?
By life and man's free will, God gave for that!
To mould life as we choose it, shows our choice:
That's our one act, the previous work's His own.
You criticise the soil? it reared this tree –
This broad life and whatever fruit it bears!
What matter though I doubt at every pore,
Head-doubts, heart-doubts, doubts at my fingers' ends,
Doubts in the trivial work of every day,
Doubts at the very bases of my soul
In the grand moments when she probes herself –
If finally I have a life to show,
The thing I did, brought out in evidence
Against the thing done to me underground
By Hell and all its blood, for ought I know?
I say, whence sprang this? shows it faith or doubt?
All's doubt in me; where's break of faith in this?
It is the idea, the feeling and the love
God means mankind should strive for and show forth,
Whatever be the process to that end, –
And not historic knowledge, logic sound,
And metaphysical acumen, sure!
'What think ye of Christ,' friend? when all's done and said,
You like this Christianity or not?
It may be false, but will you wish it true?
Has it your vote to be so if it can?
Trust you an instinct silenced long ago
That will break silence and enjoin you love
What mortified philosophy is hoarse,

And all in vain, with bidding you despise?
If you desire faith – then you've faith enough.
What else seeks God – nay, what else seek ourselves?
You form a notion of me, we'll suppose,
On hearsay; it's a favourable one:
'But still' (you add), 'there was no such good man,
Because of contradictions in the facts.
One proves, for instance, he was born in Rome,
This Blougram – yet throughout the tales of him
I see he figures as an Englishman.'
Well, the two things are reconcileable.
But would I rather you discovered that
Subjoining – 'Still, what matter though they be?
Blougram – concerns me nought, born here or there.'

   Pure faith indeed – you know not what you ask!
Naked belief in God the Omnipotent,
Omniscient, Omnipresent, sears too much
The sense of conscious creatures to be borne.
It were the seeing him, no flesh shall dare.
Some think, Creation's meant to show him forth:
I say, it's meant to hide him all it can,
And that's what all the blessed Evil's for.
Its use in time is to environ us,
Our breath, our drop of dew, with shield enough
Against that sight till we can bear its stress.
Under a vertical sun, the exposed brain
And lidless eye and disemprisoned heart
Less certainly would wither up at once
Than mind, confronted with the truth of Him.
But time and earth case-harden us to live;
The feeblest sense is trusted most; the child
Feels God a moment, ichors o'er the place,
Plays on and grows to be a man like us.
With me, faith means perpetual unbelief
Kept quiet like the snake 'neath Michael's foot
Who stands calm just because he feels it writhe.
Or, if that's too ambitious, – here's my box –

I need the excitation of a pinch
Threatening the torpor of the inside-nose
Nigh on the imminent sneeze that never comes.
'Leave it in peace' advise the simple folk –
Make it aware of peace by itching-fits,
Say I – let doubt occasion still more faith!

    You'll say, once all believed, man, woman, child,
In that dear middle-age these noodles praise.
How you'd exult if I could put you back
Six hundred years, blot out cosmogony,
Geology, ethnology, what not,
(Greek endings, each the little passing-bell
That signifies some faith's about to die)
And set you square with Genesis again, –
When such a traveller told you his last news,
He saw the ark a-top of Ararat
But did not climb there since 'twas getting dusk
And robber-bands infest the mountain's foot!
How should you feel, I ask, in such an age,
How act? As other people felt and did;
With soul more blank than this decanter's knob,
Believe – and yet lie, kill, rob, fornicate
Full in belief's face, like the beast you'd be!

    No, when the fight begins within himself,
A man's worth something. God stoops o'er his head,
Satan looks up between his feet – both tug –
He's left, himself, in the middle: the soul wakes
And grows. Prolong that battle through his life!
Never leave growing till the life to come!
Here, we've got callous to the Virgin's winks
That used to puzzle people wholesomely –
Men have outgrown the shame of being fools.
What are the laws of Nature, not to bend
If the Church bid them, brother Newman asks.
Up with the Immaculate Conception, then –
On to the rack with faith – is my advice!
Will not that hurry us upon our knees

Knocking our breasts, 'It can't be – yet it shall!
Who am I, the worm, to argue with my Pope?
Low things confound the high things!' and so forth.
That's better than acquitting God with grace
As some folks do. He's tried – no case is proved,
Philosophy is lenient – He may go!

    You'll say – the old system's not so obsolete
But men believe still: ay, but who and where?
King Bomba's lazzaroni foster yet
The sacred flame, so Antonelli writes;
But even of these, what ragamuffin-saint
Believes God watches him continually,
As he believes in fire that will burn,
Or rain that it will drench him? Break fire's law,
Sin against rain, although the penalty
Be just singe or soaking? No, he smiles;
Those laws are laws that can enforce themselves.

    The sum of all is – yes, my doubt is great,
My faith's the greater – then my faith's enough.
I have read much, thought much, experienced much,
Yet would die rather than avow my fear
The Naples' liquefaction may be false,
When set to happen by the palace-clock
According to the clouds or dinner-time.
I hear you recommend, I might at least
Eliminate, decrassify my faith
Since I adopt it; keeping what I must
And leaving what I can – such points as this!
I won't – that is, I can't throw one away.
Supposing there's no truth in what I said
About the need of trials to man's faith,
Still, when you bid me purify the same,
To such a process I discern no end,
Clearing off one excrescence to see two;
There's ever a next in size, now grown as big,
That meets the knife – I cut and cut again!
First cut the Liquefaction, what comes last

But Fichte's clever cut at God himself?
Experimentalize on sacred things?
I trust nor hand nor eye nor heart nor brain
To stop betimes: they all get drunk alike.
The first step, I am master not to take.

   You'd find the cutting-process to your taste
As much as leaving growths of lies unpruned,
Nor see more danger in it, you retort.
Your taste's worth mine; but my taste proves more wise
When we consider that the steadfast hold
On the extreme end of the chain of faith
Gives all the advantage, makes the difference,
With the rough purblind mass we seek to rule.
We are their lords, or they are free of us
Just as we tighten or relax that hold.
So, other matters equal, we'll revert
To the first problem – which if solved my way
And thrown into the balance turns the scale –
How we may lead a comfortable life,
How suit our luggage to the cabin's size.

   Of course you are remarking all this time
How narrowly and grossly I view life,
Respect the creature-comforts, care to rule
The masses, and regard complacently
'The cabin,' in our old phrase! Well, I do.
I act for, talk for, live for this world now,
As this world calls for action, life and talk –
No prejudice to what next world may prove,
Whose new laws and requirements my best pledge
To observe them, is that I observe these now,
Doing hereafter what I do meanwhile.
Let us concede (gratuitously though)
Next life relieves the soul of body, yields
Pure spiritual enjoyments: well, my friend,
Why lose this life in the meantime, since its use
May be to make the next life more intense?

Do you know, I have often had a dream
(Work it up in your next month's article)
Of man's poor spirit in its progress still
Losing true life for ever and a day
Through ever trying to be and ever being
In the evolution of successive spheres,
Before its actual sphere and place of life,
Halfway into the next, which having reached,
It shoots with corresponding foolery
Halfway into the next still, on and off!
As when a traveller, bound from north to south,
Scouts fur in Russia – what's its use in France?
In France spurns flannel – where's its need in Spain?
In Spain drops cloth – too cumbrous for Algiers!
Linen goes next, and last the skin itself,
A superfluity at Timbuctoo.
When, through his journey, was the fool at ease?
I'm at ease now, friend – worldly in this world
I take and like its way of life; I think
My brothers who administer the means
Live better for my comfort – that's good too;
And God, if he pronounce upon it all,
Approves my service, which is better still.
If He keep silence, – why for you or me
Or that brute-beast pulled-up in to-day's 'Times',
What odds is't, save to ourselves, what life we lead?

You meet me at this issue – you declare,
All special pleading done with, truth is truth,
And justifies itself by undreamed ways.
You don't fear but it's better, if we doubt,
To say so, acting up to our truth perceived
However feebly. Do then, – act away!
'Tis there I'm on the watch for you! How one acts
Is, both of us agree, our chief concern:
And how you'll act is what I fain would see
If, like the candid person you appear,
You dare to make the most of your life's scheme

As I of mine, live up to its full law
Since there's no higher law that counterchecks.
Put natural religion to the test
You've just demolished the revealed with – quick,
Down to the root of all that checks your will,
All prohibition to lie, kill, and thieve
Or even to be an atheistic priest!
Suppose a pricking to incontinence –
Philosophers deduce you chastity
Or shame, from just the fact that at the first
Whoso embraced a woman in the plain,
Threw club down, and forewent his brains beside,
So stood a ready victim in the reach
Of any brother-savage club in hand –
Hence saw the use of going out of sight
In wood or cave to prosecute his loves –
I read this in a French book t'other day.
Does law so analyzed coerce you much?
Oh, men spin clouds of fuzz where matters end,
But you who reach where the first thread begins,
You'll soon cut that! – which means you can, but won't
Through certain instincts, blind, unreasoned-out,
You dare not set aside, you can't tell why,
But there they are, and so you let them rule.
Then, friend, you seem as much a slave as I,
A liar, conscious coward and hypocrite,
Without the good the slave expects to get,
Suppose he has a master after all!
You own your instincts – why what else do I,
Who want, am made for, and must have a God
Ere I can be aught, do aught? – no mere name
Want, but the true thing with what proves its truth,
To wit, a relation from that thing to me,
Touching from head to foot – which touch I feel,
And with it take the rest, this life of ours!
I live my life here; yours you dare not live.

Not as I state it, who (you please subjoin)
Disfigure such a life and call it names,
While, in your mind, remains another way
For simple men: knowledge and power have rights,
But ignorance and weakness have rights too.
There needs no crucial effort to find truth
If here or there or anywhere about –
We ought to turn each side, try hard and see,
And if we can't, be glad we've earned at least
The right, by one laborious proof the more,
To graze in peace earth's pleasant pasturage.
Men are not gods, but, properly, are brutes.
Something we may see, all we cannot see –
What need of lying? I say, I see all,
And swear to each detail the most minute,
In what I think a man's face – you, mere cloud:
I swear I hear him speak and see him wink,
For fear, if once I drop the emphasis,
Mankind may doubt if there's a cloud at all.
You take the simpler life – ready to see,
Willing to see – for no cloud's worth a face –
And leaving quiet what no strength can move,
And which, who bids you move? who has the right?
I bid you; but you are God's sheep, not mine –
'*Pastor est tui Dominus.*' You find
In these the pleasant pastures of this life
Much you may eat without the least offence,
Much you don't eat because your maw objects,
Much you would eat but that your fellow-flock
Open great eyes at you and even butt,
And thereupon you like your friends so much
You cannot please yourself, offending them –
Though when they seem exorbitantly sheep,
You weigh your pleasure with their butts and kicks
And strike the balance. Sometimes certain fears
Restrain you – real checks since you find them so –
Sometimes you please yourself and nothing checks;
And thus you graze through life with not one lie,

And like it best.

            But do you, in truth's name?
If so, you beat – which means – you are not I –
Who needs must make earth mine and feed my fill
Not simply unbutted at, unbickered with,
But motioned to the velvet of the sward
By those obsequious wethers' very selves.
Look at me, sir; my age is double yours.
At yours, I knew beforehand, so enjoyed,
What now I should be – as, permit the word,
I pretty well imagine your whole range
And stretch of tether twenty years to come.
We both have minds and bodies much alike.
In truth's name, don't you want my bishopric,
My daily bread, my influence and my state?
You're young, I'm old, you must be old one day;
Will you find then, as I do hour by hour,
Women their lovers kneel to, that cut curls
From your fat lap-dog's ears to grace a brooch –
Dukes, that petition just to kiss your ring –
With much beside you know or may conceive?
Suppose we die to-night: well, here am I,
Such were my gains, life bore this fruit to me,
While writing all the same my articles
On music, poetry, the fictile vase
Found at Albano, or Anacreon's Greek.
But you – the highest honour in your life,
The thing you'll crown yourself with, all your days,
Is – dining here and drinking this last glass
I pour you out in sign of amity
Before we part for ever. Of your power
And social influence, worldly worth in short,
Judge what's my estimation by the fact –
I do not condescend to enjoin, beseech,
Hint secrecy on one of all these words!
You're shrewd and know that should you publish it
The world would brand the lie – my enemies first,

'Who'd sneer – the bishop's an arch-hypocrite,
And knave perhaps, but not so frank a fool.'
Whereas I should not dare for both my ears
Breathe one such syllable, smile one such smile,
Before my chaplain who reflects myself –
My shade's so much more potent than your flesh.
What's your reward, self-abnegating friend?
Stood you confessed of those exceptional
And privileged great natures that dwarf mine –
A zealot with a mad ideal in reach,
A poet just about to print his ode,
A statesman with a scheme to stop this war,
An artist whose religion is his art,
I should have nothing to object! such men
Carry the fire, all things grow warm to them,
Their drugget's worth my purple, they beat me.
But you, – you're just as little those as I –
You, Gigadibs, who, thirty years of age,
Write stately for Blackwood's Magazine,
Believe you see two points in Hamlet's soul
Unseized by the Germans yet – which view you'll print –
Meantime the best you have to show being still
That lively lightsome article we took
Almost for the true Dickens, – what's the name?
'The Slum and Cellar – or Whitechapel life
Limned after dark!' it made me laugh, I know,
And pleased a month and brought you in ten pounds.
– Success I recognise and compliment,
And therefore give you, if you please, three words
(The card and pencil-scratch is quite enough)
Which whether here, in Dublin, or New York,
Will get you, prompt as at my eyebrow's wink,
Such terms as never you aspired to get
In all our own reviews and some not ours.
Go write your lively sketches – be the first
'Blougram , or The Eccentric Confidence' –
Or better simply say, 'The Outward-bound.'
Why, men as soon would throw it in my teeth

As copy and quote the infamy chalked broad
About me on the church-door opposite.
You will not wait for that experience though,
I fancy, howsoever you decide,
To discontinue – not detesting, not
Defaming, but at least – despising me!

    Over his wine so smiled and talked his hour
Sylvester Blougram, styled *in partibus*
Episcopus, nec non – (the deuce knows what
It's changed to by our novel hierarchy)
With Gigadibs the literary man,
Who played with spoons, explored his plate's design,
And ranged the olive stones about its edge,
While the great bishop rolled him out his mind.

    For Blougram, he believed, say, half he spoke.
The other portion, as he shaped it thus
For argumentatory purposes,
He felt his foe was foolish to dispute.
Some arbitrary accidental thoughts
That crossed his mind, amusing because new,
He chose to represent as fixtures there,
Invariable convictions (such they seemed
Beside his interlocutor's loose cards
Flung daily down, and not the same way twice)
While certain hell-deep instincts, man's weak tongue
Is never bold to utter in their truth
Because styled hell-deep ('tis an old mistake
To place hell at the bottom of the earth)
He ignored these, – not having in readiness
Their nomenclature and philosophy:
He said true things, but called them by wrong names.
'On the whole,' he thought, 'I justify myself
On every point where cavillers like this
Oppugn my life: he tries one kind of fence –
I close – he's worsted, that's enough for him;
He's on the ground! if the ground should break away
I take my stand on, there's a firmer yet

Beneath it, both of us may sink and reach.
His ground was over mine and broke the first.
So let him sit with me this many a year!'

  He did not sit five minutes. Just a week
Sufficed his sudden healthy vehemence.
(Something had struck him in the 'Outward-bound'
Another way than Blougram's purpose was)
And having bought, not cabin-furniture
But settler's-implements (enough for three)
And started for Australia – there, I hope,
By this time he has tested his first plough,
And studied his last chapter of St John.

APPARENT FAILURE

'Apparent Failure' appeared in *Dramatis Personae* in 1863. It was the result of a visit to the Paris morgue in 1856 when Browning and Elizabeth were on their way back to Italy. Though his critics felt that it was further confirmation of Browning's enthusiasm for morbidity, it was one of Tennyson's favourites among his rival's work. 'I *laik* that,' Tennyson said with his Lincolnshire intonation.

'We shall soon lose a celebrated building.' – *Paris Newspaper*

I   No, for I'll save it! Seven years since,
    I passed through Paris, stopped a day
To see the baptism of your Prince;
    Saw, made my bow, and went my way:
Walking the heat and headache off,
    I took the Seine-side, you surmise,
Thought of the Congress, Gortschakoff,
    Cavour's appeal and Buol's replies,
So sauntered till – what met my eyes?

II   Only the Doric little Morgue!
    The dead-house where you show your drowned:
Petrarch's Vaucluse makes proud the Sorgue,
    Your Morgue has made the Seine renowned.
One pays one's debt in such a case;
    I plucked up heart and entered, – stalked,
Keeping a tolerable face
    Compared with some whose cheeks were chalked:
Let them! No Briton's to be baulked!

III   First came the silent gazers; next,
    A screen of glass, we're thankful for;
Last, the sight's self, the sermon's text,

The three men who did most abhor
Their life in Paris yesterday,
So killed themselves: and now, enthroned
Each on his copper couch, they lay
Fronting me, waiting to be owned.
I thought, and think, their sin's atoned.

IV Poor men, God made, and all for that!
The reverence struck me; o'er each head
Religiously was hung its hat,
Each coat dripped by the owner's bed,
Sacred from touch: each had his berth,
His bounds, his proper place of rest,
Who last night tenanted on earth
Some arch, where twelve such slept abreast, –
Unless the plain asphalte seemed best.

V How did it happen, my poor boy?
You wanted to be Buonaparte
And have the Tuileries for toy,
And could not, so it broke your heart?
You, old one by his side, I judge,
Were, red as blood, a socialist,
A leveller! Does the Empire grudge
You've gained what no Republic missed?
Be quiet, and unclench your fist!

VI And this – why, he was red in vain,
Or black, – poor fellow that is blue!
What fancy was it turned your brain?
Oh, women were the prize for you!
Money gets women, cards and dice
Get money, and ill-luck gets just
The copper couch and one clear nice
Cool squirt of water o'er your bust,
The right thing to extinguish lust!

VII It's wiser being good than bad;
It's safer being meek than fierce:
It's fitter being sane than mad.

My own hope is, a sun will pierce
The thickest cloud earth ever stretched;
That, after Last, returns the First,
Though a wide compass round be fetched;
That what began best, can't end worst,
Nor what God blessed once, prove accurst.

From THE RING AND THE BOOK

The Ring and the Book, Browning's most ambitious poem, was published in twelve books in 1868–9. Its subject is a 'Roman murder case' of 1698, whose story Browning discovered in an old parchment-covered volume on a Florentine market-stall. The case concerned Count Guido Franceschini of Arezzo, an impoverished middle-aged nobleman, who bought Pompilia Comparini as his bride when she was thirteen years old. He learnt too late that she was not the daughter of the Comparini and that they were less rich than he had hoped. Guido ill-treated his young wife, who was eventually rescued by a worldly young priest, Giuseppe Caponsacchi, with the aim of taking her home to the Comparini. The fugitives were arrested on the way, charged with adultery and convicted despite their innocence. Caponsacchi was banished, Pompilia who proved to be pregnant was sent home to her parents, after being detained for a short while in a convent. On 2 January 1698, Guido with four hired 'bravoes' came to Rome, murdered the Comparini parents and fatally stabbed Pompilia. He was tried, convicted and executed. After his conviction, he appealed unsuccessfully to Pope Innocent XII, the supreme temporal as well as spiritual power in Rome, on the grounds that natural law permitted him to kill an adulterous wife. The pope dismissed this plea and Guido was put to death.

Each book of Browning's poem presents the story in a different 'voice'. In the first and last books, he describes how he came to write the poem and he depicts the conclusion of the drama. Three books describe Roman society and its conflicting opinions on the case, some favouring Guido and some Pompilia. Counsel on either side, as well as Guido, Caponsacchi, the dying Pompilia, and Pope Innocent have their say. Among Browning's poems, it is a magnificent structure, in its portrayal of the psychopathic Guido, the radiant Pompilia, and the justice of Pope Innocent, supreme arbiter and a figure of great humanity, who defends Pompilia's innocence. Guido is dragged to his death, crying out in terror to those who can help him no longer.

> Abate, – Cardinal, – Christ, – Maria, – God, . . .
> Pompilia, will you let them murder me?

The drama of the poem and its power of description are so
intense that one can almost smell and taste Browning's Rome,
the burning tapers and the incense smoke, the waxed wood and
the hot streets. High society and common crime, political
intrigue and self-righteous sadism, mingle with innocence and
humanity. The crowds jostle for a sight of the murdered
corpses on the altar steps and take sides, for and against the
killers. In March 1869, R. W. Buchanan in the *Athenaeum*
described *The Ring and the Book* as 'the supremest poetical
achievement of our time . . . the most precious and profound
spiritual treasure that England has produced since the days of
Shakespeare.' The American poet Sidney Lanier wrote in 1870
that Browning caught and held his reader with the skill of a
lasso. Swinburne wrote to his friend Richard Monckton
Milnes.

> What a wonderful work this is of Browning's. I tore through
> the first volume in a day of careful study, with a sense of
> absolute possession. I have not felt so strongly that delightful
> sense of being mastered – dominated – by another man's
> work since I was a small boy. I always except, of course,
> Victor Hugo's which has the same force and insight and
> variety of imagination together with that exquisite bloom
> and flavour of the highest poetry which Browning's has not:
> though it has perhaps a more wonderful subtlety at once and
> breadth of humorous invention and perception. As for the
> interest, it simply kills all other matters of thought for the
> time.

In the second book of the poem, 'Half-Rome', the crowds
jostle in the church of San Lorenzo in Lucina, eager to see the
bodies of the murdered Comparini displayed on the chancel
steps of their parish church, according to tradition, and eager
to see Pompilia as well – 'and she can't outlive night.' This
Half-Rome is sympathetic to Guido and the 'baiting' he
endured as a result of Pompilia's flight. Should Guido have

trusted to the law rather than resorting to physical vengeance?
'No, take the old way trod when men were men.' Old Luca
Cini is there, an expert on dagger wounds, having seen his first
murdered corpse while holding his father's hand seventy years
before.

From dawn till now that it is growing dusk,
A multitude has flocked and filled the church,
Coming and going, coming back again,
Till to count crazed one. Rome was at the show.
People climbed up the columns, fought for spikes
O' the chapel-rail to perch themselves upon,
Jumped over and so broke the wooden work
Painted like porphyry to deceive the eye;
Serve the priests right! The organ-loft was crammed,
Women were fainting, no few fights ensued,
In short, it was a show repaid your pains:
For, though their room was scant undoubtedly,
Yet they did manage matters, to be just,
A little at this Lorenzo. Body o' me!
I saw a body exposed once . . . never mind!
Enough that here the bodies had their due.
No stinginess in wax, a row all round,
And one big taper at each head and foot.

So, people pushed their way, and took their turn,
Saw, threw their eyes up, crossed themselves, gave place
To pressure from behind, since all the world
Knew the old pair, could talk the tragedy
Over from the first to last: Pompilia too,
Those who had known her — what 'twas worth to them!
Guido's acquaintance was in less request;
The Count had lounged somewhat too long in Rome,
Made himself cheap; with him were hand and glove
Barbers and blear-eyed, as the ancient sings.

Also he is alive and like to be:
Had he considerately died, – aha!
I jostled Luca Cini on his staff,
Mute in the midst, the whole man one amaze,
Staring amain and crossing brow and breast.
'How now?' asked I. ''Tis seventy years,' quoth he,
'Since I first saw, holding my father's hand,
'Bodies set forth: a many have I seen,
'Yet all was poor to this I live and see.
'Here the world's wickedness seals up the sum:
'What with Molinos' doctrine and this deed,
'Antichrist's surely come and doomsday near.
'May I depart in peace, I have seen my see.'
'Depart then,' I advised, 'nor block the road
'For youngsters still behindhand with such sights!'
'Why no,' rejoins the venerable sire,
'I know it's horrid, hideous past belief,
'Burdensome far beyond what eye can bear;
'But they do promise, when Pompilia dies
'I' the course o' the day, – and she can't outlive night, –
'They'll bring her body also to expose
'Beside the parents, one, two, three a-breast;
'That were indeed a sight which, might I see,
'I trust I should not last to see the like!'
Whereat I bade the senior spare his shanks,
Since doctors give her till to-night to live
And tell us how the butchery happened. 'Ah,
'But you can't know!' sighs he. 'I'll not despair:
'Beside I'm useful at explaining things –
'As, how the dagger laid there at the feet,
'Caused the peculiar cuts; I mind its make,
'Triangular i' the blade, a Genoese,
'Armed with those little hook-teeth on the edge
'To open in the flesh nor shut again:
'I like to teach a novice: I shall stay!'
And stay he did, and stay be sure he will.

*   *   *

Guido Franceschini is brought before his judges. He has just been tortured on the rack to ensure that he tells the whole truth. He appears cringing and obsequious, yet vindictive towards Pompilia and her parents.

Thanks, Sir, but, should it please the reverend Court,
I feel I can stand somehow, half sit down
Without help, make shift to even speak, you see,
Fortified by the sip of . . . why, 'tis wine,
Velletri, – and not vinegar and gall,
So changed and good the times grow! Thanks, kind Sir!
Oh, but one sip's enough! I want my head
To save my neck, there's work awaits me still.
How cautious and considerate . . . aie, aie, aie,
Not your fault, sweet Sir! Come, you take to heart
An ordinary matter. Law is law.
Noblemen were exempt, the vulgar thought,
From racking, but, since law thinks otherwise,
I have been put to the rack: all's over now,
And neither wrist – what men style, out of joint:
If any harm be, 'tis the shoulder-blade,
The left one, that seems wrong i' the socket, – Sirs,
Much could not happen, I was quick to faint,
Being past my prime of life, and out of health.
In short I thank you, – yes, and mean the word.
Needs must the Court be slow to understand
How this quite novel form of taking pain,
This getting tortured merely in the flesh,
Amounts to almost an agreeable change
In my case, me fastidious, plied too much
With opposite treatment, used (forgive the joke)
To the rasp-tooth toying with this brain of mine,
And, in and out my heart, the play o' the probe.
Four years have I been operated on
I' the soul, do you see – its tense or tremulous part –

My self-respect, my care for a good name,
Pride in an old one, love of kindred — just
A mother, brothers, sisters, and the like,
That looked up to my face when days were dim,
And fancied they found light there — no one spot,
Foppishly sensitive, but has paid its pang.
That, and not this you now oblige me with,
That was the Vigil-torment, if you please!
The poor old noble House that drew the rags
O' the Franceschini's once superb array
Close round her, hoped to slink unchallenged by, —
Pluck off these! Turn the drapery inside out
And teach the tittering town how scarlet wears!
Show men the lucklessness, the improvidence
Of the easy-natured Count before this Court,
The father I have some slight feeling for,
Who let the world slide, nor foresaw that friends
Then proud to cap and kiss the patron's shoe,
Would, when the purse he left held spider-webs,
Properly push his child to wall one day!
Mimic the tetchy humour, furtive glance
And brow where half was furious half fatigued,
O' the same son got to be of middle age,
Sour, saturnine, — your humble servant here, —
When things go cross and the young wife, he finds
Take to the window at a whistle's bid,
And yet demurs thereon, preposterous fool! —

*   *   *

In a chilling revelation of self-righteous cruelty, Guido admits his error. Had he used his knife to maim Pompilia when she first transgressed, she might have avoided the misconduct which made it necessary to kill her. His words, like those of Porphyria's lover are the more chilling for being phrased in the inflexible moral logic of the psychopath.

If I, – instead of threatening, talking big,
Showing hair-powder, a prodigious pinch,
For poison in a bottle, – making believe
At desperate doings with a bauble-sword,
And other bugaboo-and-baby-work, –
Had, with the vulgarest household implement,
Calmly and quietly cut off, clean thro' bone,
But one joint of one finger of my wife,
Saying 'For listening to the serenade,
'Here's your ring-finger shorter a full third:
'Be certain I will slice away next joint,
'Next time that anybody underneath
'Seems somehow to be sauntering as he hoped
'A flower would eddy out of your hand to his
'While you please fidget with the branch above
'O' the rose-tree in the terrace!' – had I done so,
Why, there had followed a quick sharp scream, some pain,
Much calling for plaister, damage to the dress,
A somewhat sulky countenance next day,
Perhaps reproaches, – but reflections too!
I don't hear much of harm that Malchus did
After the incident of the ear, my lords!
Saint Peter took the efficacious way;
Malchus was sore but silenced for his life:
He did not hang himself i' the Potter's Field
Like Judas, who was trusted with the bag
And treated to sops after he proved a thief.
So, by this time, my true and obedient wife
Might have been telling beads with a gloved hand;
Awkward a little at pricking hearts and darts
On sampler possibly, but well otherwise:
Not where Rome shudders now to see her lie.

*   *   *

In the seventh book of the poem, the dying Pompilia recalls how
her mother, Violante Comparini, sold her in marriage to Guido, a
short, yellowed, middle-aged suitor. The brutal revelation of

sexual reality was rarely described with such skill in Victorian writing. When Guido agreed to buy Pompilia, she was thirteen years old and still playing with her toys. The wedding, with the participants hurrying through a rain-storm to the ceremony, is a horror that appears all the worse for Pompilia's uncomplaining innocence.

Beside, up to my marriage, thirteen years
Were, each day, happy as the day was long:
This may have made the change too terrible.
I know that when Violante told me first
The cavalier, – she meant to bring next morn,
Whom I must also let take, kiss my hand, –
Would be at San Lorenzo the same eve
And marry me, – which over, we should go
Home both of us without him as before,
And, till she bade speak, I must hold my tongue,
Such being the correct way with girl-brides,
From whom one word would make a father blush, –
I know, I say, that when she told me this,
– Well, I no more saw sense in what she said
Than a lamb does in people clipping wool;
Only lay down and let myself be clipped.
And when next day the cavalier who came
(Tisbe had told me that the slim young man
With wings at head, and wings at feet, and sword
Threatening a monster, in our tapestry,
Would eat a girl else, – was a cavalier)
When he proved Guido Franceschini, – old
And nothing like so tall as I myself,
Hook-nosed and yellow in a bush of beard,
Much like a thing I saw on a boy's wrist,
He called an owl and used for catching birds, –
And when he took my hand and made a smile –
Why, the uncomfortableness of it all

Seemed hardly more important in the case
Than, – when one gives you, say, a coin to spend, –
Its newness or its oldness; if the piece
Weigh properly and buy you what you wish,
No matter whether you get grime or glare!
Men take the coin, return you grapes and figs.
Here, marriage was the coin, a dirty piece
Would purchase me the praise of those I loved:
About what else should I concern myself?
So, hardly knowing what a husband meant,
I supposed this or any man would serve,
No whit the worse for being so uncouth:
For I was ill once and a doctor came
With a great ugly hat, no plume thereto,
Black jerkin and black buckles and black sword,
And white sharp beard over the ruff in front,
And oh so lean, so sour-faced and austere! –
Who felt my pulse, made me put out my tongue,
Then oped a phial, dripped a drop or two
Of a black bitter something, – I was cured!
What mattered the fierce beard or the grim face?
It was the physic beautified the man,
Master Malpichi, – never met his match
In Rome, they said, – so ugly all the same!

However, I was hurried through a storm,
Next dark eve of December's deadest day –
How it rained! – through our street and the Lion's-mouth
And the bit of Corso, – cloaked round, covered close,
I was like something strange or contraband, –
Into blank San Lorenzo, up the aisle,
My mother keeping hold of me so tight,
I fancied we were come to see a corpse
Before the altar which she pulled me toward.
There we found waiting an unpleasant priest
Who proved the brother, not our parish friend,
But one with mischief-making mouth and eye,
Paul, whom I know since to my cost. And then

I heard the heavy church-door lock out help
Behind us: for the customary warmth,
Two tapers shivered on the altar. 'Quick –
'Lose no time!' – cried the priest. And straightway down
From . . . what's behind the altar where he hid –
Hawk-nose and yellowness and bush and all,
Stepped Guido, caught my hand, and there was I
O' the chancel, and the priest had opened book,
Read here and there, made me say that and this,
And after, told me I was now a wife,
Honoured indeed, since Christ thus weds the Church,
And therefoe turned he water into wine,
To show I should obey my spouse like Christ.
Then the two slipped aside and talked apart,
And I, silent and scared, got down again
And joined my mother who was weeping now.
Nobody seemed to mind us any more,
And both of us on tiptoe found our way
To the door which was unlocked by this, and wide.
When we were in the street, the rain had stopped,
All things looked better. At our own house-door,
Violante whispered 'No one syllable
'To Pietro! Girl-brides never breathe a word!'
' – Well treated to a wetting, draggle-tails!'
Laughed Pietro as he opened – 'Very near
'You made me brave the gutter's roaring sea
'To carry off from roost old dove and young,
'Trussed up in church, the cote, by me, the kite!
'What do these priests mean, praying folk to death
'On stormy afternoons, with Christmas close
'To wash our sins off nor require the rain?'
Violante gave my hand a timely squeeze,
Madonna saved me from immodest speech,
I kissed him and was quiet, being a bride.

*   *   *

After the melodrama and the moral squalor of the crime comes the sublime and radiant judgment of Pope Innocent XII, a figure of divinity and nobility, weary of the corruption of the world. Nowhere was Browning's skill in portraying saintliness better shown than among the worldly splendour of pontifical power and disillusionment.

First of the first,
Such I pronounce Pompilia, then as now
Perfect in whiteness – stoop thou down, my child,
Give one good moment to the poor old Pope
Heart-sick at having all his world to blame –
Let me look at thee in the flesh as erst,
Let me enjoy the old clean linen garb,
Not the new splendid vesture! Armed and crowned,
Would Michael, yonder, be, nor crowned nor armed,
The less pre-eminent angel? Everywhere
I see in the world the intellect of man,
That sword, the energy his subtle spear,
The knowledge which defends him like a shield –
Everywhere; but they make not up, I think,
The marvel of a soul like thine, earth's flower
She holds up to the softened gaze of God!
It was not given Pompilia to know much,
Speak much, to write a book, to move mankind,
Be memorised by who records my time.
Yet if in purity and patience, if
In faith held fast despite the plucking fiend,
Safe like the signet-stone with the new name
That saints are known by, – if in right returned
For wrong, most pardon for worst injury,
If there be any virtue, any praise, –
Then will this woman-child have proved – who knows? –
Just the one prize vouchsafed unworthy me,
Ten years a gardener of the untoward ground,
I till, – this earth, my sweat and blood manure

All the long day that barrenly grows dusk:
At least one blossom makes me proud at eve
Born 'mid the briers of my enclosure! Still
(Oh, here as elsewhere, nothingness of man!)
Those be the plants, imbedded yonder South
To mellow in the morning, those made fat
By the master's eye, that yield such timid leaf,
Uncertain bud, as product of his pains!
While – see how this mere chance-sown, cleft-nursed seed,
That sprang up by the wayside 'neath the foot
Of the enemy, this breaks all into blaze,
Spreads itself, one wide glory of desire
To incorporate the whole great sun it loves
From the inch-height whence it looks and longs! My flower,
My rose, I gather for the breast of God,
This I praise most in thee, where all I praise,
That having been obedient to the end
According to the light allotted, law
Prescribed thy life, still tried, still standing test, –
Dutiful to the foolish parents first,
Submissive next to the bad husband, – nay,
Tolerant of those meaner miserable
That did his hests, eked out the dole of pain, –
Thou, patient thus, couldst rise from law to law,
The old to the new, promoted at one cry
O' the trump of God to the new service, not
To longer bear, but henceforth fight, be found
Sublime in new impatience with the foe!

From RED COTTON NIGHT-CAP COUNTRY

Red Cotton Night-Cap Country (1873) was Browning's modern verse novel, the true story of a contemporary international jeweller, Antoine Mellerio (Miranda in the poem), who burnt his hands off in Paris as an act of remorse for an illicit love-affair, then went back to his mistress and finally threw himself off the tower of his country house in 1870, convinced that the Virgin would bear him up and restore the age of faith by a public miracle in the skies of Normandy. A dispute over his will and his sanity was before the court at Caen, while Browning was on holiday nearby.

The poem anticipates the world of Zola, Maupassant and the new French fiction, which was itself the subject of successful criminal proceedings in England in 1888–9. The American novelist and tourist William Dean Howells dismissed the poem in the *Atlantic Monthly* for July 1873 as 'horrible and revolting in itself. . . We suppose we shall be told of power in the story; and power there undeniably is, else no one could be dragged through the book by it.' In the following month, the reviewer in *Harper's Magazine* was determined 'to enter our strong protest against the endeavour to glorify an illicit love with one who had been in succession a profligate woman and an unfaithful wife.'

Red Cotton Night-Cap Country brings full circle Browning's speculations on 'the dangerous edge of things', which had begun in 'Porphyria's Lover' almost forty years before. It evokes the boulevard life of Second Empire Paris, the music halls and fashionable society, the flat horizons of the Normandy coast, as his early poems had brought to life Renaissance Florence or the stucco and brick of Cardinal Wiseman's Westminster. Browning describes his hero, Léonce Miranda, hunting women along the music halls and dance floors of Paris, finding Clara de Millefleurs with her fashionable new apartment in the Rue du Colisée, off the Champs Elysées. Yet Miranda is both a pleasure-seeker and a susceptible Catholic, whose passions are strong in each respect.

Accordingly, on weighty business bound,
Monsieur Léonce Miranda stooped to play,
But, with experience, soon reduced the game
To principles, and thenceforth played by rule:
Rule, dignifying sport as sport, proclaimed
No less that sport was sport and nothing more.
He understood the worth of womankind, –
To furnish man – provisionally – sport:
Sport transitive – such earth's amusements are:
But, seeing that amusements pall by use,
Variety therein is requisite.
And since the serious work of life were wronged
Should we bestow importance on our play,
It follows, in such womankind-pursuit,
Cheating is lawful chase. We have to spend
An hour – they want a lifetime thrown away:
We seek to tickle sense – they ask for soul,
As if soul had no higher ends to serve!
A stag-hunt gives the royal creature law
Bat-fowling is all fair with birds at roost,
The lantern and the clapnet suit the hedge.
Which must explain why, bent on Boulevard game,
Monsieur Léonce Miranda decently
Was prudent in his pleasure – passed himself
Off on the fragile fair about his path
As the gay devil rich in mere good looks,
Youth, hope – what matter though the purse be void?
'If I were only young Miranda, now,
Instead of a poor clerkly drudge at desk
All day, poor artist vainly bruising brush
On palette, poor musician scraping gut
With horsehair teased that no harmonics come!
Then would I love with liberality,
Then would I pay! – who now shall be repaid,
Repaid alike for present pain and past,
If Mademoiselle permit the contre-danse,
Sing 'Gay in garret youth at twenty lives,'
And afterward accept a lemonade!'

Such sweet facilities of intercourse
Afford the Winter-Garden and Mabille!
'Oh, I unite' – runs on the confidence,
Poor fellow, that was read in open Court,
– 'Amusement with discretion: never fear
My *escapades* cost more than market-price!
No durably-attached Miranda-dupe,
Sucked dry of substance by two clinging lips,
Promising marriage, and performing it!
Trust me, I know the world, and know myself,
And know where duty takes me – in good time!'

Thus fortified and realistic, then,
At all points thus against illusion armed,
He wisely did New Year inaugurate
By playing truant to the favoured five:
And sat installed at 'The Varieties', –
Playhouse appropriately named, – to note
(Prying amid the turf that's flowery there)
What primrose, firstling of the year, might push
The snows aside to deck his button-hole –
Unnoticed by the outline sad, severe,
(Though fifty good long years removed from youth)
That tower and tower, – our image, bear in mind!

No sooner was he seated than, behold,
Out burst a polyanthus! He was 'ware
Of a young woman niched in neighbourhood;
And ere one moment flitted, fast was he
Found captive to the beauty evermore,
For life, for death, for heaven, for hell, her own.
Philosophy, bewail thy fate! Adieu,
Youth realistic and illusion-proof!
Monsieur Léonce Miranda, – hero late
Who 'understood the worth of womankind,'
'Who found therein – provisionally – sport,' –
Felt, in the flitting of a moment, fool
Was he, and folly all that seemed so wise,
And the best proof of wisdom's birth would be

That he made all endeavour, body, soul,
By any means, at any sacrifice
Of labour, wealth, repute, and (– well, the time
For choosing between heaven on earth, and heaven
In heaven, was not at hand immediately –)
Made all endeavour, without loss incurred
Of one least minute, to obtain her love.
'Sport transitive?' 'Variety required?'
'In loving were a lifetime thrown away?'
How singularly may young men mistake!
The fault must be repaired with energy.

Monsieur Léonce Miranda ate her up
With eye-devouring; when the unconscious fair
Passed from the close-packed hall, he pressed behind;
She mounted vehicle, he did the same,
Coach stopped, and cab fast followed, at one door –
Good house in unexceptionable street.
Out stepped the lady, – never think, alone!
A mother was not wanting to the maid,
Or, may be, wife, or widow, might one say?
Out stepped and properly down flung himself
Monsieur Léonce Miranda at her feet –
And never left them after, so to speak,
For twenty years, till his last hour of life,
When he released them, as precipitate.
Love proffered and accepted then and there!
Such potency in word and look has truth.

Truth I say, truth I mean: this love was true,
And the rest happened by due consequence.
By which we are to learn that there exists
A falsish false, for truth's inside the same,
And truth that's only half true, falsish truth.
The better for both parties! folk may taunt
That half your rock-built wall is rubble-heap:
Answer them, half their flowery turf is stones!
Our friend had hitherto been decking coat
If not with stones, with weeds that stones befit,

With dandelions – 'primrose-buds,' smirked he;
This proved a polyanthus on his breast,
Prize-lawful or prize-lawless, flower the same.
So with his other instance of mistake:
Was Christianity the Ravissante?
And what a flower of flowers he chanced on now!
To primrose, polyanthus I prefer
As illustration, from the fancy-fact
That out of simple came the composite
By culture: that the florist bedded thick
His primrose-root in ruddle, bullock's blood,
Ochre and devils'-dung, for aught I know,
Until the pale and pure grew fiery-fine,
Ruby and topas, rightly named anew.
This lady was no product of the plain;
Social manure had raised a rarity.
Clara de Millefleurs (note the happy name)
Blazed in the full-blown glory of her Spring.
Peerlessly perfect, form and face: for both –
'Imagine what, at seventeen, may have proved
Miss Pages, the actress: Pages herself, my dear!'
Noble she was, the name denotes: and rich?
'The apartment in this Coliseum Street,
Furnished, my dear, with such an elegance,
Testifies wealth, my dear, sufficiently!
What quality, what style and title, eh?
Well now, waive nonsense, you and I are boys
No longer: somewhere must a screw be slack!
Don't fancy, Duchesses descend at door
From carriage-step to stranger prostrate stretched,
And bid him take heart, and deliver mind,
March in and make himself at ease forthwith, –
However broad his chest and black his beard,
And comely his belongings, – all through love
Protested in a world of ways save one
Hinting at marriage!' – marriage which yet means
Only the obvious method, easiest help
To satisfaction of love's first demand,

That love endure eternally: 'my dear
Somewhere or other must a screw be slack!'

*   *   *

The crisis of the drama is precipitated by the death of Miranda's
ailing mother and the insistence of the priest that her son's sexual
promiscuity was the cause of her death and of the young man's
probable damnation.

> 'No flattery of self! You murdered her!
> The grey lips, silent now, reprove by mine.
> You wasted all your living, rioted
> In harlotry – she warned and I repeat!
> No warning had she, for she needed none:
> If this should be the last yourself receive?'

Harrowed by grief and remorse, Miranda performs his self-
mutilation while the rest of the family wait in another room of
their Paris house, supposing him to be burning Clara's letters.

And now let pass a week. Once more behold
The same assemblage in the same saloon,
Waiting the entry of protagonist
Monsieur Léonce Miranda. 'Just a week
Since the death-day, – was ever man transformed
Like this man?' questioned cousin of his mate.
Last seal to the repentance had been set
Three days before, at Sceaux in neighbourhood
Of Paris, where they laid with funeral pomp
Mother by father. Let me spare the rest:
How the poor fellow, in his misery,
Buried hot face and bosom, where heaped snow
Offered assistance, at the grave's black edge,
And there lay, till uprooted by main force

From where he prayed to grow and ne'er again
Walk earth unworthily as heretofore.
It is not with impunity priests teach
The doctrine he was dosed with from his youth –
'Pain to the body – profit to the soul;
Corporeal pleasure – so much woe to pay
When disembodied spirit gives account.'
However, woe had done its worst, this time.
Three days allow subsidence of much grief.
Already, regular and equable,
Forward went purpose to effect. At once
The testament was written, signed and sealed.
Disposure of the commerce – that took time,
And would not suffer by a week's delay;
But the immediate, the imperious need,
The call demanding of the Cousinry
Co-operation, what convened them thus,
Was – how and when should deputation march
To Coliseum Street, the old abode
Of wickedness, and there acquaint – oh, shame!
Her, its old inmate, who had followed up
And lay in wait in the old haunt for prey –
That they had rescued, they possessed Léonce,
Whose loathing at recapture equalled theirs
Upbraid that sinner with her sinfulness,
Impart the fellow-sinner's firm resolve
Never to set eyes on her face again:
Then, after stipulations strict but just,
Hand her the first instalment, – moderate
Enough, no question, – of her salary:
Admonish for the future, and so end. –
All which good purposes, decided on
Sufficiently, were waiting full effect
When presently the culprit should appear.

Somehow appearance was delayed too long;
Chatting and chirping sunk inconsciously
To silence, nay, uneasiness, at length

Alarm, till – anything for certitude! –
A peeper was commissioned to explore,
At keyhole, what the laggard's task might be –
What caused so palpable a disrespect!

Back came the tiptoe cousin from his quest.
'Monsieur Léonce was busy,' he believed,
'Contemplating – those love-letters, perhaps,
He always carried, as if precious stones,
About with him. He read, one after one,
Some sort of letters. But his back was turned.
The empty coffer open at his side,
He leant on elbow by the mantelpiece
Before the hearth-fire; big and blazing too.'

'Better he shovelled them all in at once,
And burned the rubbish!' was a cousin's quip,
Warming his own hands at the fire the while.
I told you, snow had fallen outside, I think.

When suddenly a cry, a host of cries,
Screams, hubbub and confusion thrilled the room.
All by a common impulse rushed thence, reached
The late death-chamber, tricked with trappings still,
Skulls, cross bones and such moral broidery.
Madame Muhlhausen might have played the witch,
Dropped down the chimney and appalled Léonce
By some proposal 'Parting touch of hand!'
If she but touched his foolish hand, you know!!

Something had happened quite contrariwise.
Monsieur Léonce Miranda, one by one,
Had read the letters and the love they held,
And, that task finished, had required his soul
To answer frankly what the prospect seemed
Of his own love's departure – pledged to part!
Then, answer being unmistakable,
He had replaced the letters quietly,
Shut coffer, and so, grasping either side
By its convenient handle, plunged the whole –

Letters and coffer and both hands to boot,
Into the burning grate and held them there.
'Burn, burn and purify my past!' said he,
Calmly, as if he felt no pain at all.

In vain they pulled him from the torture-place:
The strong man, with the soul of tenfold strength,
Broke from their clutch: and there again smiled he,
The miserable hands re-bathed in fire –
Constant to that ejaculation 'Burn,
Burn, purify!' And when, combining force,
They fairly dragged the victim out of reach
Of further harm, he had no hands to hurt –
Two horrible remains of right and left,
'Whereof the bones, phalanges formerly,
Carbonized, were still crackling with the flame,'
Said Beaumont. And he fought them all the while:
'Why am I hindered when I would be pure?
Why leave the sacrifice still incomplete?
She holds me, I must have more hands to burn!'
They were the stronger, though, and bound him fast.

Beaumont was in attendance presently.
'What did I tell you? Preachment to the deaf!
I wish he had been deafer when they preached,
Those priests! But wait till next Republic comes!'

As for Léonce, a single sentiment
Possessed his soul and occupied his tongue –
Absolute satisfaction at the deed.
Never he varied, 'tis observable,
Nor in the stage of agonies (which proved
Absent without leave, – science seemed to think)
Nor yet in those three months' febricity
Which followed, – never did he vary tale –
Remaining happy beyond utterance.
'Ineffable beatitude' – I quote
The words, I cannot give the smile – 'such bliss
Abolished pain! Pain might or might not be:

He felt in heaven, where flesh desists to fret.
Purified now and henceforth, all the past
Reduced to ashes with the flesh defiled!

*   *   *

The fragile equilibrium of Miranda's mind shifts again and he returns to Clara, living with her in his country house near the Normandy coast, while giving large sums of money to the Church with which he is no longer in communion. From the tower of the house, he can see the statue of the Virgin on the tower of the church of The Ravissante. By prayer and devotion, he hopes to win forgiveness for himself and for Clara, whose list of lovers includes Duke Hertford and Muhlhausen. By an act of faith, he will throw himself from the tower and the Virgin will bear him up. Miranda will be seen in the skies of Normandy, a miracle restoring faith in an age of unbelief. He imagines how Ernest Renan and the rationalists will repent, how the sceptical publications sold in Paris along the Seine will be burnt. Secure in faith or delusion, Miranda prepares to jump. His farewell is the soliloquy of a late-Victorian Hamlet. Is he mad? Browning thinks not. Better put faith to the proof at once than be racked with doubt for the rest of one's life.

'Thus I bestride the railing, leg o'er leg,
Thus, lo, I stand, a single inch away,
At dizzy edge of death, – no touch of fear,
As safe on tower above as turf below!
Your smile enswathes me in beatitude,
You lift along the votary – who vaults,
Who, in the twinkling of an eye, revives,
Dropt safely in the space before the church –
How crowded, since this morn is market-day!
I shall not need to speak. The news will run

Like wild-fire. "Thousands saw Miranda's flight!"
'Tis telegraphed to Paris in a trice.
The Boulevard is one buzz "Do you believe?
Well, this time, thousands saw Miranda's flight:
You know him, goldsmith in the Place Vendôme."
In goes the Empress to the Emperor:
"Now – will you hesitate to make disgorge
Your wicked King of Italy his gains,
Give the Legations to the Pope once more?"
Which done, – why, grace goes back to operate,
They themselves set a good example first,
Resign the empire twenty years usurped,
And Henry, the Desired One, reigns o'er France!
Regenerated France makes all things new!
My house no longer stands on Quai Rousseau
But Quai rechristened Alacoque: a quai
Where Renan burns his book, and Veuillot burns
Renan beside, since Veuillot rules the roast,
Re-edits now indeed "The Universe".
O blessing, O superlatively big
With blessedness beyond all blessing dreamed
By man! for just that promise has effect,
"Old things shall pass away and all be new!"
Then, for a culminating mercy-feat,
Wherefore should I dare dream impossible
That I too have my portion in the change?
My past with all its sorrow, sin and shame,
Becomes a blank, a nothing! There she stands,
Clara de Millefleurs, all deodorized,
Twenty years' stain wiped off her innocence !
There never was Muhlhausen, nor at all
Duke Hertford: nought that was, remains except
The beauty, – yes, the beauty is unchanged.
Well, and the soul too, that must keep the same!
And so the trembling little virgin hand
Melts into mine, that's back again, of course !
– Think not I care about my poor old self!
I only want my hand for that one use,

To take her hand, and say "I marry you —
Men, women, angels, you behold my wife!
There is no secret, nothing wicked here,
Nothing she does not wish the world to know!"
None of your married women have the right
To mutter "Yes, indeed, she beats us all
In beauty, — but our lives are pure at least!"
Beat witness, for our marriage is no thing
Done in a corner! 'Tis The Ravissante
Repairs the wrong of Paris. See, She smiles,
She beckons, She bids "Hither, both of you!"
And may we kneel? And will you bless us both?
And may I worship you, and yet love her?
Then!' —
      A sublime spring from the balustrade
About the tower so often talked about,
A flash in middle air, and stone-dead lay
Monsieur Léonce Miranda on the turf.

A gardener who watched, at work the while
Dibbling a flower-bed for geranium-shoots,
Saw the catastrophe, and, straightening back,
Stood up and shook his brows. 'Poor soul, poor soul!
Just what I prophesied the end would be!
Ugh — the Red Night-cap!' (as he raised the head)
'This must be what he meant by those strange words
While I was weeding larkspurs yesterday,
"Angels would take him!" Mad!'

               No! sane, I say.
Such being the conditions of his life,
Such end of life was not irrational.
Hold a belief, you only half-believe,
With all-momentous issues either way, —
And I advise you imitate this leap,
Put faith to proof, be cured or killed at once!
Call you men, killed through cutting cancer out,
The worse for such an act of bravery?
That's more than *I* know. In my estimate,

Better lie prostrate on his turf at peace,
Than, wistful, eye, from out the tent, the tower,
Racked with a doubt 'Will going on bare knees
All the way to The Ravissante and back,
Saying my Ave Mary all the time,
Somewhat excuse if I postpone my march?
– Make due amends for that one kiss I gave
In gratitude to her who held me out
Superior Fricquot's sermon, hot from press,
A-spread with hands so sinful yet so smooth?'

And now, sincerely do I pray she stand,
Clara, with interposing sweep of robe,
Between us and this horror! Any screen
Turns white by contrast with the tragic pall;
And her dubiety distracts at least,
As well as snow, from such decided black.
With womanhood, at least, we have to do:
Ending with Clara – is the word too kind?

ARNOLD

THE FORSAKEN MERMAN

Arnold's first volume of poems appeared in 1849 and his last in 1869. 'The Forsaken Merman', which he classified as one of his Narrative Poems, comes from *The Strayed Reveller, and Other Poems* (1849). Its author appeared anonymously as 'A'. 'The Forsaken Merman' is drawn from a Danish tale of a merman who married a mortal bride. Arnold's is a fine poem, a haunting fable of the young woman lured ashore at Easter by the religion of humankind.

Come, dear children, let us away;
Down and away below!
Now my brothers call from the bay,
Now the great winds shoreward blow,
Now the salt tides seaward flow;
Now the wild white horses play,
Champ and chafe and toss in the spray.
Children dear, let us away!
This way, this way!

Call her once before you go –
Call once yet!
In a voice that she will know:
'Margaret! Margaret!'
Children's voices should be dear
(Call once more) to a mother's ear;
Children's voices, wild with pain –
Surely she will come again!
Call her once and come away;
This way, this way!
'Mother dear, we cannot stay!
The wild white horses foam and fret.'
Margaret! Margaret!

Come, dear children, come away down;
Call no more!
One last look at the white-wall'd town,
And the little grey church on the windy shore;
Then come down!
She will not come though you call all day;
Come away, come away!

Children dear, was it yesterday
We heard the sweet bells over the bay?
In the caverns where we lay,
Through the surf and through the swell,
The far-off sound of a silver bell?
Sand-strewn caverns, cool and deep,
Where the winds are all asleep;
Where the spent lights quiver and gleam,
Where the salt weed sways in the stream,
Where the sea-beasts, ranged all round,
Feed in the ooze of their pasture-ground:
Where the sea-snakes coil and twine,
Dry their mail and bask in the brine;
Where great whales come sailing by,
Sail and sail, with unshut eye,
Round the world for ever and aye?
When did music come this way?
Children dear, was it yesterday?

Children dear, was it yesterday
(Call yet once) that she went away?
Once she sate with you and me,
On a red gold throne in the heart of the sea,
And the youngest sate on her knee.
She comb'd its bright hair, and she tended it well,
When down swung the sound of a far-off bell.
She sigh'd, she look'd up through the clear green sea;
She said: 'I must go, for my kinsfolk pray
In the little grey church on the shore to-day.
'Twill be Easter-time in the world – ah me!
And I lose my poor soul, Merman! here with thee.'

I said: 'Go up, dear heart, through the waves;
Say thy prayer, and come back to the kind sea-caves!'
She smiled, she went up through the surf in the bay.
Children dear, was it yesterday?

Children dear, were we long alone?
'The sea grows stormy, the little ones moan;
Long prayers,' I said, 'in the world they say;
Come!' I said; and we rose through the surf in the bay.
We went up the beach, by the sandy down
Where the sea-stocks bloom, to the white-wall'd town;
Through the narrow paved streets, where all was still,
To the little grey church on the windy hill.
From the church came a murmur of folk at their prayers,
But we stood without in the cold blowing airs.
We climb'd on the graves, on the stones worn with rains,
And we gazed up the aisle through the small leaded panes.
She sate by the pillar; we saw her clear:
'Margaret, hist! come quick, we are here!
Dear heart,' I said, 'we are long alone;
The sea grows stormy, the little ones moan.'
But, ah, she gave me never a look,
For her eyes were seal'd to the holy book!
Loud prays the priest; shut stands the door.
Come away, children, call no more!
Come away, come down, call no more!

Down, down, down!
Down to the depths of the sea!
She sits at her wheel in the humming town,
Singing most joyfully.
Hark what she sings: 'O joy, O joy,
For the humming street, and the child with its toy!
For the priest, and the bell, and the holy well;
For the wheel where I spun,
And the blessed light of the sun!'
And so she sings her fill,
Singing most joyfully,
Till the spindle drops from her hand,

And the whizzing wheel stands still.
She steals to the window, and looks at the sand
And over the sand at the sea;
And her eyes are set in a stare;
And anon there breaks a sigh,
And anon there drops a tear,
From a sorrow-clouded eye,
And a heart sorrow-laden,
A long, long sigh;
For the cold strange eyes of a little Mermaiden,
And the gleam of her golden hair.

Come away, away children;
Come children, come down!
The hoarse wind blows colder;
Lights shine in the town.
She will start from her slumber
When gusts shake the door;
She will hear the winds howling,
Will hear the waves roar.
We shall see, while above us
The waves roar and whirl,
A ceiling of amber,
A pavement of pearl.
Singing: 'Here came a mortal,
But faithless was she!
And alone dwell for ever
The kings of the sea.'

But, children, at midnight,
When soft the winds blow,
When clear falls the moonlight,
When spring-tides are low;
When sweet airs come seaward
From heaths starr'd with broom,
And high rocks throw mildly
On the blanch'd sands a gloom;
Up the still, glistening beaches,
Up the creeks we will hie,

Over banks of bright seaweed
The ebb-tide leaves dry.
We will gaze, from the sand-hills.
At the white, sleeping town;
At the church on the hill-side –
And then come back down.
Singing: 'There dwells a loved one.
But cruel is she!
She left lonely for ever
The kings of the sea.'

SHAKESPEARE and TO A REPUBLICAN FRIEND

These two sonnets appeared in *The Strayed Reveller, and Other Poems*, the first written in 1844 and the second during the year of revolutions, 1848. They represent Arnold's characteristic interests in literary tradition and modern society.

Shakespeare

Others abide our question. Thou art free.
We ask and ask – Thou smilest and art still,
Out-topping knowledge. For the loftiest hill,
Who to the stars uncrowns his majesty,

Planting his stedfast footsteps in the sea,
Making the heaven of heavens his dwelling-place,
Spares but the cloudy border of his base
To the foil'd searching of mortality;

And thou, who didst the stars and sunbeams know,
Self-school'd, self-scann'd, self-honour'd, self-secure,
Didst tread on earth unguess'd at. – Better so!

All pains the immortal spirit must endure,
All weakness which impairs, all griefs which bow,
Find their sole speech in that victorious brow.

To a Republican Friend, 1848

God knows it, I am with you. If to prize
Those virtues, prized and practised by too few,
But prized, but loved, but eminent in you,

Man's fundamental life; if to despise

The barren optimistic sophistries
Of comfortable moles, whom what they do
Teaches the limit of the just and true
(And for such doing they require not eyes);

If sadness at the long heart-wasting show
Wherein earth's great ones are disquieted;
If thoughts, not idle, while before me flow

The armies of the homeless and unfed –
If these are yours, if this is what you are,
Then am I yours, and what you feel, I share.

THE STRAYED REVELLER

Like Tennyson in 'The Lotos-Eaters', Arnold in 'The Strayed
Reveller' embellishes an incident from Homer's *Odyssey*. In this
case, Arnold alludes to a passage from Book x of Homer's poem,
in which members of Ulysses' crew are beguiled by the pleasures
offered from Circe, whose spell turns men into swine. Ulysses
himself remains immune to the effects of the spell by virtue of the
herb moly, given him by the god Hermes. In its style, Arnold's
short piece suggests the formal antithesis of dialogue in Greek
dramatic writing. The strayed reveller explains to Ulysses that his
own pleasure is in seeing visions of enchantment as clearly as no
one but the gods had been able to do. Against this Arnold
recreates vignettes of the ancient world.

THE PORTICO OF CIRCE'S PALACE. EVENING

A Youth. Circe.

The Youth.

Faster, faster,
O Circe, Goddess,
Let the wild, thronging train,
The bright procession
Of eddying forms,
Sweep through my soul!

Thou standest, smiling
Down on me! thy right arm,
Lean'd up against the column there,
Props thy soft cheek;
Thy left holds, hanging loosely,
The deep cup, ivy-cinctured,
I held but now.

Is it then evening
So soon? I see, the night-dews
Cluster'd in thick beads, dim
The agate brooch-stones
On thy white shoulder;
The cool night-wind, too,
Blows through the portico,
Stirs thy hair, Goddess,
Waves thy white robe!

Circe.

Whence art thou, sleeper?

The Youth.

When the white dawn first
Through the rough fir-planks
Of my hut, by the chestnuts,
Up at the valley-head,
Came breaking, Goddess!
I sprang up, I threw round me
My dappled fawn-skin;
Passing out, from the wet turf,
Where they lay, by the hut door,
I snatch'd up my vine-crown, my fir-staff,
All drench'd in dew —
Came swift down to join
The rout early gather'd
In the town, round the temple
Iacchus' white fane
On yonder hill.

Quick I pass'd, following
The wood-cutters' cart-track
Down the dark valley; — I saw
On my left, through the beeches,
Thy palace, Goddess,
Smokeless, empty!
Trembling, I enter'd; beheld

The court all silent,
The lions sleeping,
On the altar this bowl.
I drank, Goddess!
And sank down here, sleeping,
On the steps of thy portico.

Circe.

Foolish boy! Why tremblest thou?
Thou lovest it, then, my wine?
Wouldst more of it? See, how glows
Through the delicate, flush'd marble,
The red, creaming liquor,
Strown with dark seeds!
Drink, then! I chide thee not,
Deny thee not my bowl.
Come, stretch forth thy hand, then – so!
Drink – drink again!

The Youth.

Thanks, gracious one! –
Ah, the sweet fumes again!
More soft, ah me,
More subtle-winding
Than Pan's flute-music!
Faint – faint! Ah me,
Again the sweet sleep!

Circe.

Hist! Thou – within there!
Come forth, Ulysses!
Art tired with hunting?
While we range the woodland.
See what the day brings.

Ulysses.

Ever new magic!
Hast thou then lured hither,
Wonderful Goddess, by thy art,
The young, languid-eyed Ampelus
Iacchus' darling –
Or some youth beloved of Pan,
Of Pan and the Nymphs?
That he sits, bending downward
His white, delicate neck
To the ivy-wreathed marge
Of thy cup; the bright, glancing vine-leaves
That crown his hair,
Falling forward, mingling
With the dark ivy-plants –
His fawn-skin, half untied,
Smear'd with red wine-stains? Who is he,
That he sits, overweigh'd
By fumes of wine and sleep,
So late, in thy portico?
What youth, Goddess, – what guest
Of Gods or mortals?

Circe.

Hist! he wakes!
I lured him not hither, Ulysses.
Nay, ask him!

The Youth.

Who speaks! Ah, who comes forth
To thy side, Goddess, from within?
How shall I name him?
This spare, dark-featured,
Quick-eyed stranger?
Ah, and I see too
His sailor's bonnet,
His short coat, travel-tarnish'd,

With one arm bare! –
Art thou not he, whom fame
This long time rumours
The favour'd guest of Circe, brought by the waves?
Art thou he, stranger?
The wise Ulysses,
Laertes' son?

Ulysses.

I am Ulysses.
And thou, too, sleeper?
Thy voice is sweet.
It may be thou hast follow'd
Through the islands some divine bard,
By age taught many things,
Age and the Muses;
And heard him delighting
The chiefs and people
In the banquet, and learn'd his songs,
Of Gods and Heroes,
Of war and arts,
And peopled cities,
Inland, or built
By the grey sea – If so, then hail!
I honour and welcome thee.

The Youth.

The Gods are happy.
They turn on all sides
Their shining eyes,
And see below them
The earth and men.

They see Tiresias
Sitting, staff in hand,
On the warm, grassy
Asopus bank,
His robe drawn over

His old, sightless head,
Revolving inly
The doom of Thebes.

They see the Centaurs
In the upper glens
Of Pelion, in the streams,
Where red-berried ashes fringe
The clear-brown shallow pools,
With streaming flanks, and heads
Rear'd proudly, snuffing
The mountain wind.

They see the Indian
Drifting, knife in hand,
His frail boat moor'd to
A floating isle thick-matted
With large-leaved, low-creeping melon-plants,
And the dark cucumber.
He reaps, and stows them,
Drifting – drifting; – round him,
Round his green harvest-plot,
Flow the cool lake-waves,
The mountains ring them.

They see the Scythian
On the wide stepp, unharnessing
His wheel'd house at noon.
He tethers his beast down, and makes his meal –
Mares' milk, and bread
Baked on the embers; – all around
The boundless, waving grass-plains stretch, thick-starr'd
With saffron and the yellow hollyhock
And flag-leaf'd iris-flowers.
Sitting in his cart
He makes his meal; before him, for long miles,
Alive with bright green lizards,
And the springing bustard-fowl,
The track, a straight black line,

Furrows the rich soil; here and there
Clusters of lonely mounds
Topp'd with rough-hewn,
Grey, rain-blear'd statues, overpeer
The sunny waste.

They see the ferry
On the broad, clay-laden
Lone Chorasmian stream; — thereon,
With snort and strain,
Two horses, strongly swimming, tow
The ferry-boat, with woven ropes
To either bow
Firm-harness'd by the mane; a chief,
With shout and shaken spear,
Stands at the prow, and guides them; but astern
The cowering merchants, in long robes,
Sit pale beside their wealth
Of silk-bales and of balsam-drops,
Of gold and ivory,
Of turquoise-earth and amethyst,
Jasper and chalcedony,
And milk-barr'd onyx-stones.
The loaded boat swings groaning
In the yellow eddies;
The Gods behold them.

They see the Heroes
Sitting in the dark ship
On the foamless, long-heaving,
Violet sea,
At sunset nearing
The Happy Islands.

These things, Ulysses.
The wise bards also
Behold and sing.
But oh, what labour!
O prince, what pain!

They too can see
Tiresias; – but the Gods,
Who give them vision,
Added this law:
That they should bear too
His groping blindness,
His dark foreboding,
His scorn'd white hairs;
Bear Hera's anger
Through a life lengthen'd
To seven ages.

They see the Centaurs
On Pelion; – then they feel,
They too, the maddening wine
Swell their large veins to bursting; in wild pain
They feel the biting spears
Of the grim Lapithæ, and Theseus, drive,
Drive crashing through their bones; they feel
High on a jutting rock in the red stream
Alcmena's dreadful son
Ply his bow; – such a price
The Gods exact for song:
To become what we sing.

They see the Indian
On his mountain lake; but squalls
Make their skiff reel, and worms
In the unkind spring have gnawn
Their melon-harvest to the heart – They see
The Scythian; but long frosts
Parch them in winter-time on the bare stepp,
Till they too fade like grass; they crawl
Like shadows forth in spring.

They see the merchants
On the Oxus stream; – but care
Must visit first them too, and make them pale.
Whether, through whirling sand,

A cloud of desert robber-horse have burst
Upon their caravan; or greedy kings,
In the wall'd cities the way passes through,
Crush'd them with tolls; or fever-airs,
On some great river's marge,
Mown them down, far from home.

They see the Heroes
Near harbour; — but they share
Their lives, and former violent toil in Thebes,
Seven-gated Thebes, or Troy;
Or where the echoing oars
Of Argo first
Startled the unknown sea.

The old Silenus
Came, lolling in the sunshine,
From the dewy forest-coverts,
This way, at noon.
Sitting by me, while his Fauns
Down at the water-side
Sprinkled and smoothed
His drooping garland,
He told me these things.

But I, Ulysses,
Sitting on the warm steps,
Looking over the valley,
All day long, have seen,
Without pain, without labour,
Sometimes a wild-hair'd Mænad —
Sometimes a Faun with torches —
And sometimes, for a moment,
Passing through the dark stems
Flowing-robed, the beloved,
The desired, the divine,
Beloved Iacchus.

Ah, cool night-wind, tremulous stars!
Ah, glimmering water,

Fitful earth-murmur,
Dreaming woods!
Ah, golden-hair'd, strangely smiling Goddess
And thou, proved, much enduring,
Wave-toss'd Wanderer!
Who can stand still?
Ye fade, ye swim, ye waver before me –
The cup again!

Faster, faster,
O Circe, Goddess,
Let the wild, thronging train,
The bright procession
Of eddying forms,
Sweep through my soul!

THE SCHOLAR-GIPSY

First published in *Poems* (1853), 'The Scholar-Gipsy' has become known as one of Arnold's two so-called 'Oxford Elegies'. The other is 'Thyrsis', which he wrote on the death of his friend Clough. The story of the scholar-gipsy was recounted in Joseph Glanvill's *Vanity of Dogmatizing* (1661). The young undergraduate had been forced by poverty to leave his studies at Oxford and had joined the gipsies to learn their traditions and their mysteries. The poem shows Arnold at his best, combining a gift for landscape and mood with an idyllic evocation of Oxford and its rural surroundings, 'before this strange disease of modern life', part dream-city and part New Jerusalem. Through this landscape of the mind moves the elusive ghost of the long-dead scholar. The passage from Glanvill's book, which Arnold cited at the head of his poem, is as follows.

There was very lately a lad in the University of Oxford, who was by his poverty forced to leave his studies there; and at last to join himself to a company of vagabond gipsies. Among these extravagant people, by the insinuating subtilty of his carriage, he quickly got so much of their love and esteem as that they discovered to him their mystery. After he had been a pretty while exercised in the trade, there chanced to ride by a couple of scholars, who had formerly been of his acquaintance. They quickly spied out their old friend among the gipsies; and he gave them an account of the necessity which drove him to that kind of life, and told them that the people he went with were not such impostors as they were taken for, but that they had a traditional kind of learning among them, and could do wonders by the power of imagination, their fancy binding that of others: that himself had learned much of their art, and when he had conquered the whole secret, he intended, he said, to leave their company, and give the world an account of what he had learned.

Go, for they call you, shepherd, from the hill;
    Go, shepherd, and untie the wattled cotes!
  No longer leave they wistful flock unfed,
Nor let thy bawling fellows rack their throats,
  Nor the cropp'd grasses shoot another head;
    But when the fields are still,
And the tired men and dogs all gone to rest,
  And only the white sheep are sometimes seen
  Cross and recross the strips of moon-blanch'd green,
Come, shepherd, and again renew the quest

Here, where the reaper was at work of late —
  In this high field's dark corner, where he leaves
    His coat, his basket, and his earthen cruse,
  And in the sun all morning binds the sheaves,
    Then here, at noon, comes back his stores to use —
      Here will I sit and wait,
While to my ear from uplands far away
  The bleating of the folded flocks is borne,
  With distant cries of reapers in the corn —
All the live murmur of a summer's day.

Screen'd is this nook o'er the high, half-reap'd field,
  And here till sun-down, shepherd! will I be.
    Through the thick corn the scarlet poppies peep,
  And round green roots and yellowing stalks I see
    Pale pink convolvulus in tendrils creep;
      And air-swept lindens yield
Their scent, and rustle down their perfumed showers
  Of bloom on the bent grass where I am laid,
  And bower me from the August sun with shade;
And the eye travels down to Oxford's towers.

And near me on the grass lies Glanvil's book —
  Come, let me read the oft-read tale again!
    The story of that Oxford scholar poor,
  Of pregnant parts and quick inventive brain,
    Who, tired of knocking at preferment's door,
      One summer-morn forsook

His friends, and went to learn the gipsy-lore,
    And roam'd the world with that wild brotherhood,
    And came, as most men deem'd, to little good,
But came to Oxford and his friends no more.

But once, years after, in the country-lanes,
    Two scholars, whom at college erst he knew,
    Met him, and of his way of life enquired;
Whereat he answer'd, that the gipsy-crew,
    His mates, had arts to rule as they desired
        The workings of men's brains,
And they can bind them to what thoughts they will.
    'And I,' he said, 'the secret of their art,
    When fully learn'd, will to the world impart;
But it needs heaven-sent moments for this skill.'

This said, he left them, and return'd no more. —
    But rumours hung about the country-side,
    That the lost Scholar long was seen to stray,
Seen by rare glimpses, pensive and tongue-tied,
    In hat of antique shape, and cloak of grey,
        The same the gipsies wore.
Shepherds had met him on the Hurst in spring,
    At some lone alehouse in the Berkshire moors,
    On the warm ingle-bench, the smock-frock'd boors
Had found him seated at their entering,

But, mid their drink and clatter, he would fly.
    And I myself seem half to know thy looks,
    And put the shepherds, wanderer! on thy trace;
And boys who in lone wheatfields scare the rooks
    I ask if thou hast pass'd their quiet place;
        Or in my boat I lie
Moor'd to the cool bank in the summer-heats,
    Mid wide grass meadows which the sunshine fills,
    And watch the warm, green-muffled Cumner hills
And wonder if thou haunt'st their shy retreats.

For most, I know, thou lov'st retired ground!
    Thee at the ferry Oxford riders blithe,

Returning home on summer-nights, have met
Crossing the stripling Thames at Bab-lock-hithe,
  Trailing in the cool stream thy fingers wet,
    As the punt's rope chops round;
And leaning backward in a pensive dream,
  And fostering in thy lap a heap of flowers
  Pluck'd in shy fields and distant Wychwood bowers,
And thine eyes resting on the moonlit stream.

And then, they land, and thou art seen no more! –
  Maidens, who from the distant hamlets come
    To dance around the Fyfield elm in May,
Oft through the darkening fields have seen thee roam,
    Or cross a stile into the public way;
      Oft thou has given them store
Of flowers – the frail-leaf'd, white anemony,
  Dark bluebells drench'd with dews of summer eves,
  And purple orchises with spotted leaves –
But none hath words she can report of thee.

And, above Godstow Bridge, when hay-time's here
  In June, and many a scythe in sunshine flames,
    Men who through those wide fields of breezy grass,
Where black-wing'd swallows haunt the glittering Thames,
    To bathe in the abandon'd lasher pass,
      Have often pass'd thee near
Sitting upon the river bank o'ergrown;
  Mark'd thine outlandish garb, thy figure spare,
  Thy dark vague eyes, and soft abstracted air –
But, when they came from bathing, thou wast gone!

At some lone homestead in the Cumner hills,
  Where at her open door the housewife darns,
    Thou hast been seen, or hanging on a gate
To watch the threshers in the mossy barns.
    Children, who early range these slopes and late
      For cresses from the rills,
Have known thee eyeing, all an April day,
  The springing pastures and the feeding kine;

And mark'd thee, when the stars come out and shine,
Through the long dewy grass move slow away.

In autumn, on the skirts of Bagley Wood —
  Where most the gipsies by the turf-edged way
    Pitch their smoked tents, and every bush you see
  With scarlet patches tagg'd and shreds of grey,
    Above the forest-ground call'd Thessaly —
      The blackbird picking food
  Sees thee, nor stops his meal, nor fears at all;
    So often has he known thee past him stray,
    Rapt, twirling in thy hand a wither'd spray,
  And waiting for the spark from heaven to fall.

And once, in winter, on the causeway chill
  Where home through flooded fields foot-travellers go,
    Have I not pass'd thee on the wooden bridge,
  Wrapt in thy cloak and battling with the snow,
    Thy face toward Hinksey and its wintry ridge?
      And thou hast climb'd the hill,
  And gain'd the white brow of the Cumner range;
    Turn'd once to watch, while thick the snowflakes fall,
    The line of festal light in Christ-Church hall —
  Then sought thy straw in some sequester'd grange.

But what — I dream! Two hundred years are flown
  Since first thy story ran through Oxford halls,
    And the grave Glanvil did the tale inscribe
  That thou wert wander'd from the studious walls
    To learn strange arts, and join a gipsy-tribe;
      And thou from earth art gone
  Long since, and in some quiet churchyard laid —
    Some country-nook, where o'er thy unknown grave
    Tall grasses and white flowering nettles wave,
  Under a dark, red-fruited yew-tree's shade.

— No, no, thou hast not felt the lapse of hours!
  For what wears out the life of mortal men?
    'Tis that from change to change their being rolls;
    'Tis that repeated shocks, again, again,

Exhaust the energy of strongest souls,
    And numb the elastic powers.
Till having used our nerves with bliss and teen,
    And tired upon a thousand schemes our wit,
    To the just-pausing Genius we remit
Our well-worn life, and are – what we have been.

Thou hast not lived, why should'st thou perish, so?
    Thou hadst *one* aim, *one* business, *one* desire;
        Else wert thou long since number'd with the dead!
    Else hadst thou spent, like other men, thy fire!
        The generations of thy peers are fled,
            And we ourselves shall go;
    But thou possessest an immortal lot,
        And we imagine thee exempt from age,
        And living as thou liv'st on Glanvil's page,
Because thou hadst – what we, alas! have not.

For early didst thou leave the world, with powers
    Fresh, undiverted to the world without,
        Firm to their mark, not spent on other things;
    Free from the sick fatigue, the languid doubt,
        Which much to have tried, in much been baffled, brings.
            O life unlike to ours!
    Who fluctuate idly without term or scope,
        Of whom each strives, nor knows for what he strives,
        And each half lives a hundred different lives;
Who wait like thee, but not, like thee, in hope.

Thou waitest for the spark from heaven! and we,
    Light half-believers of our casual creeds,
        Who never deeply felt, nor clearly will'd,
    Whose insight never has borne fruit in deeds,
        Whose vague resolves never have been fulfill'd;
            For whom each year we see
    Breeds new beginnings, disappointments new;
        Who hesitate and falter life away,
        And lose to-morrow the ground won to-day –
Ah! do not we, wanderer! await it too?

Yes, we await it! – but it still delays,
   And then we suffer! and amongst us one,
     Who most has suffer'd, takes dejectedly
   His seat upon the intellectual throne;
     And all his store of sad experience he
       Lays bare of wretched days;
   Tells us his misery's birth and growth and signs,
     And how the dying spark of hope was fed,
     And how the breast was soothed, and how the head,
   And all his hourly varied anodynes.

This for our wisest! and we others pine,
   And wish the long unhappy dream would end,
     And waive all claim to bliss, and try to bear;
   With close-lipp'd patience for our only friend,
     Sad patience, too near neighbour to despair –
       But none has hope like thine!
   Thou through the fields and through the woods dost stray,
     Roaming the country-side, a truant boy,
     Nursing thy project in unclouded joy,
   And every doubt long blown by time away.

O born in days when wits were fresh and clear,
   And life ran gaily as the sparkling Thames;
     Before this strange disease of modern life,
   With its sick hurry, its divided aims,
     Its heads o'ertax'd, its palsied hearts, was rife –
       Fly hence, our contact fear!
   Still fly, plunge deeper in the bowering wood!
     Averse, as Dido did with gesture stern
     From her false friend's approach in Hades turn,
   Wave us away, and keep thy solitude!

Still nursing the unconquerable hope,
   Still clutching the inviolable shade,
     With a free, onward impulse brushing through,
   By night, the silver'd branches of the glade –
     Far on the forest-skirts, where none pursue,
       On some mild pastoral slope

Emerge, and resting on the moonlit pales
   Freshen thy flowers as in former years
   With dew, or listen with enchanted ears,
From the dark dingles, to the nightingales!

But fly our paths, our feverish contact fly!
   For strong the infection of our mental strife,
     Which, though it gives no bliss, yet spoils for rest;
   And we should win thee from thy own fair life,
     Like us distracted, and like us unblest.
       Soon, soon thy cheer would die,
   Thy hopes grow timorous, and unfix'd thy powers,
     And thy clear aims be cross and shifting made;
     And then thy glad perennial youth would fade,
Fade, and grow old at last, and die like ours.

Then fly our greetings, fly our speech and smiles!
   – As some grave Tyrian trader, from the sea,
   Descried at sunrise an emerging prow
Lifting the cool-hair'd creepers stealthily,
   The fringes of a southward-facing brow
     Among the Ægæan isles;
   And saw the merry Grecian coaster come,
     Freighted with amber grapes, and Chian wine,
     Green, bursting figs, and tunnies steep'd in brine –
And knew the intruders on his ancient home,

The young light-hearted masters of the waves –
   And snatch'd his rudder, and shook out more sail,
     And day and night held on indignantly
O'er the blue Midland waters with the gale,
   Betwixt the Syrtes and soft Sicily,
     To where the Atlantic raves
Outside the western straits, and unbent sails
   There, where down cloudy cliffs, through sheets of foam,
   Shy traffickers, the dark Iberians come;
And on the beach undid his corded bales.

PHILOMELA

First published in *Poems* (1853), 'Philomela' begins among the cedar trees of a Victorian garden by the moonlit Thames and moves into Greek legend. Tereus, king of Thrace, raped Philomela, the sister of his wife Procne. To ensure her silence, he cut out her tongue. Philomela revealed the crime by working it into her embroidery and sending it to her sister. Procne thereupon killed her own son, Itys, and served him to his unwitting father as a meal. Before Tereus could kill both sisters in revenge, the gods intervened. Tereus was turned into a hoopoe, Procne into a nightingale, and Philomela into a swallow. A variant of the legend, to be found in the sixth book of Ovid's *Metamorphoses* and used in Swinburne's poem 'Itylus', makes Philomela the nightingale and Procne the swallow.

Hark! ah, the nightingale –
The tawny-throated!
Hark, from that moonlit cedar what a burst!
What triumph! hark! – what pain!

O wanderer from a Grecian shore,
Still, after many years, in distant lands,
Still nourishing in thy bewilder'd brain
That wild, unquench'd, deep-sunken, old-world pain –
Say, will it never heal?
And can this fragrant lawn
With its cool trees, and night,
And the sweet, tranquil Thames,
And moonshine, and the dew,
To thy rack'd heart and brain
Afford no balm?

Dost thou to-night behold,
Here, through the moonlight on this English grass,
The unfriendly palace in the Thracian wild?
Dost thou again peruse
With hot cheeks and sear'd eyes
The too clear web, and thy dumb sister's shame?
Dost thou once more assay
Thy flight, and feel come over thee,
Poor fugitive, the feathery change
Once more, and once more seem to make resound
With love and hate, triumph and agony,
Lone Daulis, and the high Cephissian vale?
Listen, Eugenia –
How thick the bursts come crowding through the leaves!
Again – thou hearest?
Eternal passion!
Eternal pain!

CALAIS SANDS

First published in *New Poems* (1867), though dated 'August 1859', 'Calais Sands' recalls Arnold's courtship of Frances Wightman, whom he married in 1851. Characteristically, it mingles Arnold's Victorian observation of the 'idlers on the pier' waiting for the cross-channel steamer, whose smoke appears on the horizon, with the medieval vision of the field of the cloth of gold, war and chivalry. Yet the focus of the poem remains the portrait image of Frances Wightman with her soft brown hair and her shawl.

A thousand knights have rein'd their steeds
To watch this line of sand-hills run,
Along the never-silent strait,
To Calais glittering in the sun;

To look toward Ardres' Golden Field
Across this wide aërial plain,
Which glows as if the Middle Age
Were gorgeous upon earth again.

Oh, that to share this famous scene,
I saw, upon the open sand,
Thy lovely presence at my side,
Thy shawl, thy look, thy smile, thy hand!

How exquisite thy voice would come.
My darling, on this lonely air!
How sweetly would the fresh sea-breeze
Shake loose some band of soft brown hair!

And now my glance but once hath roved
O'er Calais and its famous plain;
To England's cliffs my gaze is turn'd,
O'er the blue strait mine eyes I strain.

Thou comest! Yes! the vessel's cloud
Hangs dark upon the rolling sea.
Oh, that yon sea-bird's wings were mine,
To win one instant's glimpse of thee!

I must not spring to grasp thy hand,
To woo thy smile, to seek thine eye;
But I may stand far off, and gaze,
And watch thee pass unconscious by,

And spell thy looks, and guess thy thoughts,
Mixt with the idlers on the pier –
Ah, might I always rest unseen,
So I might have thee always near!

To-morrow hurry through the fields
Of Flanders to the storied Rhine!
To-night those soft-fringed eyes shall close
Beneath one roof, my queen! with mine.

DOVER BEACH

Also from *New Poems* (1867), 'Dover Beach' is Arnold's classic exposition of the theme of religious faith and doubt in mid-Victorian poetry. A vignette or landscape is used to interpret the inner mood as the tide of faith withdraws into darkness. The reference to Sophocles is not specified by Arnold but seems likely to be a chorus from *Antigone*, beginning at line 583 of the play.

Blessed are they whose life has known no sorrow!
For to those whose house is shaken by the gods,
There is no lack of curse or woe,
Creeping down to future generations.
It comes like a wave, where Thracian gales blow hard
On that tempestuous shore,
Surging up from the sea's depths, where from the deep abyss
It rolls black wind-blown sand,
And every promontory that drives it back
Re-echoes with its roar.

The sea is calm to-night.
The tide is full, the moon lies fair
Upon the straits; – on the French coast the light
Gleams and is gone; the cliffs of England stand,
Glimmering and vast, out in the tranquil bay.
Come to the window, sweet is the night-air!
Only, from the long line of spray
Where the sea meets the moon-blanch'd land,
Listen! you hear the grating roar
Of pebbles which the waves draw back, and fling,
At their return, up the high strand,
Begin, and cease, and then again begin,

With tremulous cadence slow, and bring
The eternal note of sadness in.

Sophocles long ago
Heard it on the Ægæan, and it brought
Into his mind the turbid ebb and flow
Of human misery; we
Find also in the sound a thought,
Hearing it by this distant northern sea.
The sea of faith
Was once, too, at the full, and round earth's shore
Lay like the folds of a bright girdle furl'd.
But now I only hear
Its melancholy, long, withdrawing roar,
Retreating to the breath
Of the night-wind down the vast edges drear
And naked shingles of the world.

Ah, love, let us be true
To one another! for the world, which seems
To lie before us like a land of dreams,
So various, so beautiful, so new,
Hath really neither joy, nor love, nor light,
Nor certitude, nor peace, nor help for pain;
And we are here as on a darkling plain
Swept with confused alarms of struggle and flight,
Where ignorant armies clash by night.

MEMORIAL VERSES

Written on the death of Wordsworth, at the request of the poet's son-in-law Edward Quillinan, this elegy appeared in *Fraser's Magazine* for June 1850 and was reprinted in *Empedocles on Etna, and Other Poems* in 1852. It reflects Arnold's intuitive critical appreciation of European as well as English romantic tradition. In paying such a tribute to Wordsworth, he also acknowledges a debt to the great romantic whose fusion of landscape and mood was more than any other the model for Arnold's own work.

APRIL, 1850

Goethe in Weimar sleeps, and Greece,
Long since, saw Byron's struggle cease.
But one such death remain'd to come;
The last poetic voice is dumb —
We stand to-day by Wordsworth's tomb.

When Byron's eyes were shut in death,
We bow'd our head and held our breath.
He taught us little; but our soul
Had *felt* him like the thunder's roll.
With shivering heart the strife we saw
Of passion with eternal law;
And yet with reverential awe
We watch'd the fount of fiery life
Which served for that Titanic strife.

When Goethe's death was told, we said:
Sunk, then, is Europe's sagest head.
Physician of the iron age,
Goethe has done his pilgrimage.
He took the suffering human race,
He read each wound, each weakness, clear;

And struck his finger on the place,
And said: *Thou ailest here, and here!*
He look'd on Europe's dying hour
Of fitful dream and feverish power;
His eye plunged down the weltering strife,
The turmoil of expiring life –
He said: *The end is everywhere,*
Art still has truth, take refuge there!
And he was happy, if to know
Causes of things, and far below
His feet to see the lurid flow
Of terror, and insane distress,
And headlong fate, be happiness.

And Wordsworth! – Ah, pale ghosts, rejoice!
For never has such soothing voice
Been to your shadowy world convey'd,
Since erst, at morn, some wandering shade
Heard the clear song of Orpheus come
Through Hades, and the mournful gloom.
Wordsworth has gone from us – and ye,
Ah, may ye feel his voice as we!
He too upon a wintry clime
Had fallen – on this iron time
Of doubts, disputes, distractions, fears.
He found us when the age had bound
Our souls in its benumbing round;
He spoke, and loosed our heart in tears.
He laid us as we lay at birth
On the cool flowery lap of earth,
Smiles broke from us and we had ease;
The hills were round us, and the breeze
Went o'er the sun-lit fields again;
Our foreheads felt the wind and rain.
Our youth return'd; for there was shed
On spirits that had long been dead,
Spirits dried up and closely furl'd,
The freshness of the early world.

Ah! since dark days still bring to light
Man's prudence and man's fiery might,
Time may restore us in his course
Goethe's sage mind and Byron's force;
But where will Europe's latter hour
Again find Wordsworth's healing power?
Others will teach us how to dare,
And against fear our breast to steel;
Others will strengthen us to bear –
But who, ah! who, will make us feel?
The cloud of mortal destiny,
Others will front it fearlessly –
But who, like him, will put it by?

Keep fresh the grass upon his grave
O Rotha, with thy living wave!
Sing him thy best! for few or none
Hears thy voice right, now he is gone.

RUGBY CHAPEL

Arnold's tribute in *New Poems* (1863) is to his father, Thomas Arnold the great headmaster of Rugby, who had died in 1843. Thomas Arnold's work had been criticised by Fitzjames Stephen while reviewing Thomas Hughes's *Tom Brown's Schooldays* in the *Edinburgh Review* in 1852. Matthew Arnold wrote to his mother that he hoped his poem would refute Stephen's view of 'Papa being a narrow bustling fanatic ... I think I have done something to fix the true legend about Papa.' The poem, part elegy and part moral exhortation, with its austere image of the school chapel on a dark autumn evening, is a fine example of moral Victorian gothic.

NOVEMBER, 1857

Coldly, sadly descends
The autumn-evening. The field
Strewn with its dank yellow drifts
Of wither'd leaves, and the elms,
Fade into dimness apace,
Silent; – hardly a shout
From a few boys late at their play!
The lights come out in the street,
In the school-room windows – but cold,
Solemn, unlighted, austere,
Through the gathering darkness, arise
The chapel-walls, in whose bound
Thou, my father! art laid.

There thou dost lie, in the gloom
Of the autumn evening. But ah!
That word, *gloom*, to my mind
Brings thee back in the light

Of thy radiant vigour again;
In the gloom of November we pass'd
Days not dark at thy side;
Seasons impair'd not the ray
Of thy buoyant cheerfulness clear.
Such thou wast! and I stand
In the autumn evening, and think
Of bygone autumns with thee.

Fifteen years have gone round
Since thou arosest to tread,
In the summer-morning, the road
Of death, at a call unforeseen,
Sudden. For fifteen years,
We who till then in thy shade
Rested as under the boughs
Of a mighty oak, have endured
Sunshine and rain as we might,
Bare, unshaded, alone,
Lacking the shelter of thee.

O strong soul, by what shore
Tarriest thou now? For that force,
Surely, has not been left vain!
Somewhere, surely, afar,
In the sounding labour-house vast
Of being, is practised that strength,
Zealous, beneficent, firm!

Yes, in some far-shining sphere,
Conscious or not of the past,
Still thou performest the word
Of the spirit in whom thou dost live —
Prompt, unwearied, as here!
Still thou upraisest with zeal
The humble good from the ground,
Sternly repressest the bad!
Still, like a trumpet, dost rouse
Those who with half-open eyes

Tread the border-land dim
'Twixt vice and virtue; reviv'st,
Succourest! – this was thy work,
This was thy life upon earth.

What is the course of the life
Of mortal men on the earth? –
Most men eddy about
Here and there – eat and drink,
Chatter and love and hate,
Gather and squander, are raised
Aloft, are hurl'd in the dust,
Striving blindly, achieving
Nothing; and then they die –
Perish – and no one asks
Who or what they have been,
More than he asks what waves
In the moonlit solitudes mild
Of the midmost Ocean, have swell'd,
Foam'd for a moment, and gone.

And there are some, whom a thirst
Ardent, unquenchable, fires,
Not with the crowd to be spent,
Not without aim to go round
In an eddy of purposeless dust,
Effort unmeaning and vain.
Ah yes! some of us strive
Not without action to die
Fruitless, but something to snatch
From dull oblivion, nor all
Glut the devouring grave!
We, we have chosen our path –
Path to a clear-purposed goal,
Path of advance! – but it leads
A long, steep journey, through sunk
Gorges, o'er mountains in snow.
Cheerful, with friends, we set forth –
Then, on the height, comes the storm.

Thunder crashes from rock
To rock, the cataracts reply;
Lightnings dazzle our eyes;
Roaring torrents have breach'd
The track, the stream-bed descends
In the place where the wayfarer once
Planted his footstep – the spray
Boils o'er its borders! – aloft
The unseen snow-beds dislodge
Their hanging ruin; – alas,
Havoc is made in our train!
Friends, who set forth at our side,
Falter, are lost in the storm.
We, we only are left! –
With frowning foreheads, with lips
Sternly compress'd, we strain on,
On – and at nightfall at last
Come to the end of our way,
To the lonely inn 'mid the rocks;
Where the gaunt and taciturn host
Stands on the threshold, the wind
Shaking his thin white hairs –
Holds his lantern to scan
Our storm-beat figures, and asks:
Whom in our party we bring?
Whom we have left in the snow?

Sadly we answer: We bring
Only ourselves! we lost
Sight of the rest in the storm.
Hardly ourselves we fought through,
Stripp'd, without friends, as we are.
Friends, companions, and train,
The avalanche swept from our side.
    But thou would'st not *alone*
Be saved, my father! *alone*
Conquer and come to thy goal,
Leaving the rest in the wild.

We were weary, and we
Fearful, and we in our march
Fain to drop down and to die.
Still thou turnedst, and still
Beckonedst the trembler, and still
Gavest the weary thy hand.
If, in the paths of the world,
Stones might have wounded thy feet.
Toil or dejection have tried
Thy spirit, of that we saw
Nothing – to us thou wast still
Cheerful, and helpful, and firm!
Therefore to thee it was given
Many to save with thyself;
And, at the end of thy day,
O faithful shepherd! to come,
Bringing thy sheep in thy hand.

And through thee I believe
In the noble and great who are gone:
Pure souls honour'd and blest
By former ages, who else –
Such, so soulless, so poor,
Is the race of men whom I see –
Seem'd but a dream of the heart,
Seem'd but a cry of desire.
Yes! I believe that there lived
Others like thee in the past,
Not like the men of the crowd
Who all round me to-day
Bluster or cringe, and make life
Hideous, and arid, and vile;
But souls temper'd with fire,
Fervent, heroic, and good,
Helpers and friends of mankind.

Servants of God! – or sons
Shall I not call you? because
Not as servants ye knew

Your Father's innermost mind,
His, who unwillingly sees
One of his little ones lost –
Yours is the praise, if mankind
Hath not as yet in its march
Fainted, and fallen, and died!

See! In the sands of the world
Marches the host of mankind,
A feeble, wavering line.
Where are they tending? – A God
Marshall'd them, gave them their goal. –
Ah, but the way is so long!
Years they have been in the waste!
Sore thirst plagues them; the sands,
Spreading all round, overawe;
Factions divide them, their host
Threatens to break, to dissolve. –
Ah, keep, keep them combined!
Else, of the myriads who fill
That army, not one shall arrive;
Sole they shall stray; in the sands
Flounder for ever in vain,
Die one by one in the waste.

Then, in such hour of need
Of your fainting, dispirited race,
Ye, like angels, appear,
Radiant with ardour divine.
Beacons of hope, ye appear!
Languor is not in your heart,
Weakness is not in your word,
Weariness not on your brow.
Ye alight in our van! at your voice,
Panic, despair, flee away.
Ye move through the ranks, recall
The stragglers, refresh the outworn.
Praise, re-inspire the brave.
Order, courage, return;

Eyes rekindling, and prayers,
Follow your steps as ye go.
Ye fill up the gaps in our files,
Strengthen the wavering line,
Stablish, continue our march,
On, to the bound of the waste,
On, to the City of God.

CLOUGH

QUA CURSUM VENTUS

'Qua Cursum Ventus' is one of Clough's earlier and more earnest poems, published in *Ambarvalia* (1849), a volume shared with the poet Thomas Burbidge. 'Qua Cursum Ventus' takes life as a voyage, a familiar metaphor phrased here in the moral rhetoric of *Tom Brown's Schooldays*. Friends in youth are parted by life and fate to be reunited at last, in death or immortality.

As ships, becalmed at eve, that lay
   With canvas drooping, side by side,
Two towers of sail at dawn of day
   Are scarce long leagues apart descried;

When fell the night, upsprung the breeze,
   And all the darkling hours they plied,
Nor dreamt but each the self-same seas
   By each was cleaving, side by side:

E'en so – but why the tale reveal
   Of those, whom year by year unchanged,
Brief absence joined anew to feel,
   Astounded, soul from soul estranged?

At dead of night their sails were filled,
   And onward each rejoicing steered –
Ah, neither blame, for neither willed,
   Or wist, what first with dawn appeared!

To veer, how vain! On, onward strain,
   Brave barks! In light, in darkness too,
Through winds and tides one compass guides –
   To that, and your own selves, be true.

But O blithe breeze; and O great seas,
   Though ne'er, that earliest parting past,

On your wide plain they join again,
  Together lead them home at last.

One port, methought, alike they sought,
  One purpose hold where'er they fare, –
O bounding breeze, O rushing seas!
  At last, at last, unite them there!

EASTER DAY

'Nothing is more true of Clough's mind than that it worked by thesis and antithesis,' wrote John Addington Symonds in the *Fortnightly Review* in 1868. 'Easter Day', dated 'Naples, 1849', is a classic of Victorian 'honest doubt'. It suggests two voices within a single poem, a technique which Clough was to use overtly in his moral dialogue 'Dipsychus'. 'Easter Day' proclaims first that 'Christ is not risen,' but then that 'In the great gospel and true creed,/ He is yet risen.' Clough's is a powerful poem, though his philosophy is of the kind mocked by Browning the following year in *Christmas Eve and Easter Day*, where the German rationalist professor is made to argue, to a point of absurdity only possible in academic debate, that Christ 'was and was not, both together.' Browning, on behalf of Christian certainty, dismisses 'The exhausted air-bell of the Critic,' as Clough does not. Symonds saw in Clough's poem 'a mind steeped in the disintegrating solvents of nineteenth century criticism.' He thought Clough's benevolent religion had been affronted by apparent divine indifference. The poem exhibits, in Symonds's view, 'a mood of bitterness provoked by human degradation' in the Neapolitan slums.

Easter Day.

NAPLES, 1849.

Through the great sinful streets of Naples as I past,
  With fiercer heat than flamed above my head
My heart was hot within me; till at last
  My brain was lightened when my tongue had said –
        Christ is not risen!

      Christ is not risen, no –
        He lies and moulders low;
      Christ is not risen!

What though the stone were rolled away, and though
    The grave found empty there? –
    If not there, then elsewhere;
If not where Joseph laid Him first, why then
    Where other men
Translaid Him after, in some humbler clay.
    Long ere to-day
Corruption that sad perfect work hath done,
Which here she scarcely, lightly had begun:
    The foul engendered worm
Feeds on the flesh of the life-giving form
Of our most Holy and Anointed One.
    He is not risen, no –
    He lies and moulders low;
      Christ is not risen!

What if the women, ere the dawn was grey,
Saw one or more great angels, as they say
(Angels, or Him himself)? Yet neither there, nor then,
Nor afterwards, nor elsewhere, nor at all,
Hath He appeared to Peter or the Ten;
Nor, save in thunderous terror, to blind Saul;
Save in an after Gospel and late Creed,
    He is not risen, indeed, –
      Christ is not risen!

Or, what if e'en, as runs a tale, the Ten
Saw, heard, and touched, again and yet again?
What if at Emmaüs' inn, and by Capernaum's Lake,
    Came One, the bread that brake –
Came One that spake as never mortal spake,
And with them ate, and drank, and stood, and walked about?
    Ah? 'some' did well to 'doubt!'
Ah! the true Christ, while these things came to pass,
Nor heard, nor spake, nor walked, nor lived, alas!
    He was not risen, no –
    He lay and mouldered low,
      Christ was not risen!

As circulates in some great city crowd
A rumour changeful, vague, importunate, and loud,
From no determined centre, or of fact
    Or authorship exact,
    Which no man can deny
      Nor verify;
    So spread the wondrous fame;
    He all the same
    Lay senseless, mouldering low:
    He was not risen, no –
      Christ was not risen!
Ashes to ashes, dust to dust;
As of the unjust, also of the just –
    Yea, of that Just One, too!
This is the one sad Gospel that is true –
    Christ is not risen!

Is He not risen, and shall we not rise?
    Oh, we unwise!
What did we dream, what wake we to discover?
Ye hills, fall on us, and ye mountains, cover!
    In darkness and great gloom
Come ere we thought it is *our* day of doom;
From the cursed world, which is one tomb,
    Christ is not risen!

Eat, drink, and play, and think that this is bliss:
There is no heaven but this;
    There is no hell,
Save earth, which serves the purpose doubly well,
    Seeing it visits still
With equalest apportionment of ill
Both good and bad alike, and brings to one same dust
    The unjust and the just
    With Christ, who is not risen.

Eat, drink, and die, for we are souls bereaved:
  Of all the creatures under heaven's wide cope
  We are most hopeless, who had once most hope,

And most beliefless, that had most believed.
Ashes to ashes, dust to dust;
As of the unjust, also of the just –
Yea, of that Just One too!
It is the one sad Gospel that is true –
Christ is not risen!

Weep not beside the tomb,
Ye women, unto whom
He was great solace while ye tended Him;
Ye who with napkin o'er the head
And folds of linen round each wounded limb
Laid out the Sacred Dead;
And thou that bar'st Him in thy wondering womb;
Yea, Daughters of Jerusalem, depart,
Bind up as best ye may your own sad bleeding heart:
Go to your homes, your living children tend,
Your earthly spouses love;
Set your affections *not* on things above,
Which moth and rust corrupt, which quickliest come to end:
Or pray, if pray ye must, and pray, if pray ye can,
For death; since dead is He whom ye deemed more than man,
Who is not risen: no –
But lies and moulders low –
Who is not risen!

Ye men of Galilee!
Why stand ye looking up to heaven, where Him ye ne'er may
see,
Neither ascending hence, nor returning hither again?
Ye ignorant and idle fishermen!
Hence to your huts, and boats, and inland native shore,
And catch not men, but fish;
Whate'er things ye might wish,
Him neither here nor there ye e'er shall meet with more.
Ye poor deluded youths, go home,
Mend the old nets ye left to roam,
Tie the split oar, patch the torn sail:

It was indeed an 'idle tale' –
   He was not risen!

And, oh, good men of ages yet to be,
Who shall believe *because* ye did not see –
   Oh, be ye warned, be wise!
   No more with pleading eyes,
   And sobs of strong desire,
   Unto the empty vacant void aspire,
Seeking another and impossible birth
That is not of your own, and only mother earth.
But if there is no other life for you,
Sit down and be content, since this must even do:
   He is not risen!

   One look, and then depart,
   Ye humble and ye holy men of heart;
And ye! ye ministers and stewards of a Word
Which ye would preach, because another heard –
   Ye worshippers of that ye do not know,
   Take these things hence and go: –
   He is not risen!

   Here, on our Easter Day
We rise, we come, and lo! we find Him not,
Gardener nor other, on the sacred spot:
Where they have laid Him there is none to say;
No sound, nor in, nor out – no word
Of where to seek the dead or meet the living Lord.
There is no glistering of an angel's wings,
There is no voice of heavenly clear behest:
Let us go hence, and think upon these things
   In silence, which is best.
   Is He not risen? No –
   But lies and moulders low?
   Christ is not risen?

Easter Day.

II

So in the sinful streets, abstracted and alone,
I with my secret self held communing of mine own.
  So in the southern city spake the tongue
Of one that somewhat overwildly sung,
But in a later hour I sat and heard
Another voice that spake – another graver word.
Weep not, it bade, whatever hath been said,
Though He be dead, He is not dead.
     In the true creed
     He is yet risen indeed;
       Christ is yet risen.

Weep not beside His tomb,
Ye women unto whom
He was great comfort and yet greater grief;
Nor ye, ye faithful few that wont with Him to roam,
Seek sadly what for Him ye left, go hopeless to your home;
Nor ye despair, ye sharers yet to be of their belief;
     Though He be dead, He is not dead,
     Nor gone, though fled,
     Not lost, though vanished;
     Though He return not, though
     He lies and moulders low;
     In the true creed
     He is yet risen indeed;
       Christ is yet risen.

Sit if ye will, sit down upon the ground,
Yet not to weep and wail, but calmly look around.
     Whate'er befell,
     Earth is not hell;
Now, too, as when it first began,
Life is yet life, and man is man.
For all that breathe beneath the heaven's high cope,
Joy with grief mixes, with despondence hope.
Hope conquers cowardice, joy grief:

Or at least, faith unbelief.
　　Though dead, not dead;
　　Not gone, though fled;
　　Not lost, though vanished.
　　In the great gospel and true creed,
　　He is yet risen indeed;
　　　Christ is yet risen.

THE LATEST DECALOGUE

A good deal of Clough's more brittle social commentary was published after his death, including this poem by which he was best known, a cynical recasting of the Ten Commandments to match the materialism and self-interest of Victorian public morality at mid-century.

Thou shalt have one God only; who
Would be at the expense of two?
No graven images may be
Worshipped, except the currency:
Swear not at all; for, for thy curse
Thine enemy is none the worse:
At church on Sunday to attend
Will serve to keep the world thy friend:
Honour thy parents; that is, all
From whom advancement may befall;
Thou shalt not kill; but need'st not strive
Officiously to keep alive:
Do not adultery commit;
Advantage rarely comes of it:
Thou shalt not steal; an empty feat,
When it's so lucrative to cheat:
Bear not false witness; let the lie
Have time on its own wings to fly:
Thou shalt not covet, but tradition
Approves all forms of competition.

From AMOURS DE VOYAGE

Writing of *Amours de Voyage* in 1862, the *Saturday Review* ascribes its inspiration to Clough's visit to Rome in 1849. 'It is in the form of letters, supposed to be written by an English traveller to his friend, and by an English young lady to her friend. The pair gradually fall in love, although the gentleman is very long in deciding whether he feels more than the passing tenderness which results from being thrown in the way of a sympathizing and pretty girl ... He has scarcely ascertained that his feelings are serious when the young lady's family leave Rome, and he has to set off in chase of them. He visits them at Florence, at Milan, and at Como, and the story ends as a story never ended before, in the lover giving his mistress up in sheer weariness and despair, because he cannot find her direction.'

Clough's earlier novel in verse was the story of an Oxford long vacation reading-party in the Highlands, *The Bothie of Tober-na-Vuolich* (1848). Both poems are in hexametres, the metre of Homer and of Virgil's *Aeneid*, apt to sound comic in English. John Henry Newman remarked, 'If the metre can inspire anything, it is to frolic and gambol with Mr Clough.' The *Saturday Review* thought the poem's appeal lay less in the story than in 'the humorous sketches of English society abroad, of the playfulness of the young lady in her unbosomings, and in the description of the people, the city, and neighbourhood of Rome.' It embodies in English verse an urbane and sceptical observation of European society, and might claim Byron's *Don Juan* as an illustrious ancestor.

In the following three extracts, Claude arrives at Rome; he and Mary express their urbane and cautious feelings about each other; finally the romance collapses as Claude follows the Trevellyn family through Italy. The events are described against the background of Mazzini's declaration of a republic in Rome, a movement checked by the restoration of Pope Pius IX under French protection, despite Garibaldi's resistance.

254 ARTHUR HUGH CLOUGH

I. CLAUDE TO EUSTACE.

Dear Eustatio, I write that you may write me an answer,
Or at the least to put us again *en rapport* with each other.
Rome disappoints me much, – St Peter's, perhaps, in especial;
Only the Arch of Titus and view from the Lateran please me:
This, however, perhaps is the weather, which truly is horrid.
Greece must be better, surely; and yet I am feeling so spiteful,
That I could travel to Athens, to Delphi, and Troy, and Mount
    Sinai,
Though but to see with my eyes that these are vanity also.
   Rome disappoints me much; I hardly as yet understand, but
Rubbishy seems the word that most exactly would suit it.
All the foolish destructions, and all the sillier savings,
All the incongruous things of past incompatible ages,
Seem to be treasured up here to make fools of present and
    future.
Would to Heaven the old Goths had made a cleaner sweep of
    it!
Would to Heaven some new ones would come and destroy
    these churches!
However, one can live in Rome as also in London.
It is a blessing, no doubt, to be rid, at least for a time, of
All one's friends and relations, – yourself (forgive me!)
    included, –
All the *assujettissement* of having been what one has been,
What one thinks one is, or thinks that others suppose one;
Yet, in despite of all, we turn like fools to the English.
Vernon has been my fate; who is here the same that you knew
    him –
Making the tour, it seems, with friends of the name of
    Trevellyn.

II. CLAUDE TO EUSTACE.

Rome disappoints me still; but I shrink and adapt myself to it.
Somehow a tyrannous sense of a superincumbent oppression
Still, wherever I go, accompanies ever, and makes me
Feel like a tree (shall I say?) buried under a ruin of brickwork.

Rome, believe me, my friend, is like its own Monte Testaceo,
Merely a marvellous mass of broken and castaway wine-pots.
Ye gods! what do I want with this rubbish of ages departed,
Things that Nature abhors, the experiments that she has failed
　　in?
What do I find in the Forum? An archway and two or three
　　pillars.
Well, but St Peter's? Alas, Bernini has filled it with sculpture!
No one can cavil, I grant, at the size of the great Coliseum.
Doubtless the notion of grand and capacious and massive
　　amusement,
This the old Romans had; but tell me, is this an idea?
Yet of solidity much, but of splendour little is extant:
'Brickwork I found thee, and marble I left thee!' their Emperor
　　vaunted;
'Marble I thought thee, and brickwork I find thee!' the Tourist
　　may answer.

III. GEORGINA TREVELLYN TO LOUISA—.

At last, dearest Louisa, I take up my pen to address you.
Here we are, you see, with the seven-and-seventy boxes,
Courier, Papa and Mamma, the children, and Mary and Susan:
Here we all are at Rome, and delighted of course with St
　　Peter's,
And very pleasantly lodged in the famous Piazza di Spagna.
Rome is a wonderful place, but Mary shall tell you about it;
Not very gay, however; the English are mostly at Naples;
There are the A.'s, we hear, and most of the W. party.
　George, however, is come; did I tell you about his
　　mustachios?
Dear, I must really stop, for the carriage, they tell me, is
　　waiting;
Mary will finish; and Susan is writing, they say, to Sophia.
Adieu, dearest Louise, – evermore your faithful Georgina.
Who can a Mr Claude be whom George has taken to be with?
Very stupid, I think, but George says so *very* clever.

Canto I, i–iii

* * *

XIII. CLAUDE TO EUSTACE.

Wherefore and how I am certain, I hardly can tell; but it *is* so.
She doesn't like me, Eustace; I think she never will like me.
Is it my fault, as it is my misfortune, my ways are not her ways?
It is my fault, that my habits and modes are dissimilar wholly?
'Tis not her fault; 'tis her nature, her virtue, to misapprehend
    them:
'Tis not her fault; 'tis her beautiful nature, not ever to know
    me.
Hopeless it seems, — yet I cannot, though hopeless, determine to
    leave it:
She goes — therefore I go; she moves, — I move, not to lose her.

XIV. CLAUDE TO EUSTACE.

Oh, 'tisn't manly, of course, 'tisn't manly, this method of
    wooing;
'Tisn't the way very likely to win. For the woman, they tell you,
Ever prefers the audacious, the wilful, the vehement hero;
She has no heart for the timid, the sensitive soul; and for
    knowledge, —
Knowledge, O ye Gods! — when did they appreciate
    knowledge?
Wherefore should they, either? I am sure I do not desire it.
  Ah, and I feel too, Eustace, she cares not a tittle about me!
(Care about me, indeed! and do I really expect it?)
But my manner offends; my ways are wholly repugnant;
Every word that I utter estranges, hurts, and repels her;
Every moment of bliss that I gain, in her exquisite presence,
Slowly, surely, withdraws her, removes her, and severs her
    from me.
Not that I care very much! — any way I escape from the boy's
    own
Folly, to which I am prone, of loving where it is easy.
Not that I mind very much! Why should I? I am not in love,
    and

Am prepared, I think, if not by previous habit,
Yet in the spirit beforehand for this and all that is like it;
It is an easier matter for us contemplative creatures,
Us upon whom the pressure of action is laid so lightly;
We, discontented indeed with things in particular, idle,
Sickly, complaining, by faith, in the vision of things in general,
Manage to hold on our way without, like others around us,
Seizing the nearest arm to comfort, help, and support us.
Yet, after all, my Eustace, I know but little about it.
All I can say for myself, for present alike and for past, is,
Mary Trevellyn, Eustace, is certainly worth your acquaintance.
You couldn't come, I suppose, as far as Florence to see her?

XV. GEORGINA TREVELLYN TO LOUISA—.

...... To-morrow we're starting for Florence,
Truly rejoiced, you may guess, to escape from republican
        terrors;
Mr C. and Papa to escort us; we by *vettura*
Through Siena, and Georgy to follow and join us by Leghorn.
Then – Ah, what shall I say, my dearest? I tremble in thinking
You will imagine my feelings, – the blending of hope and of
        sorrow.
How can I bear to abandon Papa and Mamma and my Sisters?
Dearest Louise, indeed it is very alarming; but, trust me
Ever, whatever may change, to remain your loving Georgina.

P.S. BY MARY TREVELLYN.

...... 'Do I like Mr Claude any better?'
I am to tell you, – and, 'Pray, is it Susan or I that attract him?'
This he never has told, but Georgina could certainly ask him.
All I can say for myself is, alas! that he rather repels me.
There! I think him agreeable, but also a little repulsive.
So be content, dear Louisa; for one satisfactory marriage
Surely will do in one year for the family you would establish:
Neither Susan nor I shall afford you the joy of a second.

P.S. BY GEORGINA TREVELLYN.

Mr Claude, you must know, is behaving a little bit better;
He and Papa are great friends; but he really is too
    shilly-shally, –
So unlike George! Yet I hope that the matter is going on fairly.
I shall, however, get George, before he goes, to say something.
Dearest Louise, how delightful to bring young people together!

Canto II, xiii–xv

*   *   *

VIII. CLAUDE TO EUSTACE.

I cannot stay at Florence, not even to wait for a letter.
Galleries only oppress me. Remembrance of hope I had
    cherished
(Almost more than as hope, when I passed through Florence
    the first time)
Lies like a sword in my soul. I am more a coward than ever,
Chicken-hearted, past thought. The caffès and waiters distress
    me.
All is unkind, and, alas! I am ready for any one's kindness.
Oh, I knew it of old, and knew it, I thought, to perfection,
If there is any one thing in the world to preclude all kindness.
It is the need of it, – it is this sad, self-defeating dependence.
Why is this, Eustace? Myself, were I stronger, I think I could
    tell you.
But it is odd when it comes. So plumb I the deeps of depression,
Daily in deeper, and find no support, no will, no purpose.
All my old strengths are gone. And yet I shall have to do
    something.
Ah, the key of our life, that passes all wards, opens all locks,
Is not *I will*, but *I must*. I must, – I must, – and I do it.

———————

After all, do I know that I really cared so about her?
Do whatever I will, I cannot call up her image;

For when I close my eyes, I see, very likely, St Peter's,
Or the Pantheon façade, or Michel Angelo's figures,
Or, at a wish, when I please, the Alban hills and the Forum, –
But that face, those eyes, – ah, no, never anything like them;
Only, try as I will, a sort of featureless outline,
And a pale blank orb, which no recollection will add to.
After all, perhaps there was something factitious about it;
I have had pain, it is true: I have wept, and so have the actors.

———————————

At the last moment I have your letter, for which I was waiting;
I have taken my place, and see no good in inquiries.
Do nothing more, good Eustace, I pray you. It only will vex
    me.
Take no measures. Indeed, should we meet, I could not be
    certain;
All might be changed, you know. Or perhaps there was nothing
    to be changed.
It is a curious history, this; and yet I foresaw it;
I could have told it before. The Fates, it is clear, are against us;
For it is certain enough I met with the people you mention;
They were at Florence the day I returned there, and spoke to
    me even;
Stayed a week, saw me often; departed, and whither I know
    not.
Great is Fate, and is best. I believe in Providence partly.
What is ordained is right, and all that happens is ordered.
Ah, no, that isn't it. But yet I retain my conclusion.
I will go where I am led, and will not dictate to the chances.
Do nothing more, I beg. If you love me, forbear interfering.

IX. CLAUDE TO EUSTACE.

Shall we come out of it all, some day, as one does from a
    tunnel?
Will it be all at once, without our doing or asking,

We shall behold clear day, the trees and meadows about us,
And the faces of friends, and the eyes we loved looking at us?
Who knows? Who can say? It will not do to suppose it.

X. CLAUDE TO EUSTACE, – *from Rome*.

Rome will not suit me, Eustace; the priests and soldiers possess
    it;
Priests and soldiers: – and, ah! which is the worst, the priest or
    the soldier?
  Politics, farewell, however! For what could I do? with
    inquiring,
Talking, collating the journals, go fever my brain about things
    o'er
Which I can have no control. No, happen whatever may
    happen,
Time, I suppose, will subsist; the earth will revolve on its axis;
People will travel; the stranger will wander as now in the city;
Rome will be here, and the Pope the *custode* of Vatican
    marbles.
  I have no heart, however, for any marble or fresco;
I have essayed it in vain; 'tis in vain as yet to essay it:
But I may haply resume some day my studies in this kind;
Not as the Scripture says, is, I think, the fact. Ere our death-day,
Faith, I think, does pass, and Love; but Knowledge abideth.
Let us seek Knowledge; – the rest may come and go as it
    happens.
Knowledge is hard to seek, and harder yet to adhere to.
Knowledge is painful often; and yet when we know we are
    happy.
Seek it, and leave mere Faith and Love to come with the
    chances.
As for Hope, – to-morrow I hope to be starting for Naples.
Rome will not do, I see, for many very good reasons.
  Eastward, then, I suppose, with the coming of winter, to
    Egypt.

XI. MARY TREVELLYN TO MISS ROPER.

You have heard nothing; of course I know you can have heard
    nothing.
Ah, well, more than once I have broken my purpose, and
    sometimes,
Only too often, have looked for the little lake steamer to bring
    him.
But it is only fancy, – I do not really expect it.
Oh, and you see I know so exactly how he would take it:
Finding the chances prevail against meeting again, he would
    banish
Forthwith every thought of the poor little possible hope, which
I myself could not help, perhaps, thinking only too much of;
He would resign himself, and go. I see it exactly.
So I also submit, although in a different manner.

    Can you not really come? We go very shortly to England.

Canto V, viii–xi

SWINBURNE

From ATALANTA IN CALYDON

Swinburne's neo-Hellenic tragedy was published in 1865. Its complex subject was linked to the burning of a brand which was to measure out the life of Althea's son, Meleager, and which she snatched from the flames to prevent it being consumed. Meleager, having killed a boar which was ravaging Calydon, presented its head to Atalanta, the virgin huntress who was the first to wound it. This angered Althea's brothers and led to a dispute in which Meleager killed them. In revenge, Althea threw the brand into the fire. As it wasted away, so did Meleager's life. Outstanding in the verse drama are the energy and imagery of Swinburne's dramatic choruses.

CHORUS

When the hounds of spring are on winter's traces,
   The mother of months in meadow or plain
Fills the shadows and windy places
   With lisp of leaves and ripple of rain;
And the brown bright nightingale amorous
Is half assuaged for Itylus,
For the Thracian ships and the foreign faces,
   The tongueless vigil, and all the pain.

Come with bows bent and with emptying of quivers,
   Maiden most perfect, lady of light,
With a noise of winds and many rivers,
   With a clamour of waters, and with might;
Bind on thy sandals, O thou most fleet;
Over the splendour and speed of thy feet;
For the faint east quickens, the wan west shivers,
   Round the feet of the day and the feet of the night.

Where shall we find her, how shall we sing to her,
    Fold our hands round her knees, and cling?
O that man's heart were as fire and could spring to her,
    Fire, or the strength of the streams that spring!
For the stars and the winds are unto her
As raiment, as songs of the harp-player;
For the risen stars and the fallen cling to her,
    And the southwest-wind and the west-wind sing.

For winter's rains and ruins are over,
    And all the season of snows and sins;
The days dividing lover and lover,
    The light that loses, the night that wins;
And time remembered is grief forgotten,
And frosts are slain and flowers begotten,
And in green underwood and cover
    Blossom by blossom the spring begins.

The full streams feed on flower of rushes,
    Ripe grasses trammel a travelling foot,
The faint fresh flame of the young year flushes
    From leaf to flower and flower to fruit;
And fruit and leaf are as gold and fire,
And the oat is heard above the lyre,
And the hoofèd heel of a satyr crushes
    The chestnut-husk at the chestnut-root.

And Pan by noon and Bacchus by night,
    Fleeter of foot than the fleet-foot kid,
Follows with dancing and fills with delight
    The Mænad and the Bassarid;
And soft as lips that laugh and hide
The laughing leaves of the trees divide,
And screen from seeing and leave in sight
    The god pursuing, the maiden hid.

The ivy falls with the Bacchanal's hair
    Over her eyebrows hiding her eyes;
The wild vine slipping down leaves bare
    Her bright breast shortening into sighs;

The wild vine slips with the weight of its leaves,
But the berried ivy catches and cleaves
To the limbs that glitter, the feet that scare
   The wolf that follows, the fawn that flies.

*   *   *

CHORUS

Before the beginning of years
   There came to the making of man
Time, with a gift of tears;
   Grief, with a glass that ran;
Pleasure, with pain for leaven;
   Summer, with flowers that fell;
Remembrance fallen from heaven,
   And madness risen from hell;
Strength without hands to smite;
   Love that endures for a breath:
Night, the shadow of light,
   And life, the shadow of death.
And the high gods took in hand
   Fire, and the falling of tears,
And a measure of sliding sand
   From under the feet of the years;
And froth and drift of the sea;
   And dust of the labouring earth;
And bodies of things to be
   In the houses of death and of birth;
And wrought with weeping and laughter,
   And fashioned with loathing and love,
With life before and after
   And death beneath and above,
For a day and a night and a morrow,
   That his strength might endure for a span
With travail and heavy sorrow,
   The holy spirit of man.

From the winds of the north and the south
 They gathered as unto strife;
They breathed upon his mouth,
 They filled his body with life;
Eyesight and speech they wrought
 For the veils of the soul therein,
A time for labour and thought,
 A time to serve and to sin;
They gave him light in his ways,
 And love, and a space for delight,
And beauty and length of days,
 And night, and sleep in the night.
His speech is a burning fire;
 With his lips he travaileth;
In his heart is a blind desire,
 In his eyes foreknowledge of death;
He weaves, and is clothed with derision;
 Sows, and he shall not reap;
His life is a watch or a vision
 Between a sleep and a sleep.

ITYLUS

One of Swinburne's most accomplished pieces from *Poems and Ballads* (1866), 'Itylus' draws upon the same legend as Arnold's 'Philomela', the rape of Philomela by Tereus, her sister's revenge in feeding their child to her husband, and the conclusion in which the sisters and Tereus are changed into birds.

Swallow, my sister, O sister swallow,
   How can thine heart be full of the spring?
      A thousand summers are over and dead.
What hast thou found in the spring to follow?
   What hast thou found in thine heart to sing?
      What wilt thou do when the summer is shed?

A swallow, sister, O fair swift swallow,
   Why wilt thou fly after spring to the south,
      The soft south whither thine heart is set?
Shall not the grief of the old time follow?
   Shall not the song thereof cleave to thy mouth?
      Hast thou forgotten ere I forget?

Sister, my sister, O fleet sweet swallow,
   Thy way is long to the sun and the south;
      But I, fulfilled of my heart's desire,
Shedding my song upon height, upon hollow,
   From tawny body and sweet small mouth
      Feed the heart of the night with fire.

I the nightingale all spring through,
   O swallow, sister, O changing swallow,
      All spring through till the spring be done,
Clothed with the light of the night on the dew,
   Sing, while the hours and the wild birds follow,
      Take flight and follow and find the sun.

Sister, my sister, O soft light swallow,
    Though al! things feast in the spring's guest-chamber,
        How hast thou heart to be glad thereof yet?
For where thou fliest I shall not follow,
    Till life forget and death remember.
        Till thou remember and I forget.

Swallow, my sister, O singing swallow,
    I know not how thou hast heart to sing.
        Hast thou the heart? is it all past over?
Thy lord the summer is good to follow,
    And fair the feet of thy lover the spring:
        But what wilt thou say to the spring thy lover?

O swallow, sister, O fleeting swallow,
    My heart in me is a molten ember
        And over my head the waves have met.
But thou wouldst tarry or I would follow,
    Could I forget or thou remember,
        Couldst thou remember and I forget.

O sweet stray sister, O shifting swallow,
    The heart's division divideth us.
        Thy heart is light as a leaf of a tree;
But mine goes forth among sea-gulfs hollow
    To the place of the slaying of Itylus,
        The feast of Daulis, the Thracian sea.

O swallow, sister, O rapid swallow,
    I pray thee sing not a little space.
        Are not the roofs and the lintels wet?
The woven web that was plain to follow,
    The small slain body, the flowerlike face,
        Can I remember if thou forget?

O sister, sister, thy first-begotten!
    The hands that cling and the feet that follow,
        The voice of the child's blood crying yet
Who hath remembered me? who hath forgotten?
    Thou hast forgotten, O summer swallow,
        But the world shall end when I forget.

FAUSTINE

Faustina was the wife of the Emperor Marcus Aurelius, who ruled
Rome from AD 161–80. There is no evidence of the promiscuity,
let alone the lesbianism, alleged against her. Frederick Sandys, the
painter, described the poem's composition in 1862, when
Swinburne and several friends were on a suburban railway train.
They had a bet as to who could produce the greatest number of
rhymes for the name 'Faustine'. Swinburne, with his usual facility,
wrote the entire poem between Waterloo and Hampton Court,
winning the bet.

Ave Faustina Imperatrix, morituri te salutant.

Lean back, and get some minutes' peace;
    Let your head lean
Back to the shoulder with its fleece
    Of locks, Faustine.

The shapely silver shoulder stoops,
    Weighed over clean
With state of splendid hair that droops
    Each side, Faustine.

Let me go over your good gifts
    That crown you queen;
A queen whose kingdom ebbs and shifts
    Each week, Faustine.

Bright heavy brows well gathered up:
    White gloss and sheen;
Carved lips that make my lips a cup
    To drink, Faustine,

Wine and rank poison, milk and blood,
    Being mixed therein

Since first the devil threw dice with God
   For you, Faustine.

Your naked new-born soul, their stake,
   Stood blind between;
God said 'let him that wins her take
   And keep Faustine.'

But this time Satan throve, no doubt;
   Long since, I ween,
God's part in you was battered out;
   Long since, Faustine.

The die rang sideways as it fell,
   Rang cracked and thin,
Like a man's laughter heard in hell
   Far down, Faustine,

A shadow of laughter like a sigh,
   Dead sorrow's kin;
So rang, thrown down, the devil's die
   That won Faustine.

A suckling of his breed you were,
   One hard to wean;
But God, who lost you, left you fair,
   We see, Faustine.

You have the face that suits a woman
   For her soul's screen —
The sort of beauty that's called human
   In hell, Faustine.

You could do all things but be good
   Or chaste of mien;
And that you would not if you could,
   We know, Faustine.

Even he who cast seven devils out
   Of Magdalene
Could hardly do as much, I doubt,
   For you, Faustine.

Did Satan make you to spite God?
  Or did God mean
To scourge with scorpions for a rod
  Our sins, Faustine?

I know what queen at first you were,
  As though I had seen
Red gold and black imperious hair
  Twice crown Faustine.

As if your fed sarcophagus
  Spared flesh and skin,
You come back face to face with us,
  The same Faustine.

She loved the games men played with death,
  Where death must win;
As though the slain man's blood and breath
Revived Faustine.

Nets caught the pike, pikes tore the net;
  Lithe limbs and lean
From drained-out pores dripped thick red sweat
  To soothe Faustine.

She drank the steaming drift and dust
  Blown off the scene;
Blood could not ease the bitter lust
  That galled Faustine.

All round the foul fat furrows reeked,
  Where blood sank in;
The circus splashed and seethed and shrieked
  All round Faustine.

But these are gone now: years entomb
  The dust and din;
Yea, even the bath's fierce reek and fume
  That slew Faustine.

Was life worth living then? and now
  Is life worth sin?

Where are the imperial years? and how
    Are you Faustine?

Your soul forgot her joys, forgot
    Her times of teen;
Yea, this life likewise will you not
    Forget, Faustine?

For in the time we know not of
    Did fate begin
Weaving the web of days that wove
    Your doom, Faustine.

The threads were wet with wine, and all
    Were smooth to spin;
They wove you like a Bacchanal,
    The first Faustine.

And Bacchus cast your mates and you
    Wild grapes to glean;
Your flower-like lips were dashed with dew
    From his, Faustine.

Your drenched loose hands were stretched to hold
    The vine's wet green,
Long ere they coined in Roman gold
    Your face, Faustine.

Then after change of soaring feather
    And winnowing fin,
You woke in weeks of feverish weather,
    A new Faustine.

A star upon your birthday burned,
    Whose fierce serene
Red pulseless planet never yearned
    In heaven, Faustine.

Stray breaths of Sapphic song that blew
    Through Mitylene
Shook the fierce quivering blood in you
    By night, Faustine.

The shameless nameless love that makes
   Hell's iron gin
Shut on you like a trap that breaks
   The soul, Faustine.

And when your veins were void and dead,
   What ghosts unclean
Swarmed round the straitened barren bed
   That hid Faustine?

What sterile growths of sexless root
   Or epicene?
What flower of kisses without fruit
   Of love, Faustine?

What adders came to shed their coats?
   What coiled obscene
Small serpents with soft stretching throats
   Caressed Faustine?

But the time came of famished hours,
   Maimed loves and mean,
This ghastly thin-faced time of ours,
   To spoil Faustine.

You seem a thing that hinges hold,
   A love-machine
With clockwork joints of supple gold –
   No more, Faustine.

Not godless, for you serve one God,
   The Lampsacene,
Who metes the gardens with his rod;
   Your lord, Faustine.

If one should love you with real love
   (Such things have been,
Things your fair face knows nothing of,
   It seems, Faustine);

That clear hair heavily bound back,
   The lights wherein

Shift from dead blue to burnt-up black;
  Your throat, Faustine,

Strong, heavy, throwing out the face
  And hard bright chin
And shameful scornful lips that grace
  Their shame, Faustine,

Curled lips, long since half kissed away,
  Still sweet and keen;
You'd give him – poison shall we say?
  Or what, Faustine?

BIBLIOGRAPHY

Altick, Richard D. and James F. Loucks, *Browning's Roman Murder Story: A Reading of the Ring and the Book*, University of Chicago Press, 1968

Armstrong, Isobel (ed.), *The Major Victorian Poets: A Reconsideration*, London: Routledge and Kegan Paul, 1969
[The collection includes four essays each on Tennyson and Browning, two each on Arnold and Clough. Bernard Bergonzi on *The Princess*, Michael Mason on *Sordello*, John Killham on *The Ring and the Book*, Gabriel Pearson on *Merope*, Barbara Hardy and John Goode on Clough, and Isobel Armstrong on Browning.]

Armstrong, Isobel (ed.), *Robert Browning*, London: Bell, 1974
[A volume in the 'Writers and their Background' series, this includes essays by Michael Mason on 'Browning and the Dramatic Monologue', Barbara Melchiori on 'Browning in Italy', Leonee Ormond on 'Browning and Painting', Trevor Lloyd on 'Browning and Politics', Penelope Gay on 'Browning and Music', Roger Sharrock on 'Browning and History', and Isobel Armstrong on 'Browning and Victorian Poetry of Sexual Love'.]

Armstrong, Isobel, *Victorian Scrutinies: Reviews of Poetry 1830–1870*, London: Athlone Press, 1972

Arnold, Matthew, *Matthew Arnold*, ed. Miriam Allott and Robert H. Super, Oxford University Press, 1986 [Oxford Standard Authors]

Arnold, Matthew, *The Poems of Matthew Arnold*, ed. Kenneth Allott, London: Longmans Annotated English Poets, 1965

Biswas, Robindra Kumar, *Arthur Hugh Clough: Towards a Reconsideration*, Oxford University Press, 1972

Bradbury, Malcolm, and David Palmer, (eds), *Victorian Poetry*, London: Arnold, 1973 [Includes essays on Browning, Arnold, and Tennyson's *Idylls of the King*.]

Browning, Robert, *The Complete Works of Robert Browning*, ed. Roma A. King Jr., Ohio University Press, 1969

Browning, Robert, *Poems*, ed. John Pettigrew and Thomas J. Collins, Harmondsworth: Penguin Books, 1981

Browning, Robert, *Browning: Poetical Works, 1833–1864*, ed. Ian Jack, Oxford University Press, 1970 [Oxford Standard Authors]

Browning, Robert, *A Choice of Browning's Verse*, ed. Edward Lucie-Smith, London: Faber, 1967

Browning, Robert, and Elizabeth Barrett Browning, *The Letters of Robert Browning and Elizabeth Barrett Browning, 1845–1846*, ed. Elvan Kintner, 2 vols, Oxford University Press/ Harvard University Press, 1969

Browning, Robert, and Elizabeth Barrett Browning, *The Brownings' Correspondence*, ed. Philip Kelley and Ronald Hudson, Vols 1 & 2, Wedgestone Press, 1984 In progress

Browning, Vivienne, *My Browning Family Album*, London: Springwood Books, 1979

Buckler, William E., *On the Poetry of Matthew Arnold: Essays in Critical Reconstruction*, New York University Press, 1982
[An appreciation of structure and classicism in Arnold's poetry.]

Buckley, J. H., *Tennyson: The Growth of a Poet*, Oxford University Press/Harvard University Press, 1960
[One of the best introductions to Tennyson's work, which surveys the poetry from first to last and interweaves it with an account of Tennyson's own development.]

Bush, Douglas, *Matthew Arnold*, London: Macmillan, 1971

Carroll, Joseph, *The Cultural Theory of Matthew Arnold*, University of California Press, 1982
[An account of Arnold's cultural theory as expressed in his prose, the synthesis of Hellenism and Hebraism, with reference to his poetry.]

Christ, Carol T., *Victorian and Modern Poetics*, University of Chicago Press, 1984
[An account of the unacknowledged links between the art of the Modernists, notably Yeats, Pound and Eliot, and the Victorians whom Modernism most maligned. The book is a development of the argument that Modernism is less a rebellion against Romanticism than a continuation of it.]

Chorley, Katherine, *Arthur Hugh Clough: The Uncommitted Mind. A Study of his Life and Poetry*, Oxford: Clarendon Press, 1962

Clough, Arthur Hugh, *The Poems of Arthur Hugh Clough*, 2nd edition, ed. F. L. Mulhauser, Oxford: Clarendon Press, 1974

Clough, Arthur Hugh, *The Poems of Arthur Hugh Clough*, ed. A. L. P. Norrington, Oxford University Press, 1968 [Oxford Standard Authors – omits 'Dipsychus Continued', 'Mari Magno' and some minor poems.]

A Choice of Clough's Verse, ed. Michael Thorpe, London: Faber, 1969

Cockshut, A. O. J., *The Unbelievers: English Agnostic Thought 1840–1890*, London: Collins, 1964

Connolly, Thomas E., *Swinburne's Theory of Poetry*, University of New York/ Antioch Press, 1965

Cook, Eleanor, *Browning's Lyrics*, University of Toronto Press, 1974

Coulling, Sidney, *Matthew Arnold and his Critics: A Study of Arnold's Controversies*, Ohio University Press, 1974

Culler, A. Dwight, *The Poetry of Tennyson*, Yale University Press, 1977

Dawson, Carl (ed.), *Matthew Arnold: The Poetry. The Critical Heritage*, London: Routledge and Kegan Paul, 1973

Delaura, David J., *Matthew Arnold: Twentieth Century Views*, Englewood Cliffs: Prentice-Hall, 1973

DeVane, William Clyde, *A Browning Handbook*, London: John Murray, 1937 and reprints

Drew, Philip (ed.), *Robert Browning: A Collection of Critical Essays*, London: Methuen, 1966
[Includes major essays of the past on Browning, by Henry James, Edwin Muir, Percy Lubbock, and George Santayana.]

Drew, Philip, *The Poetry of Browning*, London: Macmillan, 1970

Dyson, Hope, and Charles Tennyson, (eds), *Dear and Honoured Lady*, London: Macmillan, 1969
[The correspondence of Tennyson and Queen Victoria.]

Eliot, T. S., *Essays Ancient and Modern*, London: Faber, 1936; *On Poetry and Poets*, London: Faber, 1957
[The essay on *In Memoriam* describes Tennyson as having the essential qualities of a great poet: abundance, variety, and complete competence, and the finest ear of any English poet since Milton. He also appears as 'the saddest of all English poets . . . the most instinctive rebel against the society in which he was the most perfect conformist.']

Elton, Oliver, *A Survey of English Literature 1830–1880*, London: Methuen, 1920 and reprints

Fletcher, Ian, *Romantic Mythologies*, London: Routledge and Kegan Paul, 1967

Ford, Boris, (ed.) *Pelican Guide to English Literature: Dickens to Hardy*, Harmondsworth: Penguin Books, rev. edn. 1982

Gosse, Edmund, *A Life of Algernon Charles Swinburne*, London: Macmillan, 1917

Gridley, Roy E., *The Brownings and France: A Chronicle with a Commentary*, London: Athlone Press, 1982

Halliday, F. E., *Robert Browning: His Life and Work*, London: Jupiter, 1976

Hassett, Constance W., *The Elusive Self in the Poetry of Robert Browning*, Ohio University Press, 1982

Henderson, Philip, *Swinburne: The Portrait of a Poet*, London: Routledge and Kegan Paul, 1974

Henderson, Philip, *Tennyson: Poet and Prophet*, London: Routledge and Kegan Paul, 1978
[A shorter, more anecdotal, and very readable biography.]

Holloway, John, *Victorian Sage: Studies in Argument*, London: Macmillan, 1953

Honan Park, *Matthew Arnold: A Life*, London: Weidenfeld and Nicolson, 1981

Irvine, William, and Park Honan, *The Ring, the Book, and the Poet: A Biography of Robert Browning*, London: Cassell, 1975

Jack, Ian, *Browning's Major Poetry*, Oxford: Clarendon Press, 1973
[A clear and specific guide to much of Browning's poetry, though excluding *The Ring and the Book*. The individual poems are discussed with cross-references to other major figures in English literature.]

Joseph, Gerhard, *Tennysonian Love: The Strange Diagonal*, Oxford University Press/ Minnesota University Press, 1969

Jump, John D., *Matthew Arnold*, London: Routledge and Kegan Paul, 1955

Jump, John D. (ed.), *Tennyson: The Critical Heritage*, London: Routledge and Kegan Paul, 1967

Kermode, Frank, *The Romantic Image*, London: Routledge and Kegan Paul, 1957

King, Roma A., Jr., *The Focusing Artifice*, Ohio University Press, 1969

Kinkaid, James R., and Albert J. Kyhn (eds.), *Victorian Literature and Society*, Ohio University Press, 1985

Leavis, F. R., *New Bearings in English Poetry*, London: Chatto and Windus, 1932 and reprints
[The first chapter contains an acerbic commentary by the author on the Victorians as the predecessors of the Moderns. It is an interesting piece, in which the author characteristically asserts rather than argues. 'Browning would have been less robust if he had been more sensitive and intelligent.' Victorian poetry was apt to make Dr Leavis cross.]

Litzinger, Boyd, and Donald Smalley (eds.), *Browning: The Critical Heritage*, London: Routledge and Kegan Paul, 1970

Martin, Robert Bernard, *Tennyson: The Unquiet Heart*, Oxford: Clarendon Press/ London: Faber, 1980
[This remains the major Tennyson biography of recent years, which adds significantly to Harold Nicolson's portrait by detailing the dark influence of childhood and heredity, in its account of Tennyson's father's epilepsy, alcoholism, opium addiction and melancholia. The postponement of the marriage to Emily Sellwood appears not as grief for Hallam but fear of heredity. A point is also made of Tennyson's inability to sustain friendship, about which he wrote so readily. He seems 'a born sprinter rather than a long-distance runner' in such relationships.]

Nicolson, Harold, *Tennyson*, London: Constable, 1923 and reprints

Page, Norman, *Tennyson: Interviews and Recollections*, London: Macmillan, 1983

Peltason, Timothy, *Reading 'In Memoriam'*, Princeton University Press, 1985

Peters, Robert L., *The Crowns of Apollo: A Study in Victorian Criticism and Aesthetics*, Detroit: Wayne State University Press, 1965

Praz, Mario, *The Romantic Agony*, Oxford University Press, 1933; London: Fontana Paperback, 1960 and reprints

Priestley, F. E. L., *Language and Structure in Tennyson's Poetry*, London: André Deutsch, 1973
[A volume in 'The Language Library', which analyses Tennyson's verse in terms of its metre, diction and structure, as well as in its philosophical and moral dimensions.]

Rader, Ralph Wilson, *Tennyson's Maud: The Biographical Genesis*, Cambridge University Press/ University of California Press, 1963

Ricks, Christopher (ed.), *The New Oxford Book of Victorian Verse*, Oxford University Press, 1987

Ricks, Christopher, *Tennyson*, London: Macmillan, 1972
[The most persuasive modern account of Tennyson's life and work, his unclamorous claim to the central humanity of a great poet. The critique of the poetry is set in the context of Tennyson's life and the development of his writing is seen in terms of the poet's progress. Succinct and incisive in its judgments by contrast with the more ponderous approach of the theoreticians.]

Russell, Bertrand, *A History of Western Philosophy*, London: George Allen and Unwin, 1946 and reprints
[Chapters 18 and 19 of Russell's book draw on poetry and fiction to demonstrate how romanticism and the example of Rousseau led to twentieth century tyranny in the Soviet Union and Nazi Germany, the link with Fascism being the stronger.]

Ryals, Clyde De L., *Browning's Later Poetry*, Cornell University Press, 1975
[An account of the less-discussed poetry following *The Ring and the Book*, this volume discusses the naturalism of *Red Cotton Night-Cap Country*, the 'cinematic' quality of *Fifine at the Fair* and the 'recognition' drama of *The Inn Album*, as well as Browning's preoccupation with criticism and reputation during the 1870s and 1880s.]

Shatto, Susan (ed.), *Tennyson's 'Maud': A Definitive Edition*, London: Athlone Press, 1986

Shatto, Susan, and Marion Shaw, (eds.), *Tennyson: 'In Memoriam'*, Oxford: Clarendon Press, 1982
[A more fully annotated edition, based upon the Tennyson manuscripts at Trinity College, Cambridge.]

Shaw, W. David, *Tennyson's Style*, Cornell University Press, 1978

Sinfield, Alan, *The Language of Tennyson's 'In Memoriam'*, Oxford: Blackwell, 1971
[A linguistic account of the poem, in terms of its diction, syntax, imagery, sound and rhythm, coupled with a perceptive valuation of it in terms of more orthodox literary criticism.]

Strange, G. Robert, *Matthew Arnold: The Poet as Humanist*, Oxford University Press/ Princeton University Press, 1967

Sullivan, Mary Rose, *Browning's Voices in the Ring and the Book*, Oxford University Press/ Toronto University Press, 1969

Swinburne, Algernon Charles, *A Choice of Swinburne's Verse*, ed. Robert Nye, London: Faber, 1973

Swinburne, Algernon Charles, *Lesbia Brandon*, ed. Randolph Hughes, London: Falcon Press, 1952

Swinburne, Algernon Charles, *New Writings by Swinburne*, ed. Cecil Y. Lang, New York: Syracuse University Press, 1965

Swinburne, Algernon Charles, *The Swinburne Letters*, ed. Cecil Y. Lang, 6 vols, Oxford University Press/ Yale University Press, 1959–62

Swinburne, Algernon Charles, *Swinburne as Critic*, ed. Clarke K. Hyder, London: Routledge and Kegan Paul, 1972

Swinburne, Algernon Charles, *A Year's Letters*, ed. F. J. Sypher, London: Peter Owen, 1975

Tennyson, Alfred, *The Letters of Alfred Lord Tennyson*, ed. Cecil Y. Lang and Edgar F. Shannon, Oxford: Clarendon Press, 1987
In progress.

Tennyson, Alfred, *The Poems of Tennyson*, ed. Christopher Ricks, 3 vols, Harlow: Longman, 1987

[This is a larger and more comprehensive edition, including variants from the Trinity College, Cambridge MSS, which were not available for publication in 1969 when the Tennyson volume of Longmans Annotated English Poets was issued.]

Tennyson, Lady Emily, *Lady Tennyson's Journal*, ed. James O. Hoge, University Press of Virginia, 1982

Tennyson, Hallam, (ed.), *Studies in Tennyson*, London: Macmillan/ New York: Barnes and Noble, 1981

Thomas, Donald, *Robert Browning: A Life Within Life*, London: Weidenfeld and Nicolson/ New York: Viking Penguin, 1982

Thomas, Donald, *Swinburne: The Poet in his World*, London: Weidenfeld and Nicolson/ New York: Oxford University Press, 1979

Thomas, Donald, *The Post-Romantics*, London and New York: Routledge, 1990
[An anthology of critical writing on the poetry of Tennyson, Browning, Arnold, Clough and Swinburne, with an introduction and a comment-ary.]

Thorlby, Anthony, *The Romantic Movement*, Harlow: Longman, 1967

Thorpe, Michael, *Clough: The Critical Heritage*, London: Routledge and Kegan Paul, 1972

Tillotson, Geoffrey and Kathleen, *Mid-Victorian Studies*, London: Athlone Press, 1966
[This includes Kathleen Tillotson, 'Tennyson's Serial Poem' on *Idylls of the King*, Geoffrey Tillotson on 'Novelists and Near-Novelists' and an analysis of Clough's *The Bothie of Tober-na-Vuolich*.]

Timko, Michael, *Innocent Victorian* [A. H. Clough], Ohio University Press, 1966

Tinker, C. B., and L. F. Lowry, *The Poetry of Matthew Arnold. A Commentary*, Oxford University Press, 1940

Tracy, Clarence (ed.), *Browning's Mind and Art*, Edinburgh: Oliver and Boyd, 1968

Trilling, Lionel, *Matthew Arnold*, London: George Allen and Unwin/ New York: W. W. Norton, 1939; rev. edn., 1949; London: Unwin University Books, 1963

Ward, Maisie, *Robert Browning and his World*, 2 vols, London: Cassell, 1968–9

Wellek, René, *A History of Modern Criticism, 1750–1950* [Volumes 3 and 4, 'The Age of Transition' and 'The Later Nineteenth Century'], London: Cape, 1966

Wheatcroft, Andrew, *The Tennyson Album: A Biography in Original Photographs*, London: Routledge, 1980

[A fascinating compendium of Tennyson photographs with an introduction by Sir John Betjeman.]

Willey, Basil, *Nineteenth Century Studies*, London: Chatto and Windus, 1949
[Basil Willey's studies of the philosophical groupings and individual beliefs inherent in Victorian literature are concise, generously informative and a pleasure to read. His account of Matthew Arnold suggests that Arnold was the elegist of a dead world but that his prose assists the birth of a new world.]

Willey, Basil, *More Nineteenth Century Studies: A Group of Honest Doubters*, London: Chatto and Windus, 1956

Williams, David, *Too Quick Despairer*, London: Rupert Hart-Davis, 1969 [A biography of Arthur Hugh Clough]

DRAMA
IN EVERYMAN

The Oresteia
AESCHYLUS
New translation of one of the greatest Greek dramatic trilogies which analyses the plays in performance
£5.99

Everyman and Medieval Miracle Plays
edited by A. C. Cawley
A selection of the most popular medieval plays
£4.99

Complete Plays and Poems
CHRISTOPHER MARLOWE
The complete works of this great Elizabethan in one volume
£5.99

Restoration Plays
edited by Robert Lawrence
Five comedies and two tragedies representing the best of the Restoration stage
£7.99

Female Playwrights of the Restoration: Five Comedies
edited by Paddy Lyons
Rediscovered literary treasures in a unique selection
£5.99

Plays, Prose Writings and Poems
OSCAR WILDE
The full force of Wilde's wit in one volume
£4.99

A Dolls House/The Lady from the Sea/The Wild Duck
HENRIK IBSEN
introduced by Fay Weldon
A popular selection of Ibsen's major plays
£4.99

The Beggar's Opera and Other Eighteenth-Century Plays
JOHN GAY et. al.
Including Goldsmith's She Stoops To Conquer *and Sheridan's* The School for Scandal, *this is a volume which reflects the full scope of the period's theatre*
£6.99

Female Playwrights of the Nineteenth Century
edited by Adrienne Scullion
The full range of female nineteenth-century dramatic development
£6.99

SHORT STORY COLLECTIONS
IN EVERYMAN

The Strange Case of Dr Jekyll and Mr Hyde and Other Stories
R. L. STEVENSON
An exciting selection of gripping tales from a master of suspense
£1.99

Nineteenth-Century American Short Stories
edited by Christopher Bigsby
A selection of the works of Henry James, Edith Wharton, Mark Twain and many other great American writers
£6.99

The Best of Saki
edited by MARTIN STEPHEN
Includes Tobermory, Gabriel Ernest, Svedni Vashtar, The Interlopers, Birds on the Western Front
£4.99

Souls Belated and Other Stories
EDITH WHARTON
Brief, neatly crafted tales exploring a range of themes from big taboo subjects to the subtlest little ironies of social life
£6.99

The Night of the Iguana and Other Stories
TENNESSEE WILLIAMS
Twelve remarkable short stories, each a compelling drama in miniature
£4.99

Selected Short Stories and Poems
THOMAS HARDY
Hardy's most memorable stories and poetry in one volume
£4.99

Selected Tales
HENRY JAMES
Stories portraying the tensions between private life and the outside world
£5.99

The Best of Sherlock Homes
ARTHUR CONAN DOYLE
All the favourite adventures in one volume
£4.99

The Secret Self 1: *Short Stories by Women*
edited by Hermione Lee
'A superb collection' The Guardian
£4.99

All books are available from your local bookshop or direct from:
Littlehampton Book Services Cash Sales, 14 Eldon Way, Lineside Estate,
Littlehampton, West Sussex BN17 7HE (*prices are subject to change*)

To order any of the books, please enclose a cheque (in sterling) made payable to
Littlehampton Book Services, or phone your order through with credit card details (Access,
Visa or Mastercard) on 01903 721596 (24 hour answering service) stating card number
and expiry date. (*Please add £1.25 for package and postage to the total of your order.*)

In the USA, for further information and a complete catalogue call 1-800-526-2778

CLASSIC FICTION
IN EVERYMAN

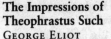

**The Impressions of
Theophrastus Such**
GEORGE ELIOT
*An amusing collection of character
sketches, and the only paperback
edition available*
£5.99

Frankenstein
MARY SHELLEY
*A masterpiece of Gothic terror in
its original 1818 version*
£3.99

East Lynne
MRS HENRY WOOD
*A classic tale of melodrama,
murder and mystery*
£7.99

**Holiday Romance and
Other Writings for Children**
CHARLES DICKENS
*Dickens's works for children,
including 'The Life of Our Lord'
and 'A Child's History of England',
with original illustrations*
£5.99

The Ebb-Tide
R. L. STEVENSON
*A compelling study of ordinary
people in extreme circumstances*
£4.99

The Three Impostors
ARTHUR MACHEN
*The only edition available
of this cult thriller*
£4.99

Mister Johnson
JOYCE CARY
*The only edition available of this
amusing but disturbing twentieth-
century tale*
£5.99

The Jungle Book
RUDYARD KIPLING
*The classic adventures of Mowgli
and his friends*
£3.99

Glenarvon
LADY CAROLINE LAMB
*The only edition available of the
novel which throws light on the
greatest scandal of the early nineteenth century – the infatuation of
Caroline Lamb with Lord Byron*
£6.99

**Twenty Thousand Leagues
Under the Sea**
JULES VERNE
*Scientific fact combines with
fantasy in this prophetic tale
of underwater adventure*
£4.99

All books are available from your local bookshop or direct from:
Littlehampton Book Services Cash Sales, 14 Eldon Way, Lineside Estate,
Littlehampton, West Sussex BN17 7HE (*prices are subject to change*)

To order any of the books, please enclose a cheque (in sterling) made payable to
Littlehampton Book Services, or phone your order through with credit card details (Access,
Visa or Mastercard) on 01903 721596 (24 hour answering service) stating card number
and expiry date. (*Please add £1.25 for package and postage to the total of your order.*)

In the USA, for further information and a complete catalogue call 1-800-526-2778

CLASSIC NOVELS
IN EVERYMAN

The Time Machine
H. G. WELLS
*One of the books which defined
'science fiction' – a compelling
and tragic story of a brilliant
and driven scientist*
£3.99

Oliver Twist
CHARLES DICKENS
*Arguably the best-loved of
Dickens's novels. With all the
original illustrations*
£4.99

Barchester Towers
ANTHONY TROLLOPE
*The second of Trollope's
Chronicles of Barsetshire,
and one of the funniest of all
Victorian novels*
£4.99

The Heart of Darkness
JOSEPH CONRAD
*Conrad's most intense, subtle,
compressed, profound and
proleptic work*
£3.99

Tess of the d'Urbervilles
THOMAS HARDY
*The powerful, poetic classic
of wronged innocence*
£3.99

Wuthering Heights and Poems
EMILY BRONTË
*A powerful work of genius – one of
the great masterpieces of literature*
£3.99

Pride and Prejudice
JANE AUSTEN
*Proposals, rejections, infidelities,
elopements, happy marriages –
Jane Austen's most popular novel*
£2.99

North and South
ELIZABETH GASKELL
*A novel of hardship, passion
and hard-won wisdom amidst the
conflicts of the industrial revolution*
£4.99

The Newcomes
W. M. THACKERAY
*An exposé of Victorian polite
society by one of the nineteenth-
century's finest novelists*
£6.99

Adam Bede
GEORGE ELIOT
*A passionate rural drama enacted
at the turn of the eighteenth
century*
£5.99

All books are available from your local bookshop or direct from:
Littlehampton Book Services Cash Sales, 14 Eldon Way, Lineside Estate,
Littlehampton, West Sussex BN17 7HE (*prices are subject to change*)

To order any of the books, please enclose a cheque (in sterling) made payable to
Littlehampton Book Services, or phone your order through with credit card details (Access,
Visa or Mastercard) on 01903 721596 (24 hour answering service) stating card number
and expiry date. (*Please add £1.25 for package and postage to the total of your order.*)

In the USA, for further information and a complete catalogue call 1-800-526-2778

WOMEN'S WRITING
IN EVERYMAN

Poems and Prose
CHRISTINA ROSSETTI
A collection of her writings, poetry and prose, published to mark the centenary of her death
£5.99

Women Philosophers
edited by Mary Warnock
The great subjects of philosophy handled by women spanning four centuries, including Simone de Beauvoir and Iris Murdoch
£6.99

Glenarvon
LADY CAROLINE LAMB
A novel which throws light on the greatest scandal of the early nineteenth century – the infatuation of Caroline Lamb with Lord Byron
£6.99

Women Romantic Poets
1780–1830: An Anthology
edited by Jennifer Breen
Hidden talent from the Romantic era rediscovered
£5.99

Memoirs of the Life of Colonel Hutchinson
LUCY HUTCHINSON
One of the earliest pieces of women's biographical writing, of great historic and feminist interest
£6.99

The Secret Self 1: Short Stories by Women
edited by Hermione Lee
'A superb collection' The Guardian
£4.99

The Age of Innocence
EDITH WHARTON
A tale of the conflict between love and tradition by one of America's finest women novelists
£4.99

Frankenstein
MARY SHELLEY
A masterpiece of Gothic terror in its original 1818 version
£3.99

The Life of Charlotte Brontë
ELIZABETH GASKELL
A moving and perceptive tribute by one writer to another
£4.99

Victorian Women Poets
1830–1900
edited by Jennifer Breen
A superb anthology of the era's finest female poets
£5.99

Female Playwrights of the Restoration: Five Comedies
edited by Paddy Lyons
Rediscovered literary treasure in a unique selection
£5.99

All books are available from your local bookshop or direct from:
Littlehampton Book Services Cash Sales, 14 Eldon Way, Lineside Estate,
Littlehampton, West Sussex BN17 7HE *(prices are subject to change)*

To order any of the books, please enclose a cheque (in sterling) made payable to
Littlehampton Book Services, or phone your order through with credit card details (Access,
Visa or Mastercard) on 01903 721596 (24 hour answering service) stating card number
and expiry date. *(Please add £1.25 for package and postage to the total of your order.)*

In the USA, for further information and a complete catalogue call 1-800-526-2778